Children in Trouble

The Role of Families, Schools and Communities

Carol Hayden

palgrave
macmillan

First published 2007 by
PALGRAVE MACMILLAN
Houndmills, Basingstoke, Hampshire RG21 6XS and
175 Fifth Avenue, New York, N.Y. 10010
Companies and representatives throughout the world

PALGRAVE MACMILLAN is the global academic imprint of the Palgrave Macmillan division of St. Martin's Press, LLC and of Palgrave Macmillan Ltd. Macmillan® is a registered trademark in the United States, United Kingdom and other countries. Palgrave is a registered trademark in the European Union and other countries.

ISBN-13: 978 1–4039–9486–8 paperback
ISBN-10:   1–4039–9486–2 paperback
ISBN-13: 978 1–4039–9485–1 hardback
ISBN-10:   1–4039–9485–4 hardback

This book is printed on paper suitable for recycling and made from fully managed and sustained forest sources.

A catalogue record for this book is available from the British Library.

A catalog record for this book is available from the Library of Congress.
10   9   8   7   6   5   4   3   2   1
16   15   14   13   12   11   10   09   08   07

Printed in China

Children in Trouble

to my family

Contents

List of Figures and Tables

Figures

Tables

Acknowledgements

The ideas in this book have been influenced by many people. First, my family and friends with whom I have had numerous conversations over the years. Thanks to Judith Smyth who read an early version of the book and was brave enough to comment on it in detail. Thanks, also, to the two anonymous referees who helped suggest improvements for the final version of the text. Colleagues at the University of Portsmouth and people from external agencies who worked with me as contemporaries or in some cases as research assistants on some parts of the original research projects (included within Chapters 4, 5 and 6) deserve a particular mention, especially Carol Lupton, Tim Martin and Renate Prowse. Others involved include Jo Goodship, Liz Holton, Julie Lawrence, Sandra Lemon, George Matthews, Sue Pike, Kate Ramsell, Dwynwyn Stepien and Dave Turner. Mikey Johns undertook the original research on young people and anti-social behaviour included in Chapter 6.

Abbreviations

ABC	Acceptable Behaviour Contract
ADHD	Attention Deficit and Hyperactivity Disorder
ADSS	Association of Directors of Social Services
ASB	anti-social behaviour
ASBO	Anti-Social Behaviour Order
ASBU	Anti-Social Behaviour Unit
BCS	British Crime Survey
BEST	Behaviour and Education Support Team
BIP	Behaviour Improvement Project
CAMHS	Child and Adolescent Mental Health Services
CHE	Community Home with Education
CPR	Child Protection Register
CRAE	Children's Rights Alliance for England
CSR	Comprehensive Spending Review
CtC	Communities that Care
CYP	Children and Young Persons (record)
DES/WO	Department of Education and Science/Welsh Office
DfE	Department for Education
DfEE	Department for Education and Employment
DfES	Department for Education and Skills
DoH, DH	Department of Health
DSM	Diagnostic Statistical Manual
DSRU	Dartington Social Research Unit
EBD; SEBD	emotional and behavioural difficulties; social, emotional and behavioural difficulties
EP	educational psychology
EPPI Centre	Evidence for Policy and Practice Information Co-ordinating Centre
ESRC	Economic and Social Research Council
EWS	Education Welfare Service
FE	further education
FGC	Family Group Conference
GCSE	General Certificate of Secondary Education
IBP	Individual Behaviour Plan
IRT	Identification, Referral and Tracking
ISSP	Intensive Supervision and Support Programme
IT	intermediate treatment
JSFST	Joint School and Family Support Team
LAC	looked-after child

LASCH	Local Authority Secure Children's Home
LEA	local education authority
LSU	learning support unit
MORI	Market and Opinion Research International
NACRO	National Association for the Care and Resettlement of Offenders
NAHT	National Association of Head Teachers
NAI	non-accidental injury
NAS/UWT	National Association of Schoolmasters/Union of Women Teachers
NSPCC	National Society for the Prevention of Cruelty to Children
NUT	National Union of Teachers
OCJS	Offending, Crime and Justice Survey
Ofsted	Office for Standards in Education
PEP	Personal Education Plan
PRU	Pupil Referral Unit
PSHE	Personal Social and Health Education
PSP	Pastoral Support Plan
PYO	persistent young offender
RCT	Randomised Control Trial
RIP	Research in Practice
SCIE	Social Care Institute for Excellence
SDQ	Strengths and Difficulties Questionnaire
SEBD	social, emotional and behavioural difficulties
SEN	special educational needs
SEU	Social Exclusion Unit
SIPS	Social Inclusion Pupil Support
SPECTR	social, psychological, educational and criminological-controlled trials register
SSD	Social Services Department
SSLP	Sure Start local programme
STC	Secure Training Centre
TWOC	taking a vehicle without the owner's consent
YCS	Youth Cohort Study
YIP	Youth Inclusion Programme
YISP	Youth Inclusion Support Panel
YJB	Youth Justice Board
YOI	young offenders institution
YOP	Youth Offender Panel
YOT	Youth Offending Team

Introduction and Overview

Children in trouble, or troublesome children, occupy the energies of all professionals in contact with them, to varying degrees. They are an issue of concern to parents, both the parents of these children and the parents of their contemporaries who may be concerned about the impact on their own children. The media delights in stories of extreme cases or particular emblems of youth dress and attitude. The debate is perennial, although the language, form and focus shift. Centrally the issue is one of balancing the care and control of children.

This book is an attempt to make sense of the contradictory ways in which we have come to view and respond to children in trouble in different contexts. It is the culmination of 17 years of research at the University of Portsmouth, following a 10-year career in secondary-school teaching. The latter occupation and continuing belief in the power of education to transform lives inevitably informs the emphasis on education and schooling that will be found throughout this volume. However, other influences have been important, including an ongoing research programme for Social Services departments during the period 1989–2003, as part of the Social Services Research and Information Unit (SSRIU). Researching children known to social services departments meant focusing on the most vulnerable children and was a stark reminder of the hurdles some children overcome. More recently, working in the Institute for Criminal Justice Studies (ICJS) has refocused the emphasis of my research in the direction of offending behaviour. In many ways the criminal justice system is the final destination for children in serious trouble, or what is likely to happen if attempts to get them back on track fail.

The choice of title – '*Children in Trouble*' – already suggests that children are at odds with society in some way. Although the starting point for this book is children *in trouble*, a consistent feature will be to point to the well-documented evidence of 'troubles', difficulties and abuse elsewhere in the lives of many (Goldson and Peters, 2000), persistent young offenders in particular (Hagell and Newburn, 1994; Arnull *et al.*, 2005). This book supports the argument that we need to retain a focus on children 'in need' when providing services for children 'in trouble' (Goldson, 1997, p. 86). Indeed, the Children Act 1989 recognized this in imposing preventative and diversionary duties on local authorities in relation to offending. The focus in the book is on children and young people up to the age of 18, all of whom are still 'children'. The use of the word 'children' in the title is deliberate; it is there to remind the reader that we are talking about children who should be entitled to be children and make some mistakes in the course of growing up (Stephen and Squires, 2004). A key point that the book sets out to make is that it is within the capacity of adults to respond to children in trouble in a way that can ameliorate, stabilize or entrench their difficulties. Piper (2001) writes of the importance of the words we use to describe young offenders: 'children are given another chance; for "youths", as for adults, there are no more excuses' (p. 37).

By emphasizing the overlap between children *in trouble* and seen as 'troublesome' and those who are also 'troubled', the book argues that we need to consider ways of addressing both the troubled and troublesome aspects of their behaviour. This necessitates developing a better understanding of why children behave the way they do. The scale, nature and interpretation of troublesome behaviour in different contexts – family, school and community – is the ongoing theme of the book. It is a theme that we explore in more depth in the sections where original research evidence is presented.

The issues considered in this book are a part of growing up and childhood in any society. However, the particular level of development, culture and legal context have an important influence on how problems might develop, be understood and responded to. This book centrally concerns itself with England in terms of the specific legal definitions, and so on, and does not attempt to explain the differences across the UK, Europe, or, indeed, the rest of the world. Making comparisons and investigating differences between countries is an interesting area of research which is left open for the reader to pursue. The book provides some organising principles and a conceptual framework for this undertaking.

The book is organised into eight chapters. *Chapter 1* presents an overview of historical, theoretical and conceptual perspectives on children's behaviour and particularly those in trouble. This chapter sets out to try and explain how our ideas about children in trouble have developed and it illustrates the ongoing tensions between welfare and justice and care and control in our responses. *Chapter 2* looks at more contemporary perspectives and the shifts in approach that are creating the responses to children in trouble. *Chapter 3* reviews the evidence about the scale, level and nature of the different ways in which children may be in trouble. Boys and young men are shown overall to be more likely to find themselves in serious trouble, especially through instances of aggressive and violent behaviour, in comparison with girls and women. Most young people in trouble are also white. However, the picture in relation to both gender and ethnicity is complex. Girls and women are involved in and suffer from specific forms of problematic behaviour. Young people from minority ethnic backgrounds are more likely to be convicted of a criminal offence, and they are also more likely to experience many of the risk factors associated with the development of criminal behaviour and to have to deal with the additional adversities of prejudice and discrimination. Gender, ethnicity and being 'in trouble' are issues that deserve books in their own right – these issues will be addressed in this text, but the reader particularly interested in them should also look at texts written specifically on these issues.

A theme throughout the book is an evaluation of the different sources of evidence about children in trouble and especially evidence from empirical research. *Chapters 4, 5 and 6* in turn deal with the key themes of the text: children in trouble, at home, in school and in the community. Each chapter reviews key research evidence in the field and then draws on original research, mostly presented as case studies or examples that explore or illustrate in more depth the nature of the issues that need to be addressed or different types of response that set out to address different aspects or level of problem, as they manifest themselves in different parts of the system.

Chapter 7 explores an important contemporary question in relation to the evidence about what to do about children in trouble – the 'what works' debate. The chapter reviews the main methodological arguments, as well as the political and practical ones that need to be considered. It highlights some of the key evidence about where to focus and how to work with children in trouble. *Chapter 8* concludes the book by presenting a view on the evidence and development of the contemporary responses to children in trouble. It also looks to the future and the increasing integration of children's services, and considers the balance and practicalities of responsibilities that face families, schools and communities and the variety of sources of evidence about what to do. The chapter highlights the ongoing shifts in the nature of the response to children in trouble and notes the political imperative to balance populist rhetoric against the desire to improve services for the most needy and troublesome children.

The overall message of the book is that 'children in trouble' do not present a simple set of problems that can be solved by a few well-evidenced interventions. Even programmes that 'work' don't work for everybody, and only work to the extent that they do when the intervention is appropriate to the young person's needs and practitioners are motivated, appropriately trained and resourced. Children in any society will continue to tax adults as they grow up and adults are always likely to vary in their capacity to respond in helpful and nurturing ways. Nevertheless, this book is based on both a belief that we could and should do better and a review of the evidence that suggests this is a reasonable belief.

1

Children in Trouble – Historical, Theoretical and Conceptual Perspectives

Our earth is degenerate – children no longer obey their parents.

> – 6,000-year-old inscription of an Egyptian priest,
> cited in D. Jones, 2001, p. 45

Winchester [the public school] was often hit by serious disturbances; one rising there in 1818 required the intervention of soldiers armed with fixed bayonets before order was restored.

> – Tubbs, 1996, p. 12

It is probably a minority of children who grow up without ever behaving in ways which may be contrary to the law.

> – HMSO, 1969, p. 3

Childhood and Trouble

Every new generation of adults tends to complain about the behaviour of children and young people. Most parents will have at least some problems in bringing up their children; most teachers will experience difficulties in managing the behaviour of some pupils and most of us are likely to witness or experience behaviour from children and young people in the community that is at the least lacking in civility, and may sometimes feel threatening. We hear less about the everyday difficulties children and young people have living with and responding to the expectations and behaviours of their parents and other adults, although we know more about cases of identified neglect and abuse. It is interesting to reverse the narrative for a moment and remember that some parents are 'in trouble' too, and may also be instrumental in the trouble presented by their children. At the start of this book, it is a good time for you to consider your own experiences and beliefs about the behaviour of children and young people. It will be useful then to evaluate the nature

1

of your evidence – to what extent has it been influenced by a particular event, perhaps a work role in a particular setting, or cases presented by the media? Notice when your preconceptions are challenged or changed by evidence presented in this book.

For most children and young people, getting into trouble is part of the normal business of growing up, testing the boundaries and finding one's place in the world. The extent to which this normal process is viewed as a problem is one of the issues we will consider in this chapter. The question often asked is whether the behaviour of children and young people has actually deteriorated, or whether social norms have changed. This is a complex question to answer, for a variety of reasons. The position of children and young people within the family and community is continually evolving in response to changing family forms, expectations about how children and young people should spend their time and, of course, the policing and recording of information about this. This chapter sets out to outline how our thinking about what adults want and expect in terms of the behaviour of children and young people has evolved. It will briefly outline key theoretical and conceptual perspectives in relation to children's behaviour.

'Childhood' as a distinct phase of life can be viewed from a variety of different perspectives: as a developmental or physiological phase (or series of phases); as a moral or legal construction; as a period that relates to educational, social and economic imperatives; and as a political or popular construction that befits a period in history. Child development theorists, such as Piaget, have been influential. Piaget saw childhood as a period of identifiable stages of development towards adulthood, in which 'egocentrism, dependency, incompetence, and irrationality eventually give way to adult independence, competency, ability to reason and act responsibly' (Haydon and Scraton, 2000, p. 417). Modern UK law acknowledges childhood immaturity as part of the reason why children are not treated like adults by the criminal justice system. However, by the age of 10 in England, Wales and Northern Ireland (8 in Scotland) children are held to be criminally responsible, indicating that in this respect at least, childhood ends early in the UK; certainly earlier than much of Europe, where the age of criminal responsibility ranges from 12 (in the Netherlands) to 18 (in Belgium). The principle of *doli incapax* (incapable of evil), established in a law dating back to Edward III, ameliorated the situation to a degree until the Crime and Disorder Act 1998. Under this principle, children aged 10 to 13 were presumed to be incapable of criminal intent unless this intent was proved 'beyond reasonable doubt'. Since the 1998 Act there is no longer any legal requirement for the criminal courts to take formal account of a child's age (when they are aged 10 or over) when assessing their culpability.

A number of sources have alerted us to the fact that childhood, youth and adolescence have not always been recognised as distinct phases of life that are necessarily problematic, despite the opening quotation from our Egyptian priest. Muncie (2004, p. 51) presents a useful overview of the 'invention' of childhood and youth in which he notes that for most of human history ordinary children and young people generally had to grow up in the world of adults, joining in whatever work and activities happened around them. In this setting the most meaningful distinction was between 'infancy', associated with physical immaturity and dependence on parents and carers for life's necessities, and a more capable state when a child became a person who could contribute to the work needed to support a family. There was no possibility of 'childhood' in the modern sense for children of the labouring classes. Education and leisure were pursuits of children of those with money and power. From the late Middle Ages, children of the aristocracy and nobility began to be seen differently; sometimes as innocents and objects of affection, sometimes as wilful and in need of discipline and moral guidance. Ariès (1960) notes that before the seventeenth century children were often portrayed as a small but inadequate adult: paintings frequently depicted children as miniatures of their elders. Prolonged periods of childhood were a luxury for all but the elite until relatively recently.

In pre-industrial and early industrial Britain the majority of households had to contribute to the family resources and income, with child labour from the age of 4 or 5 being usual in agricultural communities. Children formed the bulk of factory labour in the industrial revolution: 80 per cent of workers in English cotton mills were children (Muncie, 2004, p. 53). Orphaned and deserted children, as well as children of parents unable to maintain them, were 'boarded out' to whoever would take them. This was, in effect, a system of apprenticeship under the Poor Law Act of 1601. It was an attempt to deal with rural forms of poverty in a predominantly rural society, but also, in Elizabethan times, reflected a concern about increasing vagrancy. A key principle of the Poor Law and the associated workhouse system was that of 'less eligibility'. This principle was based on the belief that those in the workhouse should experience conditions worse than those outside. The 1834 Poor Law Amendment Act led to a partial shift to 'indoor' industrial training in buildings separate from workhouses, but was not greatly dissimilar to the earlier legislation. Being 'in trouble' in the nineteenth century was synonymous with being in trouble with the law and being poor, and both were connected to families who were variously described as 'feckless', 'neglectful' or 'destitute'. The interconnection between being poor, being found to break the law and having parents who could not or would not fulfil their responsibilities was established early on.

In keeping with more adult-style work roles, children were held to be adult above the age of 7 in terms of responsibility for misdemeanours. Punishment was harsh. For example, in one day in 1814 five children were condemned to death for the burglary of a dwelling: they ranged in age from 8 to 12. Children could be sentenced to transportation to the colonies at this time, and were accommodated in hulks on the Thames or Medway or at Portsmouth while they awaited this fate (Hyland, 1993). By the early nineteenth century concern was evident about the cruel and harsh treatment of young delinquents, and in 1815 a group was formed to consider more humane ways of dealing with them. This was known as 'The Society for Investigating the Causes of the Alarming Increase in Juvenile Delinquency in the Metropolis'. This Society believed that most children could be reformed by more enlightened treatment. Parallel with these concerns about children who had offended in some way was the growth of notions of childhood innocence. The latter was important in motivating a child protection and welfare response to children in trouble (Piper, 2001). However, it was not until 1889 that cruelty to children became a specific criminal offence (Muncie, 2004, p. 53).

The twentieth century saw extensions to childhood and the period of transition to adult status for young people. From the middle of the century 'youth' increasingly became categorised as an unstable period between childhood and adulthood. Yet during the 1960s and 1970s, Spence (2005, pp. 49–50) argues that youth was 'thought of much more as a period of life to be celebrated and enjoyed for its own sake'. Youth unemployment in the 1980s can be seen as undermining the relative freedom of young people, as they became more economically dependent on their families and the state. In 1986 access to social benefits for young people was redefined, with the dependency of young people on adults ending at ages ranging from 16 to 24. In practice this has resulted in a prolonged financial reliance of young people on their parents, an uncomfortable situation for many and a precarious one for young people with difficult relationships, or estranged from their parents. The concept of 'youth transition' rose into the ascendancy in the 1980s and 1990s and has been an important influence on government thinking, with an increasing emphasis on the 'risks' in this transitional period. Theories of transition emphasise the importance of processes and structures outside young people's control in determining their opportunities and choices, or lack of them. This way of thinking is amenable to policy decisions that shape young people's opportunities and choices (Spence, 2005).

Postman (1982), like many other writers on the subject, sees 'childhood' as a social artefact but focuses his theory of change on communications systems. He sees infancy as ending when the child is able to use words to communicate sufficiently with the adult world, with face-to-face communication being the norm for most of human history. The advent of the printing press in the sixteenth century is seen as bringing about changes in communication that ultimately led to literacy becoming important and schools developing as special places in which children learned to be literate. Postman focuses on television (to which we can now add the internet) as giving access to all sorts of knowledge and information – 'the secrets of adult life' – ahead of a child's capability of assimilating it. This he sees as leading to the disappearance of childhood. Developing this viewpoint, we could say that for most children access to the media has probably contributed to the loss of innocence ascribed to idealised pictures of childhood; most apparent perhaps in relation to infants. Further biological maturity occurs earlier, adding to a complex mix of knowledge, feelings, expectations and conflicts in status for young people trying to find their place in the world.

By the end of the twentieth century Coleman (1997) writes that 'adolescence is becoming stretched at both ends, creating an artificially long period of dependence and semi-independence, and leading to all sorts of doubts and uncertainties about the entry into adulthood' (p. 45). Many parents have difficulty in communicating effectively with their sons and daughters when they reach adolescence. Young people will not so readily accept adult authority at this stage, and many adults feel reluctant to relinquish some of the power they have exercised when their child was younger. In a sense this might be seen as part of the collective anxiety that the older generation feel about children and young people. Coleman (1997) concludes that adolescence is often viewed within an 'overwhelmingly negative stereotype' (p. 45).

More broadly, the social position of children and young people in contemporary economically developed societies is complex and has negative consequences for some. Rutter and Smith (1995) argue that the evidence about increasing 'psychosocial disorders' experienced by young people is explained in part by their cultural position in society, a position that is fraught with difficulties because of the possibilities available alongside the reality that 'the glittering prizes' are only available to the few. Children and young people today are more exposed than any previous generation to the promise and expectations generated by the media and ready availability of rapidly changing technology. The overall evidence is that in terms of psychosocial disorders, the situation of young people has generally deteriorated since the mid-twentieth century. Increased rates of depressive illnesses, eating disorders, suicide, substance misuse, and so on are evident. Whether the latter trends are because we have become better at detecting and recording these problems is always worth considering, of course. The evidence of increased psychosocial disorders in young people across much of the developed world is important, however, because of the established connection between some of the acting-out behaviours and anti-social and criminal behaviour.

Residential and Community Options for Children in Trouble

Residential options for children in trouble, whether primarily for care or control, were a common response in the nineteenth and early twentieth centuries. The merging of purpose between everyday care, control, education and training was a common part of the debate. Children were imprisoned with adults, with an early attempt in 1821 to introduce separate provision for young offenders failing. Ensuing debate on provision took two main approaches: one advocated the establishment of juvenile prisons, the other educational and home-like reformatories. This early split in approach reflects modern concerns about responding to children who have committed serious offences as well as those who are 'at risk', or have committed minor offences. This split also reflects different traditions in terms of the nature and purpose of responding to young people in trouble. The industrial schools focused on welfare and the provision of opportunities for future employment for those considered to be 'at risk', or who had committed minor offences. Although reformatories originated from humanitarian ideals, many were in practice run in a punitive and restrictive way; they were supposed to be focused on more serious offenders. Sadly, echoing modern debate in relation to the Thompson and Venables case,[1] concern was expressed about the supposed educational advantage gained by children being sent to reformatories, compared with 'ordinary' children. Awareness of this issue led educational provision in reformatories to be harsh and often of poor quality.

The rapid expansion of reformatories and industrial schools was matched by an equally rapid decline: in 1865 around 7,000 children were in these schools; in 1912 about 26,000 and in 1926 about 7,000 (Hyland, 1993, pp. 7–21). The reasons for this decline were varied, ranging from concern about harsh punishments to the belief that they were not structured and punitive enough. There was also concern about the nature and quality of education provided in these institutions, an issue still in evidence (see Stephenson *et al.*, 2001). Increasing provision of universal education and smaller families also changed the emphasis of the debate.

While the reduction in the number of children sent to prison in Victorian Britain may seem a positive indication of the undoubted reforming zeal of the time, enforced emigration offered a one-off solution to dealing with children who were thought to need a 'fresh start'. Although children had been sent to the colonies since the early seventeenth century, the practice began on a large scale in the 1860s, being partly evangelical in motivation. Barnardo's was active in this field, sending children to Canada, South Africa, Australia and New Zealand. It has been estimated that at least 150,000 children were subject to enforced emigration (Pinchbeck and Hewitt, 1969).

By the end of the nineteenth century various child-care charities had been established, including Barnardo's (1870), the National Children's Home (1869), the Church of England Waifs and Strays Society (1881), the Catholic Children's Society (1887) and the NSPCC (1884). Although philanthropy is often seen as a prime motive behind these societies, it is also clear that protecting the Christian faith was another. Nevertheless, a focus on child welfare was developing with these charities, reflected in the Prevention of Cruelty to Children Act of 1889 and strengthened in the Children Act of 1908. The latter led to the creation of juvenile courts, with a focus on treatment and rehabilitation rather than punishment. The Act also abolished imprisonment for children and young people.

From the 1930s 'approved schools' were formed through the merger of reformatories and industrial schools and approved by the Home Office. Their purpose was short-term training for boys and girls of 10 years and older, up to a maximum period of three years. Their philosophy tended towards child welfare, but they were also based on the notion that children with ineffectual parents should be removed from them. The majority of approved schools were situated in the countryside. A series of events and circumstances gradually led to growing criticism of the approved school system – scandals to do with harsh and inappropriate punishment, concerns about staff quality and a reducing 'success rate' in terms of reoffending, as well as concerns about cost (Hyland, 1993).

The ideas of Burt (1925) and Bowlby (1951) became influential in the mid-twentieth century; their work suggested that juvenile crime could be traced back to early childhood relationships and circumstances. This led to links being made between state child-care provision and the juvenile justice system; in part an attempt to divert young offenders away from the juvenile justice system and into the state child-care system. This helped to create a common perception that children looked after by the state are also there because of what they have done, rather than what their parents have done, been unable or failed to do. Diverting young offenders into the state child-care system was based on the belief that a welfare-orientated children's service was needed and that problems should be dealt with within the community, rather than in residential establishments.

The government paper *Children in Trouble*, first published in 1968, showed understanding of the multiple causes of juvenile delinquency, as well as recognition (shown in the quotation at the start of this chapter) that most children are likely to do something that is contrary to the law in the course of growing up. *Children in Trouble* recognised the need for alternatives to custody or simply remaining in the community. Intermediate treatment (IT) was introduced, the aim of which was 'to bring the young person into contact with a new environment, and to secure his participation in some constructive activity' (HMSO, 1969, p. 10). However, it was some time before intermediate treatment became a real alternative to detention centres. Bottoms *et al.* (1990) note that it was not until the late 1970s that there was a concerted push, from both the Personal Social Services Council and a group of academics, to use IT with offenders, as opposed to those 'at risk'. *Children in Trouble* removed the Approved Schools Order[2] and merged approved schools into community homes, and approved schools became part of children's departments. Head teachers of approved schools were resistant to this, wanting to retain 'school' in the title. Community Homes with Education (CHE) came to be used to distinguish the old approved schools from other children's residential homes. The peak occupancy for CHEs was 1973, with 7,100 children in residence, declining to 1,149 in 1990 (Hyland, 1993, p. 117).

The Seebohm report, in 1968, marked the shift away from residential options as a way of responding to children in trouble. This report placed greater emphasis and responsibility on society, rather than on institutions coping with problems. The Children and Young Persons Act 1969 followed, advocating more care and management of young offenders in the community. All types of residential accommodation for children reduced in the decade 1979–89: for example, the number of children in care reduced from about 100,000 in 1979 to about 66,000 in 1989. Proportionately, the use of foster care rose from about a third to over half of all provision within this ten-year period (Hyland, 1993, p. 117.)

Overall, the 1970s and 1980s have been characterised as a period in which the diversion of young offenders became increasingly important. 'Labelling' and 'stigma' as a consequence of prosecution were well recognised as harmful to the future prospects of young offenders (Piper, 2001). The 1982 Criminal Justice Act contained certain restrictions on the custodial sentencing of young people under 21 and gave courts greater powers to impose conditions on Care and Supervision Orders,[3] including a new supervised activities requirement (Bottoms *et al.*, 1990). Arguments to support more community-based facilities also used favourable cost comparisons with residential care in their argument to support the development of intermediate treatment.

Pitts (2001, p. 6) highlights the large reduction in the number of young people sentenced to custody in juvenile courts during the 1980s: the number fell from 7,700 in 1981 to 1,900 in 1990. Pitts (2001, p. 7) describes how the number of young people sentenced in juvenile courts halved during the 1980s; in effect starving the courts of juvenile offenders owing to a combination of police cautioning and other forms of pre-court diversion. Thus an apparently draconian law and order mandate for right-wing governments in the 1980s actually presided over a halving of young people sentenced in juvenile courts and a reduction to a quarter of the number in youth custody in 1990, compared with 1981. No doubt part of this situation can be explained by the cost-cutting imperatives of the era, which were also high on the political agenda. The notion of radical non-intervention was also influential (Pitts, 2001). This complex array of influences, perspectives and types of evidence about the increased emphasis on community alternatives reminds us of the issues of evaluation and success criteria, as well as any assurances particular types of research can offer. The latter are crucial issues in the 'what works' debate (see Chapter 7).

Attempts were made to 'get tough' at various points throughout the 1980s and 1990s. Experiments such as the 'short, sharp shock' were introduced, then abandoned, and were found in any case to have no effect on reconviction rates (YJB, 2001a). Still, the continued move towards more community-based alternatives and away from institutional care or control was in the ascendant until the early 1990s, when a series of circumstances and events helped to create a climate change in responses to young people in trouble.

Children, Behaviour and Schooling

Parallel to concerns about children at home and in the community, the history of formal schooling has tended to show that wherever records have been kept, there has been evidence of concern about the care and control of some children and young people. Formal schooling has always had a number of aims, beyond the more obvious ones of imparting knowledge and developing abilities. Keeping children occupied and encouraging conforming behaviour are also part of what schools do. Schooling did not begin to become available to ordinary children until Forster's Elementary Education Act of 1870, after which education was provided out of national funds. Schooling to the age of 10 was made compulsory in 1880. Early schooling can be seen as primarily focused on the control of children in terms of the methods used to suppress nonconforming behaviour.

School was a privilege for the minority before Forster's Act, much of it either provided by the Church and monasteries, or paid for privately by those who could afford it. In the monasteries of the Middle Ages, physical punishment was routine and was passed on to the emerging church schools of that time. McManus (1989) observes that most sixteenth- and seventeenth-century pictures of schoolmasters portrayed them holding a birch or rod. Serious riots in schools are documented which involved shootings and even deaths, with intervention from the army (as in one of the opening quotations to this chapter). In 1818 in Eton, for example, a riot among pupils occurred in which pupils smashed their headmaster's desk. This latter headmaster has been described as a 'champion flogger' who, even in his sixtieth year, is said to have found the energy to flog 80 boys in one day (Tubbs, 1996). Lawrence *et al.* (1984) confirm these types of stories and observe that canings and beatings were the only way in which some level of order was maintained in schools in the past.

We know, therefore, that adult concern about pupil behaviour and attendance at school is not new. What has gradually changed is the length of time young people spend in formal education, and thus there is more potential time for conflict when the expectations of the institution are at odds with those of the individual and the home and/or community. One response in the school system has been to segregate and send the badly behaved children somewhere else. This latter tendency became more apparent from the 1970s onwards, with debates about disruptive and disaffected pupils becoming increasingly common. Following the raising of the school-leaving age in 1972, from 15 to 16, there was a marked growth in off-site 'special units'. Many schools also developed on-site withdrawal rooms or on-site units in the 1970s. Off-site units were aimed at pupils who (it was believed) could not be contained in ordinary or mainstream schools because of their behaviour or because they regularly truanted (chose not to attend school). The first 'special unit' for disruptive and truanting pupils was established in 1961, but by 1969 there were still only 20 nationally. Rapid growth came in the 1970s so that by 1977 there were 239 special units. Two-thirds of all local education authorities (LEAs) in England and Wales had these special units – they were spread throughout the country and not confined to inner-city areas. However, London could still be seen as the 'capital of the disruptive industry', with over half the nationally available places by 1980 (Basini, 1981, p. 192). Essentially, special units were where pupils went following exclusion from school. The use of these units was criticised for segregating pupils, for the limited role models they could provide and the content and breadth of the curriculum. The over-representation of black pupils was also noted (Basini, 1981).

Parallel to the growth in special units for disruptive and truanting pupils, there was a growth in residential and day schools for 'maladjusted' children, especially in the 1970s. The distinction made between 'disruptive' children and those deemed 'maladjusted' is an interesting one, not least because it brought with it a different response, although Laslett (1998) comments that 'while maladjusted children are not the same as disruptive children, they resemble them in many ways' (p. 12). From 1945 to 1970 it was common to use medical terminology in relation to maladjusted children, with a tendency to see them as ill or sick in some way. Gradually a distinction was made between emotional maladjustment and social maladjustment. In relation to the latter group home and community conditions were believed to explain their behaviour. The Warnock report (DES/WO, 1978) is often seen as the watershed in relation to the concept and use of the term 'maladjusted'. The report replaced the concept of handicap with 'special educational needs' and 'educationally subnormal' with the term 'learning difficulty'. The report also marks a move away from separate and specialist provision for such children.

Laslett (1998, p. 13) estimates that around 8,000 children attended day or residential state schools for maladjusted children in 1980. However, around a third of this type of provision comes from the independent sector, which then (as now) makes it difficult to estimate state precisely how many children are educated in these types of school. Grimshaw with Berridge (1994) cite an estimate of 12,609 maladjusted children resident in special boarding schools and CHEs in England in 1983.

General concern about pupil behaviour continued to grow throughout the 1980s, culminating in a government enquiry known as the Elton report (DES/WO, 1989). The teaching profession at the time was of the view that disruptive, even violent, behaviour was becoming more apparent in schools. However, a key finding from this enquiry was that the biggest problem for teachers was the cumulative effect of everyday minor acts of misbehaviour. The growth of whole-school behaviour policies (now expected in all schools) and training in pupil behaviour management can be seen as developing from the recommendations of the Elton report.

Important to the emerging educational policy context of the late 1980s was the Education Reform Act 1988, which introduced the National Curriculum, linked with attainment targets and testing. This led to a more competitive and image management-driven ethos developing in schools. The Ofsted (Office for Standards in Education) inspection system, with its publication of reports, further added to the pressure on schools to focus on measurable results. The pace of change and pressures to perform and 'deliver' the National Curriculum helped to create behaviour problems in the classroom, as well as limit the possibility of more flexible responses to them.

Behaviour that is seen as problematic in school is a theme we will return to a number of times in this volume. Aside from the more everyday issues of adolescence, school culture or ethos and individual teacher ability to keep order in the classroom, serious behaviour problems in school can result in other problems associated with poor prospects and an increased likelihood of criminal behaviour. Equally, good experiences in the education system and the opportunities for achievement can be important as protection against adverse outcomes, as we will expand on later in this chapter.

Understanding Children's Behaviour

Whether behaviour is viewed as 'a problem' – indeed, whether it is viewed as 'normal' – will always be a matter of some dispute. It is important to note at this point that this book is based on the premise that the extent to which behaviour is viewed as problematic is partly a matter of perception; it is context-dependent and the result of interaction. However, perceptions are important because they tend to shape our responses. So, what we believe is normal or reasonable behaviour from a child in a particular context is likely to shape our interactions with that child. This in turn will shape their response to us.

It is well recognised that most children present some level of behaviour problems as a normal part of their development and that the majority grow out of them. Parenting and family interaction factors are said to account for between 30 and 40 per cent of behaviour viewed as 'anti-social' in children (Barlow, 1999). Judgements about particular behaviours can be subjective and are necessarily context- and culturally specific: for example, whether or not a child makes eye contact when an adult in authority is speaking to them. There are various validated psychological instruments that purport to identify and measure the extent of particular behavioural problems in children in specified contexts and time periods (see, for example, Goodman, 1997, the SDQ or Strengths and Difficulties Questionnaire and the research example using this questionnaire in Chapter 4 in this volume). Behaviour-rating scales, such as the SDQ, measure 'caseness' or the extent to which a particular set of behaviours constitutes a problem that is outside the 'normal' range of behaviours for an age group. Behaviour-rating scales can measure both internalising problems, such as anxiety, depression, autism and attention-deficit disorders, and externalising problems, such as conduct disorders, aggression, sleeplessness, and so on. Emotional and behavioural problems are common in childhood, but estimates of prevalence vary, partly in relation to definitions and partly in relation to locality. For example, the prevalence of emotional and behavioural problems in children has been estimated to be as high as 20 per cent in urban areas, using clinical criteria for establishing 'problems' (Charlton *et al.*, 1995).

Children in trouble generally present externalising problems and behave in ways that attract adults' attention. 'Conduct disorder' (DSM-111) is the frequent diagnosis for behaviour in which major societal or interpersonal rules are continuously broken; for example through fighting, temper tantrums, destruction of property, stealing and fire-setting (Linfoot *et al.*, 1999). Conduct disorder includes problems that are defined as 'oppositional' in character, including disobedience, provocative opposition to authority figures, argumentativeness, non-compliance and violation of minor rules (Barlow, 1999). The proportion of children thought to be 'conduct disordered' varies with population area: estimates vary from around 6 per cent of boys and 3 per cent of girls aged 5–10 (Meltzer *et al.*, 2000) to as many as 10 to 15 per cent of young children, with even higher estimates for children in poor neighbourhoods (Linfoot *et al.*, 1999). We focus on childhood behaviour here because of the associations found between behaviour problems in childhood and negative outcomes for the child, family and community, including high levels of public expenditure (see also Scott *et al.*, 2001 and the section on early intervention in Chapter 7, this volume). Problem behaviour can lead to interruptions in social development and education, as well as peer-group problems and distress to other children. Longer-term problems include criminal behaviour, drug and alcohol misuse, mental health difficulties, relationship breakdown and poor work histories. The likelihood of these outcomes is greater for individuals whose behaviour problems start in early childhood, rather than in adolescence (Rutter *et al.*, 1998).

Children's behaviour is explained and responded to differently according to both the various theoretical models developed to try and understand it, as well as the particular remit of the agencies that come into contact with this behaviour. The terminology varies with perspective, as well as agency and profession, so behaviour that might be seen as 'disruptive' in a school may be seen as 'anti-social' in the community, or indeed as indicative of 'mental health needs', 'neglect' or even 'abuse', depending on the perspective of the observer and indicators used. Traditionally, explanations of and interventions with a child's behaviour tended to locate the problem with the individual child, as in the concept of 'maladjustment'. This approach drew heavily from medical, psychological and psychiatric models (Cooper, 1998). The response was psychoanalysis and psychotherapy, approaches that by their nature could only reach small numbers of children, who either met strict organisational criteria, or had parents who could afford to pay privately for help. Therapeutic residential care is based around these kinds of psychotherapeutic approaches (see also Chapter 4). Psychodynamic theory was first developed by Freud. Practitioners working with this model view behaviour as a visible symptom of internal conflict, and their central task becomes one of enabling the child to resolve their inner conflict. The psychodynamic approach thus sees change being brought about through individuals identifying and understanding links between present events and past experience (Cooper, 1998). Thus the behaviour itself is not the focus, but the underlying issues that might explain and resolve it. These sorts of approaches lend themselves to longer-term intervention and one-to-one relationships between the child and therapist.

Behavioural approaches (or learning theory) are more pragmatic and start with the behaviours seen as a problem in a particular context (Laslett, 1998). This approach is based on the belief that all behaviour is learnt; behaviourists look for what is reinforcing problem behaviour, so that it can be 'unlearned'. Rewards (for wanted behaviour) and sanctions (for unwanted behaviour) are often part of this approach. Behavioural approaches lend themselves more readily to larger group settings, and they are often used in schools as well as in children's residential care. Indeed, many parents are well aware of the principles behind this approach and some parenting programmes will incorporate elements of learning theory.

Labelling theory takes another approach again. 'Problem' behaviour is seen as socially defined, as opposed to inherent in the behaviour itself (Lemert, 1951). So, for example, behaviour that used to be labelled 'maladjusted' may be viewed as such in a school environment, yet may serve the individual well in the home and community. Teachers (as with other professionals working with children) may come to typify pupils based on particular observations and respond accordingly in a way that may entrench problems and differences (Hargreaves *et al.*, 1975).

Ecosystemic approaches locate children and their behaviours within the key systems that surround them – home, school, community – and try to view these behaviours in context within these interrelated systems (Cooper and Upton, 1990). Change from this perspective is problematic if approached in only one area of an individual's life and may not be sustainable. Thus some programmes with younger children would try to work with both home and school, so that the child experiences more consistency in the way adults respond to their behaviour.

Much of the behaviour of young people that especially troubles adults in the community is referred to as 'anti-social'. However, there are different interpretations of this term. Rutter *et al.* (1998) use the term 'anti-social behaviour' in a very specific way, to cover behaviour that is a criminal offence, whether or not the behaviour results in detection or conviction. Their use of the term in relation to criminal behaviour is chosen in order to make the distinction between this behaviour and the various diagnostic categories used by clinicians when referring to behaviour considered to be outside the norm (such as conduct or oppositional disorders). Rutter *et al.* remind us that the various clinical disorders are *not* synonymous with criminal behaviour; neither is criminal behaviour synonymous with social or psychological dysfunction. In contrast, the Home Office definition and use of the term is wider: 'it is behaviour which causes or is likely to cause harassment, alarm or distress to one or more people who are not in the same household as the perpetrator' (2003, p. 5). Examples of anti-social behaviour (using the Home Office definition) include graffiti, abusive and intimidating language, excessive noise, dropping litter, drunken behaviour in the street and dealing drugs. Such behaviour is explicitly linked with family and community issues and blamed for holding back the regeneration of the most disadvantaged areas and creating an environment conducive to crime. Research evidence on the persistence and desistence of anti-social behaviour (as defined by Rutter *et al.*, 1998) would indicate that the more serious and persistent forms can be detected as early as the age of 3, in the form of oppositional and hyperactive behaviour. The distinction is made between 'adolescent-limited' and 'life-course persistent' anti-social behaviour, although it is emphasised that 'nothing is cast in stone' and a range of life events and other opportunities and circumstances can play a part in helping anti-social behaviour to continue or cease (Rutter *et al.*, 1998, p. 307).

Social Control

An alternative perspective to the attempt to define and pinpoint types of behaviour that are problematic and to explain their origins is to question why we might want to define 'normality' in the first place. Normality is a contested concept, although in popular discourse it is often invoked to express disapproval of those who are believed to be acting outside an assumed norm. At the same time it is well known that different cultures and age groups have different views about what they might consider 'normal'. In this context social control is not a neutral concept, although it may have some value for general descriptive purposes. Social control varies in meaning and purpose according to the perspective of the writer using the term. Essentially it is about how and why social order is maintained and how co-operation and social integration are achieved. Viewpoints range across a spectrum in which social control is seen as self-evidently necessary and essentially benign (as in the work of Parsons, 1939) to being a form of organised repression (as in the work of Marx and Engels, 1968). Foucault (1977) would see the central task of the 'dispersed disciplinary complex'[4] in modern societies as the control of citizens, so that they are well-behaved, hard-working and conform to expectations about being a citizen. Thinking about what constitutes 'problem' behaviour, in turn, defines what is not problematic. This thinking tends to produce dichotomies of what is 'normal' and what is 'deviant', 'deserving' and 'undeserving', 'sane' and 'insane'. The production of these dichotomies is typical of much political posturing on crime and disorder in liberal democracies, so that 'the criminal process is disingenuously described as a contest between the citizen-victim and the criminal' (Kennedy, 2004, p. 10). As Kennedy warns, in a culture that encourages us to consider ourselves the potential victims of the 'other', 'we easily forget that the state is capable of victimising us more effectively' (*ibid.*).

A labelling perspective is particularly useful for looking at how young people come to be seen as a problem, arguably 'the problem' for society in an everyday sense. Labelling theory views social reality as not objectively measurable and straightforward; it is viewed as socially constructed, problematic and open to interpretation. According to Lemert (1951), labelling a behaviour or a group, or other identifiable characteristic, as 'a problem' or 'deviant' is a process that is socially defined, but may have consequences that trap individuals in that identity. The concept of labelling is common in studies of deviancy and has also been used in other settings, such as the classroom. For example, anti-school cultures have been viewed as a group response to ability grouping and the feeling of academic failure (Ball, 1981), as well as pupil perceptions of teacher expectation and cultural attitudes – of particular relevance in relation to race (Wright, 1986). According to labelling theory, the label can become a self-fulfilling prophecy, both for individuals and communities. In the community the belief that some young people are 'in trouble' and 'out of control' can leave adults feeling powerless and threatened. A reaction to this might be for those who can move away from the situation to leave, ultimately contributing to the decline of a neighbourhood (Loader *et al.*, 1998).

Risk, Protection and Resilience

The concept of 'risk' has come to be used in different ways in relation to children in trouble. Risk is both a metanarrative that refers to a view that risk and uncertainty is now a generalised state; as well as the use of risk in the more actuarial sense of calculating the risk posed by and to individuals. In the former sense it is common to talk of 'the risk society' (Beck, 1992) in which young people have to negotiate a set of risks unknown to previous generations. It is argued that changes in employment, housing and welfare have created conditions of uncertainty and protracted youth transitions to adulthood. These debates characterise old solidarities as having broken up, alongside a tendency to see crises and setbacks as personal shortcomings, rather than events beyond individual control. Fergusson (2004) shows, in his analysis of transitions to adulthood, that for some young people this will inevitably be partly trial and error, when the options available are already

Individual
- Being male
- Cognitive ability, impairment
- Hyperactivity, impulsivity
- Alienation, lack of social commitment
- Attitudes – condoning of offending, drug misuse
- Peer group – involved in offending, drug misuse

Family
- Prenatal and perinatal problems
- Poor parental supervision, no discipline
- Low income, poor housing, large family
- Low attachment to parents
- Family conflict
- Family history of criminal activity
- Attitudes – condoning of anti-social and criminal behaviour

School
- Low achievement (beginning in primary
- Lack of commitment/connection (incl. truancy)
- Aggressive behaviour (incl. bullying)
- School organisation and ethos (punitive, poor leadership, disorganised)

Community
- Disadvantaged neighbourhood
- High turnover, lack of neighbourhood attachment
- Community disorganisation, neglect
- Availability of drugs

Figure 1.1 Risk factors for youth crime
Source: Farrington, 1996; YJB, 2001a.

constrained by the belief that further training and education beyond the age of 16 should be the norm. Beck (1992, p. 21) defines risk as 'a systematic way of dealing with hazards and insecurities induced and introduced by modernization itself'. Yet risk is differentially distributed and continues to replicate established social divisions of class, race and gender (Furlong and Cartmel, 1997).

When applied to individuals and families, risk is often used in the actuarial sense of calculating specific risks to individuals or types of individuals. This, in turn, tends to create a focus on individual (rather than social) change as the appropriate response. There are various levels at which this concept of being 'at risk' can be considered. Children and young people may be 'at risk' *from others* (both adults and other children/young people); they may pose a risk *to others* (both adults and other children/young people) or be a risk *to themselves* (through risk taking behaviour and deliberate self-harm). The 'risk factors' commonly employed when talking about children and young people tend to be similar for a range of adverse outcomes, including failure or rejection from school, being 'looked after' by the local authority, or criminal involvement, as well as broader processes of marginalisation and social exclusion.

Prospective longitudinal studies, such as the Cambridge Study in Delinquent Development, are often quoted when particular 'risk factors' are cited and justified. This was a survey of approximately 400 London males, first interviewed at the age of 8, and subsequently interviewed a number of times

Absence of 'risks' (see Figure 1.1)

Individual
- Being female*
- Resilient temperament
- Sense of self-efficacy
- Positive, outgoing disposition
- High intelligence

Family/school/community
- Opportunities for positive social bonds
- Warm, affectionate relationship with at least one parent
- Parents who maintain a strong interest in a child's education
- Parents who provide effective supervision and consistent discipline
- Healthy communities
- Opportunities for involvement, using social and reasoning skills, getting recognition and due praise

Figure 1.2   Protective factors against youth crime
Notes: *up to adolescence, Rutter *et al.*, 1998.
Source: Farrington, 1996; YJB, 2001b.

until adulthood (Farrington, 2002). The risk factors identified by such research converge with greater force in particular neighbourhoods and more specifically in relation to 'anti-social behaviour'. For example, the report of Policy Action Team 8 on Anti-Social Behaviour notes that such behaviour appears more prevalent in 'deprived neighbourhoods' where there are wider issues of poverty, family stress, truancy and school exclusion, drug dependency and community disorganisation (Stephen and Squires, 2004, p. 353).

Farrington (1996) and the YJB (2001a) identify a number of protective factors, including a resilient temperament, a warm, affectionate relationship with at least one parent, parents who provide effective supervision, pro-social beliefs, consistent discipline, and parents who maintain a strong interest in their child's education (see Figure 1.2). However, it is worth sounding some words of caution against over-simplistic interpretations of concepts of 'risk' and 'protection'. McCarthy *et al.* (2004: pp. ix–x) argue that risks are 'context-dependent and vary over time and with different circumstances'. Further, CtC (2005) maintains that protection is not simply the opposite of risk and that it is possible for a young person (or population of young people) to be simultaneously at high risk, but also highly protected. It is also known that children vary in their resilience to difficult circumstances. Children with a stronger sense of attachment to other people, with a more positive outlook on life, more plans for the future and more control over their lives are more likely to demonstrate resilience (Rutter *et al.*, 1998).

Some risk and protective factors are individual characteristics. The idea of 'being male' as a risk factor and 'being female' as a protective factor is one such issue, which in some ways can also seem somewhat ridiculous and cause one to question the meaning of 'risk' and 'protection'. However, gender, like other risk and protective factors, is part of a wider dynamic that can operate positively or negatively for individuals, as part of wider social processes. Rutter *et al.* (1998) found that there is little difference in the tendency of men and women to get into interpersonal conflicts, either as children or as adults. However, men are more likely to commit theft, show persistent symptoms of attention-deficit hyperactivity disorders and to commit seriously aggressive and violent acts, in comparison with women. The impact of negative peer-group pressure for males may in part explain some of the difference.

Resilience and self-efficacy are concepts that have a growing currency within the debate about risk and protective factors, inasmuch as the development of resilience and self-efficacy might be encouraged or enhanced by the actions of others. Rutter *et al.* (1998) advise that we must avoid mistaking risk factors for causal mechanisms and focus instead on ways of reducing risk and enhancing protection. Although they describe the evidence about what actually constitutes 'resilience' as sparse, they suggest that it especially relates to the qualities that elicit positive responses from others. Resilient children tend to have better problem-solving skills and a sense of self-efficacy (Rutter, 1985). Resilient children are often easily likeable and thus easier to parent or teach; responses to them are self-reinforcing. A sense of self-efficacy has also been linked to an ability to plan ahead, foresee consequences and find positive solutions to problems (Bandura, 1995). Overall, research on resilience underlines the central importance of relationships in childhood. Close attachments to one or two significant adults, not necessarily parents, appear to play a key protective role.

It is important to understand critiques of this psychological approach to the development of criminality. Bradford (2005) sees 'risk' as the way young people's identities are constructed and involves limitless possibilities and justifications for professional intervention and 'multi-agency' approaches. In a sense, he argues, this is 'making up people' (Bradford, 2005, p. 62). Ethnographic and more in-depth approaches allow people to tell their own stories and provide a different insight. Studies such as those of Foster (1990) and Craine and Coles (1995) illustrate an alternative interpretation, where people in particular circumstances may be making understandable and rational choices to the restricted opportunities available in some communities.

Problem Construction

Children in trouble are likely to become known to several key agencies. Often their behaviour is interpreted with a different emphasis, according to the agency that comes up against it. Figure 1.3 depicts this for 'aggressive and impulsive' behaviour. Research by The Children's Society in the early 1990s (Malek, 1993, p. 20) found, in relation to referral and routes for admission into residential care, that 'underlying causes and expressions of difficult behaviour were often similar. Moreover, young people's needs were seen to be similar.' Furthermore, this research showed that availability of provision-influenced

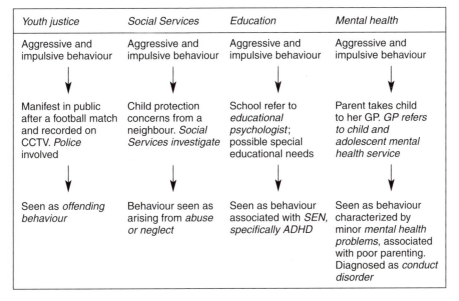

Youth justice	Social Services	Education	Mental health
Aggressive and impulsive behaviour	Aggressive and impulsive behaviour	Aggressive and impulsive behaviour	Aggressive and impulsive behaviour
↓	↓	↓	↓
Manifest in public after a football match and recorded on CCTV. *Police involved*	Child protection concerns from a neighbour. *Social Services investigate*	School refer to *educational psychologist*; possible special educational needs	Parent takes child to her GP. *GP refers to child and adolescent mental health service*
↓	↓	↓	↓
Seen as *offending behaviour*	Behaviour seen as arising from *abuse or neglect*	Seen as behaviour associated with *SEN, specifically ADHD*	Seen as behaviour characterized by minor *mental health problems*, associated with poor parenting. Diagnosed as *conduct disorder*

Figure 1.3 Aggressive and impulsive behaviour – different agency, different response?
Source: Developed from Malek, 1993, p. 5.

decisions about the nature of provision and placement breakdown in one service could lead to admission to another service. Inter-agency co-operation 'at the point at which difficulties surface' was one of the recommendations of this report (p. 22). Although Malek's report was published in the early 1990s, in many ways it encapsulates the different routes children in trouble have always taken and still take, in differing volumes, with changing labels and destinations, institutional care being only one possible destination. Indeed, diverting children and young people from various types of institutional care or specialist facility is a theme evident within debates in all four types of service. Children in enough trouble so that they come to the attention of one of these agencies, however, are likely to have needs that could be helped by more than one of these agencies, although all carry with them a degree of stigma.

This is not a new observation, although the nature and configuration of services changes. Hyland (1993), in writing about nineteenth-century provision for children who were viewed as 'a problem' or in need of care outside their families, says: 'All were vulnerable and their categorisation was often dependent on whatever arms of society they initially fell into, for example the police, education authorities, voluntary organisations, or the "Parish"' (p. 10).

One way that we can conceptualise the source and impact of the trouble children might be in is to configure it in relation to the key aspects of their lives: at home, at school and in the community. The degree of overlap in contexts in relation to the trouble children are in tends to exacerbate the problem. Children in trouble in more than one aspect of their lives are likely to get a great deal of negative feedback that may in turn serve to entrench and perpetuate their behaviour. It is also likely to be related to the degree and level of troublesomeness they display. In other words, those in most trouble in one context are likely to have difficulties in the rest of their lives as well. On the other hand, a large proportion of children in trouble are likely to be having lesser problems in only one area of their life – they may not like school, or have conflicts at home.

Responses to children in trouble across different contexts are influenced by perennial debates about the extent to which it is a care or control, welfare or justice issue. In reality these concepts are part of a continuum. Care and control, welfare and justice are needed wherever children are in trouble, albeit in different measures. Indeed, it could be argued that we have to care enough in order to be able to exercise appropriate control. The recognition that the welfare of children should be considered within any system that attempts to address the issue of justice likewise has a long history, as we have seen in this chapter. The punitive and retributive streak is apparent throughout, as is the desire to understand the needs of children in trouble and help make possible an alternative future. As Hylands' (1993) work on schools for young offenders illustrates, it is this punitive streak that, coupled with concerns about cost, has constantly limited possibilities by restricting the availability of help that might be effective. Arguments about the 'undeserving' getting a better deal than those who play by the rules have a long history, yet still have a contemporary ring to them.

An enduring theme in much of the writing on responding to children in trouble is the recognition that this is an issue inextricably bound up with poverty and lack of legitimate opportunity. The old adage that 'the devil makes work for idle hands' shows an early recognition that a lack of opportunities or alternatives is a potentially dangerous situation. The overlap in concerns about the material and moral welfare of children was very apparent in the desire to remove children from their home circumstances and bring them under the controlled conditions of reformatories and industrial schools. Schools have always provided a potential route out of poverty and the opportunity to experience alternative ways of behaving and preparing for the future, as well as fulfilling the more mundane role of 'keeping children off the streets'. The history of debate about children in trouble is also explicitly one in which the state has intervened in the families of children in trouble; whether parents were deemed unwilling or incapable of exercising appropriate care and control of their children. Indeed, 'outside parental control' or simply 'out of control' have been common ways of describing children in trouble.

Having set the scene on the way thinking about and responding to children in trouble has developed, it is probably time to make explicit the way this book approaches the issue. Fundamentally, it takes a left realist stance. It is 'realist' in the sense that it acknowledges that some children are indeed 'troublesome'; that this is not merely some media construction or political trick designed to suppress young people, or certain groups of young people in particular areas. It can be described as 'left' in the sense that inequality and poverty are viewed as important drivers for some, although not all, seriously troublesome behaviour. The book takes more account of individual situations and conditions than is typical of this approach. The position of young people in contemporary society is viewed as a problem in and of itself. It is connected in part to problematic relationships created by enforced and prolonged dependency, as well as adult frustrations and assertions of power connected to this situation. The focus on children and young people's behaviour is a theme that will be found throughout the book, for ultimately it is adult responses to their behaviour that help to construct the degree of 'trouble' they are in. Understanding influences on children's behaviour is crucial to understanding how to prevent and reduce serious trouble. The fundamental issues that the book seeks to address are how as a society we balance responsibilities for helping children grow up into well-adjusted adults; how we reduce the incidence of major problems in childhood; and, when they occur how we reduce the likelihood that they reoccur or get worse. The book sets out to review the different types of research evidence we have to inform what we do. It takes a critical look at the 'what works' debate, particularly the methodological issues that underpin it and the practical and political considerations that complicate its use and value. The book is written at a time when great political interest and energy is being expended on these issues and the move towards more integrated children's services is under way. In the next two chapters we will look at contemporary debates about children in trouble and outline the evidence about the scale and nature of the issues involved.

Notes

1   Thompson and Venables were the 10-year-old boys who abducted and killed 2-year-old Jamie Bulger in February 1993. There was later some popular and political debate about the extent to which they had a better chance educationally because of the 'five-star treatment' they received in secure accommodation.

2   A legal order whereby children were sent to residential approved schools; 'approved' by the Home Office.

3   A legal order whereby children were cared for in the community, by a combination of visits from social workers and activities and programmes.

4   The *dispersed disciplinary complex* is where punitive discipline is dispersed from the prison, so that not only does formal punishment and control take place in many tiny 'theatres of punishment' throughout society, but all social relations become relationships of control, infused with disciplinary power (Hudson, 2002, p. 241).

2

Children in Trouble – Contemporary Perspectives

Recent years have witnessed an increasingly punitive attitude towards children in trouble. There is an apparent widespread belief that only harsh punishment will stem the perceived increase in youth crime and related forms of anti-social behaviour. This belief extends beyond public opinion, however, and cuts to the core of policy responses to children in trouble.

— Goldson and Peters, 2000, p. 1

In the communal garden where I live, one bad boy terrorised all the younger children for months while their parents stood around powerless to stop him for fear of the law. It wasn't until a brave dad clipped the boy around the ear, to general astonishment, that the problem was solved – illegally. If community responsibility means anything that ought to have been legal. On the same principle it ought to be possible for two or three teenage thugs to be marched forcibly out of the classroom without the threat of legal action. There ought to be more big brawny men around in schools.

— Marrin, 2005, p. 19

To assume that a three-year-old child shows symptoms of criminality seems to me so ridiculous that I can hardly find words for it. I am shocked by the mere idea. Most of the three-year-olds I have known have had aggressive tendencies from time to time.

— Sereny, 2005, p. 2

Contemporary Debates

It can be argued that children and young people are centre stage in much of contemporary social policy and that this is both a major departure in terms of state intervention and support for the family, as well as a shift in cultural attitudes towards children and young people (Williams, 2004). Policy relating to better child-care support and provision for working parents, improving the school system, or addressing the quality of life in certain neighbourhoods is part of this mainstream response. While much of this debate is forward-looking and positive, the spectre of unruly children and youth is never far away from any of these discussions, either as part of the rationale for extended schools and community projects, or indeed almost any service for children and families. As a nation, Britain has very divided viewpoints about the nature of the problem and the response to it. So while Marrin (2005), in one of the opening quotations above, might advocate a degree of force and smacking as a way of controlling the behaviour of children and young people, she is at the same time at pains (elsewhere in this article) to explain that she is not an advocate of corporal punishment. Marrin is, however, part of a common popular perspective – those who think 'something must be done' and that some children and young people are out of control. A logical consequence of the evidence about early aggressive behaviour might be very early intervention. However, Sereny (2005) expresses shock at the possibility of early behavioural screening of children in nursery school, a proposal that focuses on identifying aggressive and bullying behaviour. Certainly the latter idea is likely to make many people feel uncomfortable because of the age of the children, although it could be equally presented as an attempt at 'nipping problems in the bud' (James, 2005). We do know much more now about risk factors for various adverse outcomes: they are remarkably similar whether we are looking at aggressive behaviour, problems in school or in relationships with others, and criminality. However, we also know that risk factors are not causal mechanisms. Indeed, we also know that 'labelling' can have adverse consequences. In other words, contemporary perspectives are somewhat conflicted, although they do share continuities with the kinds of historical debates that we noted in Chapter 1. One of the things we highlighted at the end of the last chapter was the growing understanding about the way children in a lot of trouble tend to have needs that cross service-sector boundaries. Often the families of these children also have their own complex and cross-sector needs. This understanding has led to the increasing focus on inter-agency and multi-agency work, as well as to the development of children's services departments.

Joined-up Government, Joined-up Service Delivery?

The recognition that many perennial social problems, such as children in trouble, were intractable through single agencies led to the coining of the phrase 'joined-up government' (Cabinet Office, 1999, p. 5). Reforms to make government more joined-up are not new features of public policy (Cope and Goodship, 1999), but previous attempts have been dogged by problems linked to the structure of government itself, particularly the separation of departments and allocation of budgets to them. A key problem is links across departments.

The contemporary push towards more joined-up government can be distinguished from earlier attempts in that it involves a 'move away from coordination through hierarchy or competition and towards networks and partnerships', and represents 'a more explicit focus on partnership as a way of governing' (Newman, 2001, pp. 104–5). New forms of 'partnership' between public service delivery agencies were developed in the 1980s and 1990s, mostly at the local level. Multifaceted social problems prompted many local authorities to work with other delivery agencies (no longer located exclusively in the public sector, but also increasingly to be found in the private and voluntary sectors) to provide public services better tailored to meet local needs. These developing partnerships, however, encountered several barriers which limited the extent to which effective collaboration and co-operation were achieved. Barriers included diverse organisational and professional cultures, vested interests, short-termism, and the sheer complexity of resolving some problems (Hambleton *et al.*, 1996).

An important influence in the argument for more 'joined-up government' and service delivery for young people in trouble was the Audit Commission (1996) report *Misspent Youth*. The Audit Commission was established to promote economy, efficiency and effectiveness in public services and, as such, represents another of the contemporary favourites in social policy – the influence of managerialism.[1] The Audit Commission has been influential in the picture presented on the scale of youth crime, the connection with deprived areas, wasted resources and the barriers and misunderstandings between agencies working with young offenders. The solutions suggested by the earlier reports emphasised crime prevention through a range of types of community-based support, such as parenting programmes and more support for schools to help them keep difficult pupils, as well as community safety strategies.

The Audit Commission has emphasised the particular problem of persistent young offenders and observed that young males were not 'growing out' of offending behaviour as they used to. However, Audit Commission reports about youth justice have been criticised for their use of their own surveys to back up assertions made, rather than more detailed research, and for their 'cavalier use of statistics' (D. Jones, 2001, p. 364), as well as for the lack of explanation as to how estimates of costs to the public service were made. Undoubtedly the early reports helped provide the rationale for the change in the system brought about by the Crime and Disorder Act 1998 and Youth Justice and Criminal Evidence Act 1999, as well as the increased emphasis on performance targets.

A later review of the reformed Youth Justice System by the Audit Commission (2004) concludes overall that the new system is a considerable improvement on the old one. This report, in effect, indicates that 'something is being done' and that it is being done more quickly. The proportion of young offenders reporting that 'nothing happened' to them after they were caught by the police has reduced: from one in four in 2001 to one in ten in 2003. In January 1997 the average time between arrest and sentence was 142 days; by August 2001 it had been halved to 71 days. There are other indications within this report of improvements, many of them related to performance management targets. However, in terms of levels of offending the Audit Commission (2004) concludes that things have remained stable, taking into account self-reported offending. There appears to have been a slight fall in reconviction rates or those given alternatives such as Final Warnings, Reparation Orders and Action Plan Orders. The number of young people in the secure estate[2] has remained fairly stable since 1997, at around 3,000 at any one time. A key issue remains making possible the provision of constructive activities and addressing the multiple needs of young offenders.

The Children's Fund was set up in 2000 to finance new projects working with children aged 5–13 and their families. The Children's Fund provides for a range of preventative projects and represents new money in this area. It aims to bridge the gap between *Sure Start* (0–4-year-olds) and *Connexions* (13–19-year-olds). Behaviour Improvement Projects (BIPs) and Behaviour and Education Support Teams (BESTs) focus on support for schools, through a variety of partnerships, programmes and projects. The crime prevention agenda is explicit, with BIPs including police officers working directly with schools in crime hotspots. Concepts such as 'hate crime' are coming to be used in relation to bullying and discriminatory behaviour from children in school. The Youth Justice System, and specifically Youth Offending Teams (YOTs), work with children who have already been convicted or cautioned for a criminal offence.

Other services might be better described as having the overall objective of promoting social inclusion, as in Youth Inclusion Programmes (YIPs) – and Connexions. Connexions is a service which has been available to all young people since April 2003, although personal advisers are focused on the most vulnerable children and young people. Looked-after children and children with disabilities have access to the service up to the age of 25. Connexions is a partnership of organisations which provide access to support, information, advice and guidance; specifically on careers, education and training. The service aims to bring together all existing available services to help and support young people.

By 2005 a range of new services and umbrella organisations had been established, working with children living in poverty and need, or considered to be 'at risk'. Some were clearly already 'in trouble'. All incorporate either inter-agency work (work that includes work across agencies, e.g. Safer Schools Partnerships) or involve multi-agency (work that involves the input of a range of agencies, e.g. Children's Fund projects) or multi-professional working (where the service or team is made up of people of different professional backgrounds, e.g. Sure Start or Youth Offending Teams). The overlap in concern between poverty and need/risk and trouble is very apparent, as is the explicit encroachment of the crime prevention agenda into the world of welfare.

Co-ordination and information-sharing are key to the development of these services. Indeed, the lack of both has been a finding of all the major inquiries into child deaths, as in the Victoria Climbié case. Preventative strategies now include an emphasis on improved systems for information-sharing about vulnerable children and young people aged 0–19.

Poverty and Social Exclusion

The historical interconnection between social and economic inequalities and children in trouble was noted in Chapter 1. Contemporary political debate reconceptualises poverty and inequality as social exclusion. Social exclusion can be defined as a shorthand label for what can happen when individuals or areas suffer from a combination of problems that include unemployment, poor housing, high crime levels, poor health, high levels of family breakdown, a low skill base and low incomes for those in work (Hayden, 2001). The connection to locality quickly linked action to tackle social exclusion with neighbourhood renewal (SEU, 2001). The specific links between disorder, crime and general neighbourhood decline were highlighted in New Labour thinking while still in opposition (Straw and Michael, 1996). Thus what was once the domain of social welfare has become redefined in terms of the potential contribution to crime control (Hughes *et al.*, 2002). A Social Exclusion Unit (SEU) was established in December 1997 and a report on school exclusion and truancy was the focus of the first report (SEU, 1998). Excluded young people were also the first to be targeted through the New Deal programme for the young unemployed.

With this focus on social exclusion youth work has increasingly concentrated on specific groups of young people, rather than on the provision of a universal service. *Transforming Youth Work* (DfES, 2002b) has changed the broader educational tradition of youth work to one that is strongly connected to the management of problematic youth, promoting social inclusion and working in ways that are more accountable to performance management targets. Youth work has become closely associated and integrated with the Connexions service focus of managing transitions to the labour market.

Although MacDonald and Marsh (2001) are critical of the concept of social exclusion, saying that its meaning remains open to interpretation, they nevertheless state they believe that it is of some worth because of its emphasis on processes, how circumstances operate over time and also because locality is recognised as important. In short, the concept offers a general metaphor that is understood to describe the sets of circumstances that young people might face in poor areas. Young (2002) is also critical, warning of the dangers of using the social exclusion concept in that it can carry with it a series of false binaries, ignoring the problems of the included majority. So while problems might well be concentrated in particular areas, locations or social groups, they are not exclusive to them. Furthermore, viable 'solutions' to the problems of unemployment may well be drug dealing and engaging in the hidden economy, rather than becoming one of the working poor. Yet by choosing these alternatives, the solution becomes one of the problems identified by the Social Exclusion Unit (Young, 2002).

'Education, education, education' is often quoted to emphasise the three top priorities of the incoming Blair government in 1997. Education is viewed as a critical vehicle in countering social exclusion and creating an opportunity society. Targets were set by the 1997 Labour government for a one-third reduction in both truancy and exclusion from school by September 2002. A plethora of programmes that broadly interrelated on the issue of fighting social exclusion through educational initiatives were linked to achieving these targets. Many of these initiatives cut across an already complex system of targets and priorities at school level, and are widely acknowledged to have led to initiative overload as well as an increase to teacher workloads (Watkins, 2004).

In 1999 the *Social Inclusion Pupil Support* (SIPS) guidance was introduced which, in an effort at 'joined-up government', was endorsed by the SEU, the Home Office and the Department of Health, as well as the Department for Education and Employment (DfEE, 1999). This guidance represented the early expectations that explicit procedures, inter-agency co-operation and pastoral support for 'at-risk' pupils was the way to reduce exclusion from school. However, the resources to do what was suggested were not immediately available, and a great deal of resentment was generated in schools at a time when concerns about teacher recruitment and retention were increasing (Gillen, 2002). A series of amendments to the guidance and a consultation exercise were undertaken so that by 2002 a more conciliatory tone towards schools was in evidence. In essence this change in emphasis can be seen as a response to pressures from teaching unions; it reinforced head teachers' powers to exclude pupils for a first-time offence such as carrying a weapon, serious actual or threatened violence, sexual misconduct, or supplying an illegal drug. Persistent and defiant behaviour, including bullying, is similarly seen as reasonable grounds for exclusion.

Victims and Perpetrators

The foundations to contemporary debates about children in trouble are well documented. Repeat offenders who appeared to be 'getting away with it' led to headlines about 'Spiderboy' and 'Ratboy' in the 1990s and the well-rehearsed arguments about the unruly and 'anti-social' children of the underclass from sink estates, and so on. Between 1991 and 1992, 13 violent disturbances were recorded: 12 of these occurred in social housing estates, and involved groups of young men clashing with the police in chaotic street battles. All the areas had been part of major government programmes before the disturbances. Young men attacked and destroyed shops, community facilities and the improved amenities that had been built up, often with the dedicated involvement of local community leaders (Power and Tunstall, 1997). These 'disturbances' helped lay the foundations of increasing concern about 'disorder' and the connection with disadvantage and locality.

Specific events have received extensive media coverage and popular analysis. In particular, some of the images generated have become emblematic of dangerous and 'evil' children who are out of control. The CCTV camera-still of the abduction of James Bulger (1993) from a shopping centre by two 10-year-old boys, who were truanting from school at the time, is particularly memorable. The murder of head teacher Philip Lawrence (1995) at the school gates, by a 15-year-old so-called 'gang leader' from another school, helped create another unsafe space. CCTV footage of Damilola Taylor (2000) presented a picture of a child on his way home from school before he was stabbed and killed. The stabbing and death of 14-year-old Luke Walmsley (2003) by a fellow pupil brought fatal attacks into the school corridor of a rural secondary school.

An alternative series of events, however, would show children as victims of adults, as in the Dunblane killings (1996), in which 16 primary-school children and their teacher were shot by a local man and former scout leader; or the machete attack on a nursery teacher and her class in 1996. The torture and slow death of Victoria Climbié (2000) was particularly influential in leading to the development of the Green Paper, *Every Child Matters*. The murder of Holly Wells and Jessica Chapman by their school caretaker in the school summer holidays of 2002 led to renewed emphasis on Criminal Records Bureau checks for people working with children. In all, the latter events have contributed to our heightened concerns about risks *to* children.

Young people are more likely to be victims of crime, compared with adults. Numerous sources of evidence illustrate this situation. Overall Youth Justice Board (YJB) self-report data on young people aged 11–16 show that they are about twice as likely to be victimised as people over 16, as indicated by the British Crime Survey (BCS) (NACRO, 2003). We will return to this evidence in more depth in Chapter 3. In explaining why young people are more likely than adults to be victims, NACRO (2003) puts forward two key explanations. First, young people are physically immature and so often less able to defend themselves from attack, in comparison with adults. Secondly, they have less choice about with whom they associate – in that they have little control over where they live or go to school. Indeed, MORI (2004) has shown, in the surveys conducted for the YJB, that school is where many young people are victimised, a theme we will return to in Chapter 5.

The conflicting picture of young people as both perpetrators and victims is a recurring theme throughout all the literature dealing with children in trouble. Overlying these different forms of evidence about the scale and nature of the issue is the influence of the media.

Populist Punitiveness

Newburn (2002) argues that there was already a noticeable change in the general tenor of official concern about juvenile offending in the early 1990s, before the key event that the Bulger killing came to be. There was also a renewal of concern about pupil behaviour in school – notably due to the publication of the first national statistics on school exclusion (DfE, 1992). The connections between Thompson and Venables being out of school (truanting) at the time they abducted James Bulger in February 1993 resonated with and amplified a popular belief that children were out of control and that the authorities were doing little about it. One of the opening quotations to this chapter exemplifies the view that 'populist punitiveness' typifies contemporary responses to children in trouble. As a concept, popular punitiveness is based on the claim that it is one of the main components of sentencing and penal policy, alongside concerns about human rights, community and managerialist imperatives (Matthews, 2005). It is easy to find examples to support this view – notably the overall increase in the number of children in young offenders institutions since the early 1990s and the use of Anti-Social Behaviour Orders (ASBOs) and Acceptable Behaviour Contracts (ABCs). ASBOs in particular have been characterised as 'that emblem of punitive populism' (Burney, 2002, p. 469) and as 'the modern equivalent of the stocks' (CRAE, 2004, p. 7).

Talk from both Labour and Conservative politicians about 'zero tolerance' of various behaviours presented by young people is common. However, it is equally possible to find more liberal responses in the numerous Youth Inclusion Support Panels (YISPs) and in services like Connexions. Matthews (2005) queries the extent to which the reality of policy development in crime and justice differs from the political rhetoric and the near-consensus among academics that policy and practice in this field are indeed 'punitive'. Rather than simply seeing policy and practice in relation to crime as punitive overall, Matthews argues that this is a one-sided view. Reality is more complex. Instead, the diverse, uneven and contradictory nature of responses to troublesome behaviour, whether criminal or not, is a more realistic account. This is also what a democracy is about – people do not agree about the appropriate response.

Risk and Fear

We have already touched on the notion of risk factors in Chapter 1. We will now explore the concept of risk a little further in terms of the way it is increasingly used and understood in contemporary society and, specifically, we note how it relates to fear *of* and *for* young people and their behaviour in public. It is hard for anybody in contemporary society to be unaware of the presence and potential of risk and to feel sometimes fearful of, sometimes fearful about young people. We are constantly made aware of the possible risks we might be taking, or the consequences of the risks taken by others. This not only serves to help create a generalised sense of worry, even fear, but also clearly locates the responsibility with individuals and families. Individuals take risks, so individuals can be held responsible. Risk assessments of individuals, families, working environments and events (such as school trips) are the norm. This can be both restrictive and misleading: restrictive in that 'taking risks' becomes implicitly something to worry about, rather than a normal feature of human activity; misleading in that it can fuel belief that we can eliminate risk. Further, Taite (1995) has argued that at-risk discourses provide a rationale for regulating a potentially endless list of behaviours and dispositions of young people that may be worrying or offensive to others.

Fearfulness might seem the obvious and logical corollary to an increased awareness of risk. Certainly, fear of crime and anti-social behaviour specifically has increased in prominence since the early 1990s, in terms of government recognition of the issues and the way they tend to resonate with the population at large. These issues also delight the national media which, in turn, help to influence popular perception of the issues. An increasingly strict regulatory framework is apparent that attempts to set controls on anti-social behaviour, alongside attempts to foster a greater capacity in the most affected communities to address these issues themselves. Altheide (2002) argues that a key element in the contemporary discourse of fear involves images of children and actions towards and by children. He notes that this discourse of fear is so widespread that it often replaces parallel terms such as concern or worry. Fear about and for children operates as a common perspective or way of talking about and referring to children in the public domain. Altheide differentiates between 'altruistic fear' for those you love, or for whom you are responsible, and fear as a social narrative, that is less specific, more generalised and encompassing. It can be argued that fear is also a powerful form of social control in that 'directing fear in a society is tantamount to controlling that society' (Altheide, 2002, p. 247).

It has become commonplace in recent years to associate incivilities in public places and fear of crime with the activities of young people. Loader *et al.* (1998), in conducting an 'ethnography of anxiety' in an English 'middletown', illustrate some of the complexities that may be behind this perception of young people. They illustrate different perceptions of the issue in the same place, related both to age as well as the level of connection and expectations of place. Older long-term residents with a greater investment of self in the place tended to be more critical of the public behaviour of young people. Young professionals whose reference points were not as strongly connected to place were able to be more 'matter-of-fact' about the situation. There was also a sense among some residents that by buying into a more expensive small town, away from the problems of the city, they had also bought themselves out of the latter problems. Thus incivilities in such a place were a greater affront. Interestingly, Loader *et al.* (1998) did not discover a harsh exclusionary response to teenage incivilities from the adults in their study; a viewpoint often demonstrated by the media and politicians. What adults seemed to want was young people who were willing to live by adult rules and prescriptions. This latter desire can be interpreted as ultimately about adult power and control and the presumption that adults should set the rules by which young people live. This is the uneasy tension of most adult–child/young person relationships, but on a larger scale. Loader *et al.* (1998) found that when adults actually met young people in structured debate within their research study, there was a tendency to see them as different in some way (as 'good kids') to distinguish them from the 'other' young people (not present at the meeting) who were viewed as troublemakers. They conclude that people respond in more complex ways to events in which they are personally implicated, in comparison with those about which they are more abstractly aware, reminding us that the dominant discourse about young people presented by the media and politicians may only be shared in the abstract by the general public, rather than in the specific sense.

For young people themselves there can be varying accounts and perspectives on how they perceive risk and negotiate their environments. Taite (1995) argues that young people are experiencing a heightened sense of risk. However, Green *et al.* (2000, p. 121) show in their study of 'Townville' that 'risk, danger and pleasure were interwoven within many young men's lives'. In this context an element of danger was important, providing excitement and an alternative to boredom, while Cahill (2000) writes about how young people in urban areas have a highly developed sense of negotiating their environment, for which she uses the term 'street literacy'.

Crime, Disorder and the New Youth Justice

The focus on 'disorder' as well as crime was an increasing feature of 1990s social policy. The Crime and Disorder Act received royal assent in July 1998. The central thrust of this Act in relation to young people relates to crime prevention, reducing delays in the system, setting up multi-disciplinary teams in the form of YOTs and creating a series of new orders, including ASBOs, reparation orders, action plan orders, supervision orders, detention and training orders, drug testing and training orders, and parenting orders. The YJB was created in 1999, as a non-departmental public body to oversee the youth justice system, which comprises YOTs, custodial institutions, youth courts and the police. Key to the performance targets for YOTs is preventing crime and fear of crime, as well as reducing offending (Audit Commission, 2004).

The Youth Justice and Criminal Evidence Act 1999 followed. It comprises two parts. Part One deals with referrals to youth offender panels and Part

Two deals with the giving of evidence for the purposes of criminal proceedings. The Referral Order is established as the standard sentence imposed by the Youth Court, or a Magistrates' Court, for children who have been convicted of an offence for the first time. Children who plead guilty to an offence must be referred by the court to a Youth Offender Panel (YOP) unless the sentence is fixed by law, or the court imposes a custodial sentence, or the court deals with the case by means of absolute discharge. Children who have been previously bound over in criminal proceedings, together with those who have been conditionally discharged by the court, will be treated as having a previous conviction and will not be eligible for the new sentence.

YOTs are responsible for YOPs. Children are referred to YOPs for a period of between three and twelve months, and YOPs have to establish a programme of behaviour with which the child must comply. The programme should be informed by restorative justice principles of restoration, reintegration and responsibility. Typical components of a 'programme of behaviour' may include reporting conditions to persons or places, prohibition from association with specified persons and/or places, specified activities to address behaviour, unpaid work as a service to the community, and so on.

Some criticisms of the Referral Order focus on the issue of proportionality, legal safeguards and contracts. In relation to proportionality the issue is whether the wide-ranging powers available to a YOP are proportionate to a child convicted of one offence. There is no legal representation at the YOP, and children as young as 10 are required to sign a contract agreeing to the programme of behaviour it specifies. The ethics and justice of this have been questioned (Goldson, 2000a). Muncie (2004) has also outlined criticisms about the coercive nature of some aspects of restorative justice, the problems of low rates of victim participation and the lack of resources to enable offenders to become stakeholders in community life following this approach.

Extending Controls on Anti-social Behaviour

We discussed some of the definitional issues of anti-social behaviour in Chapter 1. The Home Office definition of anti-social behaviour can be seen as a response to a more generalised concern about 'disorder' and the specific perception of the connection to young people with public places. For example, the BCS found that 22 per cent of respondents perceived a high level of disorder in their neighbourhood, with a third (33 per cent) citing teenagers 'hanging around' the streets as a big problem (Home Office, 2004). The Home Office definition of anti-social behaviour is important. Some of the behaviour viewed as 'anti-social' according to the Home Office and viewed as problematic by respondents to the BCS is not criminal, yet ASBOs can be served on children committing 'nuisance' activities from the age of 10. Breach of an ASBO is a criminal offence. These orders have been available since

April 1999 and are used for adults as well as young people. The most common types of behaviour for which ASBOs have been served are 'general loutish[3] and unruly conduct such as verbal abuse, harassment, assault, graffiti and excessive noise' (Home Office, 2003, p. 11). The Children's Rights Alliance for England (CRAE, 2004) estimates that 81 children were imprisoned following the breach of an ASBO between June 2000 and December 2002. Many of these imprisonments arising from breaches of ASBOs related to behaviour that would not otherwise have met the seriousness threshold for custody (CRAE, 2004, p. 48).

ABCs have created another tier in the system since 2003: they constitute 'a written agreement between a person who has been involved in anti-social behaviour and one or more agencies whose role it is to prevent such behaviour' (Home Office, 2003, p. 52). ABCs are designed for young people (10–18) and they can be effected more quickly and cheaply than ASBOs (Stephen and Squires, 2003). It is advocated that the ABC should be well publicised among young people, in particular within schools. Information from the education service about truancy and school exclusion is explicitly cited as a potential source of evidence when identifying individuals for ABCs. Stephen and Squires (2003, p. 11) note that 'not only can almost any behaviour potentially be regarded as "anti-social" but there is a much lower standard of proof; a situation that can be viewed as criminalisation by stealth'. That is, as some of the behaviour which is the focus of ASBOs and ABCs is not criminal, the process could be argued to be having a 'net-widening' effect of bringing young people who would not previously have been in this situation into the criminal justice system.

In January 2003, the Home Office created its own Anti-Social Behaviour Unit (ASBU), quickly followed by the White Paper *Respect and Responsibility* (two important watchwords in the ensuing debate), leading to the Anti-Social Behaviour Act 2003. This Act extended existing sanctions such as ASBOs, parenting orders and child curfews. This extension of existing controls and, indeed, the prominence given to the issue by enacting legislation give an indication of the level of concern. Indeed, the importance attached to addressing anti-social behaviour has been described by one Labour politician as 'nothing less than a war for civilisation as we know it' (Field, 2003, p. 18). For example, parenting contracts allow local authorities or school-governing bodies to enter into voluntary contracts with parents whose child is truanting from school, or is excluded because of their behaviour. If parents refuse to engage with a contract this can result in a formal parenting order. The remit of parenting orders has been extended so that they can be issued at an earlier stage, for example, before a young person has appeared in court. LEA and school staff can issue parents with fixed-penalty notices which entail a fine, if parents do not take action to address their child's truancy. The reduction in numbers defined as a 'public assembly' (down from 20 or more to 2 or more) or a 'rave' (down from 100 or more to 20 or more) is seen as controversial in its extension of police powers into smaller groupings. The police are also given the power to enact child curfews by returning children to their homes at night (Callaghan, 2004).

By 2003 it was estimated that around 60 per cent of ASBOs were for juveniles. The focus of concern about anti-social behaviour had already become predominantly about controlling the behaviour of young people and parental responsibility. It is common for ASBOs to be accompanied by publicity about the individuals, including the use of photographs and details of past behaviour and current restrictions on their behaviour. The consequences of these actions are debated, with some commentators being of the view that ASBOs are likely to be a badge of honour in some communities or for some individuals; rather than (as intended) something that might induce shame and remorse. Criticisms of the increasing focus on anti-social behaviour and young people are numerous. They include the pseudo-legality of parenting contracts, and so on, and the reduction in focus on the welfare aspect of work with young people, as well as the increasing use of publicity we have already noted (Grier and Thomas, 2004). With regard to the latter, Grier and Thomas have noted that the 'publicity attendant upon young people who are anti-social and receive Anti-Social Behaviour Orders is greater than that accorded those who appear in the Youth Court on straight charges of criminality' (p. 14).

Every Child Matters and *Youth Matters* Too

Every Child Matters (DfES, 2003a) continues the themes already highlighted: reducing poverty and social exclusion, developing the role of schools, inter-agency co-operation, early intervention and a strong emphasis on supporting the role of parents and carers. Although *Every Child Matters* emerged from the Laming enquiry into the child protection system and how it operated prior to and surrounding the death of 8-year-old Victoria Climbié in February 2000, its remit is much broader than this. In 2001 a National Service Framework was announced for children, to set in place standards against which services would be inspected. Responsibility for children's social services was transferred from the Department of Health to the DfES in 2003, making the explicit link between child welfare and broader issues of education and skills.

Five key outcomes for all children are listed at the beginning of *Every Child Matters*. These are:

> *Being healthy* – enjoying good physical and mental health and living a healthy lifestyle.
> *Staying safe* – being protected from harm and neglect and growing up able to look after themselves.

Enjoying and achieving – getting the most out of life and developing broad skills for adulthood.

Making a positive contribution – to the community and to society and not engaging in anti-social or offending behaviour.

Economic well-being – overcoming socioeconomic disadvantages to achieve their full potential in life. (Para 1.3)

The rest of the document focuses mainly on children most at risk, within a framework of universal services and the rights and responsibilities agenda.

The thrust of proposals is around multi-disciplinary teams carrying out assessments under a common framework co-located around schools, Sure Start centres and primary care. Schools are the focus as universal support centres, and education is the main principle around which children's services are organised. The location of a Ministry for Children, Young People and Families within the DfES further emphasises the centrality of education in the overall plan; arguably underlining the link between supporting children and families and between the economy and productivity, the connections being that education is the basis to employability, employability is the route out of poverty, and this, in turn, reduces crime. The aim is for information to be stored and accessed electronically by a range of agencies, based on national standards capable of interaction with other datasets. *Every Child Matters* has been seen as 'the biggest shake-up of statutory children's services since the Seebohm Report of the 1960s' (Williams, 2004, p. 406).

The Children Act 2004 provides the legislative spine for the wider strategy for improving children's lives. The Act sets out to be enabling rather than prescriptive, so that local authorities have a considerable amount of flexibility in the way they implement its provisions. The overall aim is to encourage integrated planning, commissioning and delivery of services as well as to improve multi-disciplinary working, remove duplication, increase accountability and improve the coordination of individual and joint inspections in local authorities (DH, 2005). While the specifics of this vision are likely to be more complex, these ideals seem to make sense at the strategic level.

Youth Matters (DfES, 2005a) sets out to build on *Every Child Matters*, focusing on 'teenagers'. Following the format of its predecessor, this Green Paper sets out four key issues, referred to as 'challenges': they are easy to agree with but will also mean more service reform, pilot programmes and developments. The four key challenges are:

Engaging young people in *positive activities.*

Encouraging more young people to *volunteer and become involved* in their communities.

Providing better *information, advice and guidance* to young people.

Providing better and more *personalised intensive support* for young people with serious problems or who are in trouble.

Youth Matters starts out as a very upbeat and positive document and is, like *Every Child Matters*, directed at services and opportunities for all young people, while also recognising that some will need much more intensive support.

Children's Rights

'Children's rights' were once described as a slogan in search of a definition (Rodham, 1973). Indeed there are very different strands of thinking about what 'children's rights' actually means. A protectionist approach sees adults as the guardians or protectors of children' rights with some writers suggesting that children have the right to autonomous parents and no state interference in their family life. The liberationist approach is radical and based on the idea that children need to be empowered and given more autonomy. Pragmatists have attempted to establish a compromise between these two extremes, emphasising the need to ensure children have the opportunity to express their views, participate and know how to get help when they need it.

Land (2004) outlines the different forms children's rights can take: *welfare rights*, which involve the protection from abuse or neglect from carers, as well as the rights to education, medical care, and so on – and *freedom rights* – which involve the assertion of the child's own autonomy. However, alongside these rights are the limits set by the state and the notion of what is 'in the child's best interests' – a judgement made by adults. Minow (1996) concludes that because both the state and parents are interested in controlling and guiding children, the notion of children's individual rights is limited.

Nevertheless, the recognition that children do have individual rights (and responsibilities) is an important principle informing the way we think about how to respond to children in trouble. The UK is a signatory, along with over 190 other countries, to the Convention on the Rights of the Child, which was adopted by the UN General Assembly in November 1989. The Human Rights Act 1998 is primarily concerned with guaranteeing respect for civil and political rights, and there are few mentions of children's rights specifically. However, there are a number of important issues that do impinge more specifically on children in trouble and their families:

Article 2   (First Protocol) guarantees the right to education;
Article 3   prohibits torture, inhuman and degrading treatment or
            punishment;
Article 6   guarantees the right to a fair and public hearing;
Article 8   guarantees the right to respect for private and family life.

There is increased emphasis on the role of the state in protecting children from abuse, with more possibilities of claims of negligence where the state fails to fulfil its duties. Yet Kilkelly (2001, p. 2) concludes that the Human Rights Act is 'unlikely to change dramatically the way children are treated in the legal system'.

The Children Act 2004 established a Children's Commissioner for England. Unlike Commissioners in the rest of the UK, the English Children's Commissioner must 'promote awareness of the views and interests of children, rather than protect their rights' (CRAE, 2004, p. 6). Areas in which the CRAE is particularly critical about England's record include the high rate of child imprisonment, deaths in custody, high levels of physical restraint for children in custody, child imprisonment for breaches of ASBOs, the continued sanctioning of physical punishment by parents (usually referred to as 'smacking', the treatment of asylum-seeking children, school exclusion and segregated education, and child poverty.

Land (2004, p. 66) writes of 'the fundamental tension between children's and parents' rights and responsibilities'. As a society we want parents to fulfil their responsibilities but we also want to ensure that children have fundamental rights. We want to instil a sense of responsibility in children and achieve a balance between the rights of parents and the expectations of that role from the state. These tensions are especially highlighted in relation to certain key issues – such as physical punishment, child curfews, ABCs and ASBOs, as well as school attendance. We will return to these issues elsewhere in the book. Physical punishment is a particular case in point in terms of how different cultures draw the line between the rights of children and parents and the point at which the state might intervene. Physical punishment of children by parents in Sweden has been illegal for over twenty years and is illegal in other European countries as well.

Children as Investments, Children as Threats and Children as Victims

Skevik (2003) has characterised contemporary political debates about children in the following way: 'children as investments, children as threats and children as victims' (p. 426). Children patently are our investment in the future and we are understandably concerned that as a society we do the best to invest in them as the future. However, there is a sharp divide between those individual children who have the advantage of optimal investment made in them in all respects and those who do not. More recently, this concept of 'investment' has been characterised as part of the 'social investment state' (Lister, 2003) in which investment in children is an investment in the 'citizen-worker of the future' and is achieved by a combination of anti-poverty strategies and educational measures. The notion of partnership between the state and families, as well as between business, voluntary and statutory service sectors in relation to children and families is part of this overall strategy.

We should also remember that the key concern for many is about boys and young men – they are proportionately more likely than girls and young women to get into trouble in various contexts because of their behaviour. Girls outperform boys at school and are less likely to be excluded because of their behaviour. Although they are probably equally likely to find themselves in conflict with their peers and others, they appear to more often resolve situations without aggression. Yet girls and women are more worried about victimisation. Research by Frosh *et al.* (2002) on young masculinities demonstrates that teenage boys are acutely aware of being seen as socially and educationally problematic and of being disparaged by adults. It is young men who are most often seen as the main source of threat, although they are also the most likely to be victimised in terms of recorded crime. However, the picture of the nature and prevalence of different types of victimisation experienced by boys and girls becomes more complex when we start to look at specific forms of child abuse or bullying in schools, for example. There are also some important differences in the experiences of minority ethnic groups.

While there is a discernible and often progressive vision in the attempts in contemporary policy to increase opportunity for those in poor areas and circumstances, the politics of making this happen is pragmatic. Children in the worst circumstances are victims of these circumstances to some extent; they are also potential threats, as the disaffected and troublesome youth of the future. Sound political judgement from all political parties is likely to agree to a large degree about this. It is in the question of where and how to invest in the future and respond in the present that the specific political and policy questions arise. Chapter 3 will look at estimates of the scale, nature and needs indicated by evidence about children in trouble.

Notes

1   *Managerialism* is the process through which the public sector has become subjected to regimes predicated on efficiency, value for money, performance targets, auditing, quality of service monitoring and an expectation that they should be consumer-responsive (Loader and Sparks, 2002, p. 88).

2   The *secure estate* is an amalgam of institutions (see Chapter 3 for more details) in which some children are incarcerated after being convicted of a criminal offence. A minority, in Local Authority Secure Children's Homes (LASCHs), are there for welfare reasons.

3   A *lout* has been defined as an ill-mannered, aggressive or awkward man or youth, and *loutish* as awkward, ill-mannered and coarse (*Chambers Concise Dictionary*). Note the assumptions and meaning of the term in relation to antisocial behaviour (ASB).

3

Children in Trouble – What Kind of Trouble?

It is crucial not to demonise children ... There are issues of behaviour that need to be addressed but the vast majority of children are as supportive, idealistic and inspirational as young people have ever been.

– Sir Alan Steer, leader of the school disciplinary task force, quoted in Taylor, 2005, para. 7

Children often don't view themselves as victims of crime, they seem to be resigned to it and think it's just the way life is. They develop their own strategies for dealing with threat, yet they feel adults rarely listen to their suggestions about how crime could be prevented.

– Howard League, 2002, para. 4

Before long we began to hear about cases of children with learning difficulties receiving ASBOs which appeared to take no account of the fact that the child's condition was directly responsible for their behaviour.

– Bright, 2005a, p. 7

Estimating the Number and Proportion of Different Types of 'Trouble'

The information presented in this chapter sets out to look at the official records that indicate various levels of 'trouble' in a young person's life, as well as evidence from self-report studies and other types of survey. It is important when looking at any of this evidence to be clear about sources and the generalisability of the data, and it should be noted that much of this evidence is regularly updated, often annually. All government departments and organisations like the Youth Justice Board (YJB) have websites where annual statistics are made available, so it is easy to get up-to-date information and often past statistics as well. There is no shortage of data. For example, YJB statistics give us a very specific picture of the nature of detected offending and the response to these offences. The YJB has also commissioned a number of youth surveys in which the experiences of 11–16-year-olds in mainstream schools and 11–17-year-olds in education projects and facilities for those excluded from school are compared (see, for example, MORI, 2004). The Home Office undertook a survey of offending, anti-social behaviour and drug use of 10–25-year-olds in 2003: the *Offending, Crime and Justice Survey* (OCJS). This comprises both a longitudinal element which will trace the development, escalation, de-escalation and desistence of these behaviours over time, as well as trends and prevalence. The DfES provides annual statistics on exclusion from school and non-attendance at school, as well as the *Youth Cohort Study* (YCS). The YCS surveys the education, training and work experience of young people and thus gives us a picture of the overall pattern of young people's participation in these areas. The DfES also collates figures on Children in Need[1] and, within this group, those who are looked after and/or on the Child Protection Register (CPR). Statistics from a variety of other agencies (e.g. children's charities such as the NSPCC) present figures and perspectives on trends on whatever aspect of the issue we chose to focus.

However, we should proceed cautiously in the matter of interpreting official statistics as well as self-report surveys. Official statistics are clearly influenced by any changes in decisions about how to report on and respond to children's behaviour. For example, Estrada (2001) writes of the move away from the informal towards more formal controls of aggressive and violent behaviour during the twentieth century, arguing that this accounts in part for the increased levels of recorded violence from young people. Awareness-raising about issues, such as bullying, is likely to lead to increased recognition, detection and reporting of bullying in surveys, and so on. This does not necessarily mean that more bullying is happening. Also, what constitutes 'trouble' is itself not unproblematic, not least because of such disputed concepts as 'anti-social behaviour' but also because of the strong association between being 'troublesome' and being 'troubled'. Some families as a whole cross these latter two categories. The extreme upset and disruption connected to being abused and taken into care can precipitate very difficult behaviour that may be interpreted and responded to in various ways. With these issues in mind, we will now set out to review the evidence about the kind of trouble in which many children find themselves and the relative scale or prevalence of issues that are an indication of the number and proportion of children in trouble.

According to the 2001 Census there were 11.7 million children in England and Wales. Children attending school number some 8.4 million, over half a million of whom are in independent or private schools (582,990). A minority attend special schools (93,880) and Pupil Referral Units, or PRUs (12,010) (DfES, 2005c). As we saw in Chapters 1 and 2, the associations between being 'in need' and being 'in trouble' are well known. One way this can be understood is in relation to risk and protective factors, as presented in Chapter 1. The current chapter ends with a typology of children *and* trouble. The categories in this typology are inevitably fluid, but are designed to give some sense of the proportion of young people who are in different levels of 'trouble' in their lives, at a point in time.

Youth Crime and Victimisation

Youth crime is a problem and young people commit a disproportionate amount of crime. We noted in Chapter 2 that there is widespread concern among adults about youth crime and anti-social behaviour, although most criminals are adults (NACRO, 2004). It is estimated that about 25 per cent of known offenders are under 18. Around 5 per cent of 10–17-year-olds will come into contact with the criminal justice system through arrest for a notifiable offence[2] in a single year (Audit Commission, 2004). Over a quarter of a million (287,883) offences by 10–17-year-olds resulted in a disposal of some sort in 2003–04 (YJB, 2004). The highest proportion (23 per cent) was for motoring offences, followed by theft and handling stolen goods (16.9 per cent) and violence against the person (14.1 per cent). More than four in five offences (83.5 per cent) were committed by males and less than one in five (16.5 per cent) by females; nearly three-quarters are between the ages of 15 and 17. More than four in five (84 per cent) offences are committed by young white people. The ethnicity of 4 per cent of offenders is not known: the rest are of mixed parentage and minority ethnic backgrounds (YJB, 2004).

The way the media treats the issue of youth crime tends to fuel concern that youth crime is getting worse, with their focus on the most extreme cases, street crime and violent crime. Yet overall trends in terms of convictions or cautions (more recently known as reprimands and warnings) of 10–17-year-olds for an indictable offence show a downward trend. They fell from 143,600 to 105,700 from 1992 to 2002, a drop of 36 per cent (NACRO, 2004). The Audit Commission (2004) does note, however, that detection rates have also fallen: from 29 per cent in 1991 to 23 per cent in 2001, although the latter may be due to a tighter definition of 'detection'. Hough and Roberts (2004), in a national survey conducted in 2003, explore public opinion about youth crime and youth justice. They show that people are generally ill-informed about youth crime trends and that their dissatisfaction with the youth justice system reflects this lack of knowledge and the belief that sentences are too lenient. The media focus on the most extreme cases is criticised, as well as the lack of analysis of the issues involved. Most positively, the study highlights the potential for public support for new approaches to sentencing, including restorative justice.

Since April 2000, the YJB has been responsible for commissioning and purchasing all places for 10–17-year-olds committed to custody by the courts. The 'secure estate' consists of three main types of facility: Young Offenders Institutions (YOIs); Secure Training Centres (STCs) and Local Authority Secure Children's Homes (LASCHs). Just under 3,000 children were in these

Table 3.1 Occupancy and provision in the secure estate (October 2004)

Type of facility	Boys (% by type of facility)	Girls (% by type of facility)	Total (% of all facilities)
YOI places	2,612 (96.7)	88 (3.3)	2,700 (84)
LASCH places	182 (77.4)	53 (22.6)	235 (7)
STC places	174 (63.5)	100 (36.5)	274 (9)
Total	2,968 (92.5)	241 (7.5)	3,209 (100)

Source: YJB, 2004.

facilities in a snapshot survey undertaken in 2003, with around 6,000 young people passing through these facilities in a year. About two-thirds are there under a Detention and Training Order (YJB, 2004).

Table 3.1 illustrates the uneven balance between the different types of facility that make up the secure estate, as well as the different balance in the way that facilities are used for boys and girls. More than nine in ten young people in the secure estate are male and they are proportionately more likely to be sent to YOIs than girls. Girls are most likely to go to STCs, followed by LASCHs. The three types of facility are very different environments with different types of facilities and resourcing, notably in relation to expenditure and provision of education (Stephenson *et al.*, 2001). Furthermore, some children placed in LASCHs are there for welfare reasons, rather than because of offending behaviour. Of particular note is the fact that half of the YOIs are on split sites, shared with young adults in prison (YJB, 2004). Both the YJB (2004) and CRAE (2004) highlight the fact that England and Wales make greater use of custody for children than in most industrialised, democratic countries.

Figure 3.1 illustrates the trends in custodial sentences of boys and girls between 1993 and 2003. For both boys and girls the number given custodial sentences has increased overall, with the proportionate increase being greatest with girls – from 114 in 1993 to 424 in 2003, or an almost fourfold increase in custodial sentences. In 1993, 4,109 boys were given custodial sentences and 5,776 in 2003, although the 2003 figure represents a reduction from 6,886 in 2002. Rates of reconviction following time in custody are worse for young people leaving the secure estate than for adults leaving prison: 59 per cent of all prisoners are reconvicted within two years of their release from prison, in comparison with 80 per cent of 14–17-year-olds (NACRO, 2003).

Self-report studies and cross-sectional surveys, such as the annual MORI Youth Survey conducted for the YJB, add a further dimension to the picture. There are also longitudinal self-report studies, such as the Edinburgh study of youth transitions and crime, that add an individual trajectory or pathway to this overall picture. Less frequent studies, such as the *Youth Lifestyles Survey* and

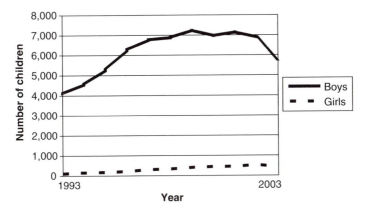

Figure 3.1 Children aged 10–17 given custodial sentences (1993–2003)
Source: From figures in de Silva, 2005, p. 38.

particular Home Office studies, such as *Young People and Crime* (Graham and Bowling, 1995), add further to what we know about the prevalence of particular behaviours and experiences.

Overall we know that offending behaviour is relatively common in young people: well over half admit to at least one offence in self-report studies. Proportions, age groups and timescales vary according to the particular report. For example, East and Campbell (2001) found that 47 per cent of 12–30-year-olds had committed at least one offence; Flood-Page *et al.* (1999) found that 60 per cent of 16–17-year-olds and 66 per cent of 18–20-year-olds admitted to ever having committed an offence. The peak age for offending in 2002 was 19 for males and 15 for females (NACRO, 2004). However, most young people commit relatively low-level offences. Of most interest to policy-makers are the persistent and prolific offenders, around 2 per cent of men and 1 per cent of women, who account for about half of all offences committed (East and Campbell, 2001).

The MORI (2004) survey conducted for the Youth Justice Board comprises samples from two populations: mainstream school pupils aged 11–16 (4,715 pupils in 192 schools) and excluded pupils aged 11–17 attending various special projects and educational provisions (687 young people attending 85 projects). The comparative element in this study is important in that it makes possible the comparison of experiences of young people in mainstream schools and those who have been excluded. It includes questions on fears, victimisation and offending and also questions to do with detection, alcohol and drug use.

Overall, what these studies show is that offending levels are higher among excluded young people, as are levels of victimisation. Excluded young people are more likely to commit very serious offences, such as breaking and entering, carrying weapons, fire-setting, TWOC (taking a vehicle without the owner's

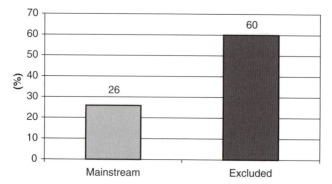

Figure 3.2 Offending levels – young people of school age
Source: Developed from figures in MORI, 2004.

consent), robbery, beating up or hurting people sufficiently for them to require medical treatment, and so on. Interestingly, excluded young people feel safer at their educational project than do their counterparts in mainstream schools, and a smaller proportion report victimisations occurring in the educational settings they attend. Excluded young people are more likely to experience victimisation outside these settings, in comparison with young people in mainstream schools. Excluded young people are less likely to report fears and worries about victimisation, in comparison with mainstream pupils. Offenders are more likely to be victims, but less likely to be concerned about the possibility (MORI, 2004, p. 52). The Home Office survey of 10–25-year-olds found that around a quarter (26 per cent) of children and young people admitted to one of 20 types of offence in a one-year period, with 8 per cent committing an offence six or more times. Two per cent were classified as frequent serious offenders, committing a more serious offence[3] at least six times in the preceding year (Budd *et al.*, 2005, p. I).

Within this overall picture there are important differences in the proportion of offenders who are male or female or from different ethnic groups. Girls are less likely to offend: one in five girls (20 per cent) in mainstream schools reported committing an offence in the previous 12 months, compared with just under a third (31 per cent) of boys. Nearly half (48 per cent) of excluded girls admitted committing an offence in the previous 12 months, compared with two-thirds (65 per cent) of excluded boys. In mainstream schools, a higher proportion (37 per cent) of black pupils report having committed an offence, compared with either white (26 per cent) or Asian (20 per cent) pupils. The number of minority ethnic young people in the exclusion comparison group is too small to draw conclusions (MORI, 2004, p. 15).

As we already noted in Chapter 2, young people are more likely to be the victim of crime, compared with adults, although estimates vary according to the nature of the population sampled, the age range and the types of victimisations included. The data in Table 3.2 come from nationally representative surveys,

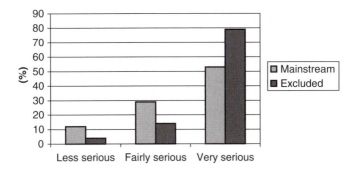

Figure 3.3 Severity of offence (offending pupils in mainstream schools compared with offending excluded pupils)
Source: Developed from figures in MORI, 2004.

Table 3.2 Victimisation – comparing adults and young people of secondary-school age

Group	% victimised in a year
Adults in BCS	24
11–16-year-olds in school in MORI survey	49
11–17-year-olds excluded from school in MORI survey	55
10–25-year-olds in OCJS survey	31

Source: From figures in Budd *et al.*, 2005; Clegg *et al.*, 2005; MORI, 2004.

so it is reasonable to generalise from these figures. For young people in school the most common victimisation experiences are being threatened by others (26 per cent), having something other than a mobile phone stolen (15 per cent), and being physically attacked (13 per cent). For excluded young people the pattern is: being threatened by others (33 per cent), being physically attacked (23 per cent), and having something other than a mobile phone stolen from them (19 per cent) (MORI, 2004, p. 51). The range of victimisations is greater in the MORI survey and includes incidents of bullying and verbal threats, whereas the OCJS survey focuses on assaults and personal thefts.

Patterns of victimisation across gender and race are also discernible. In general boys and young men are more likely to be the victim of a crime or incivility. In the OCJS survey over a third of males aged 10–25 were victims of personal crimes, compared with around a quarter of females (26 per cent) (Budd *et al.*, 2005). In the MORI (2004) survey girls in school are slightly less likely than boys to be the victim of any offence (48 per cent of girls compared with 51 per cent of boys); whereas slightly more excluded girls than boys report the same (57 per cent of girls compared with 55 per cent of boys). Girls are more concerned about something happening to them. The one area in which girls in mainstream education are more likely to be victims is bullying (25 per cent compared with 20 per cent of boys). Boys are significantly more likely to be a victim of all other offences. They are more than twice as likely to be physically attacked (18 per cent compared with 8 per cent of girls). No significant differences by gender are reported by excluded young people (MORI, 2004, p. 52).

Generally, young people from minority ethnic groups are slightly more likely to be victims of any offence in mainstream school (51 per cent minority ethnic compared with 49 per cent white) and slightly less likely when in exclusion projects (48 per cent minority ethnic compared with 57 per cent white). Young black people are more likely to be the victim of particular types of offence – such as theft of something other than a mobile phone (19 per cent black; 15 per cent white; 11 per cent Asian). Both Asian and African-Caribbean students are much more likely to be victims of racial abuse (18 per cent and 20 per cent, compared with 2 per cent of white young people) (MORI, 2004, p. 53).

Longitudinal cohort studies are another important source of information about the factors associated with the development of what has often been termed 'criminal careers'. They provide evidence for the prevalence of criminal behaviour at different ages as well as a source of evidence about the risk and protective factors discussed in Chapter 1. Prospective longitudinal studies are important in that they eliminate the possibility of retrospective bias when people are asked to recall aspects of their lives in cross-sectional surveys. Prospective longitudinal studies also help determine the order in which risk factors or events present themselves in an in individual's life (YJB, 2001a). The Cambridge Study of Delinquent Development is the best known early British study, also referred to in Chapter 1. This research shows that by the age of 40, 40 per cent of the London males that make up this study were convicted of a criminal offence, excluding minor offences such as traffic offences and drunkenness (Farrington, 2002). Most of the largest-scale longitudinal criminological research has been undertaken in Britain, Scandinavia, New Zealand and the United States (YJB, 2001a). However, much of this research is now relatively old, so it might be argued that more modern studies are needed. For example, the Cambridge study found that adolescents with tattoos were more likely to commit crime (West and Farrington, 1973); this finding may now seem rather quaint. Tattoos in the 1970s could be seen as indicative of the daring and risk-taking behaviour associated with offending, not the commonplace fashion symbol they are for young people in contemporary Britain (YJB, 2001a).

The Edinburgh youth transitions and crime study is a more recently initiated longitudinal study which began in 1998 with 4,469 children aged around 12 (Smith and McVie, 2003). The study aims to follow up these individuals until they reach the age of 30. The focus is on transitions during adolescence rather than childhood influences and, unlike the Cambridge study, it includes girls as well as boys. Early findings from this study confirm the association between offending and impulsivity; parental supervision; offending peers; use of alcohol and illicit drugs at the age of 12 and what they term 'moral disengagement'. One of the objectives of the study is to explore the link between offending and self-control. The concept of moral disengagement relates to this latter objective and to the capacity of individuals to temporarily free themselves from the constraints of particular beliefs or principles that may later come back into play. In the first sweep of this study (i.e. with the 12-year-olds) young people were asked whether they had ever committed one of 15 offences: the mean score over the whole cohort was 8.29 offences (10.77 boys; 5.79 girls). There were strong differences when the family and living circumstances of children were compared. Children who had ever been in care reported a higher mean volume of offending (19.77); children of single fathers (13.28) reported the highest level compared with other family forms. A clear socio-economic gradient is evident in the study, with the highest mean volume of offending being reported by children from Class 5 (unskilled manual) (13.15) and households where no parent works (11.25).

Drug and alcohol (substance) use can be associated with a range of problematic behaviours from young people. In the OCJS survey nearly a quarter (22 per cent) of all young people aged 10–25 reported taking a drug in the preceding year, with 8 per cent having taken a Class A drug.[4] Cannabis was the drug used in nine out of ten cases (Budd *et al.*, 2005). The MORI (2004) youth survey once again provides some useful insights into the different levels of substance use from young people in mainstream schools, compared with those already in more serious trouble through exclusion from school. This survey shows excluded young people as much more likely to use cannabis, ecstasy, amphetamines, solvents and so on, compared with young people in mainstream schools. While there are obvious issues to do with age and the use of alcohol as a legal substance, there are clearly other issues to do with the use of and access to illegal substances at a young age. Other nationally representative research has shown that four in ten Year 10 pupils (14–15-year-olds) and over half of Year 11 pupils (15–16-year-olds) acknowledged 'binges' where they consumed five or more alcoholic drinks in a session (Beinart *et al.*, 2002).

Problem Behaviour in School

We have already seen from YJB surveys that self-reported offending behaviour by young people of secondary-school age is quite common; especially for those attending facilities for excluded pupils. We have also seen earlier in this text that problems in school are one of the risk factors for criminal involvement and that exclusion and truancy are specifically associated. Behaviour that stands out in a school environment can be an important warning or barometer that something is going wrong for a young person. However, as with information about the prevalence of offending behaviour in young people generally, we do need

Table 3.3 Teachers' experiences of problematic behaviour in school

Type of behaviour/problem	% teachers experiencing in a school week
Possession of offensive weapon (pupil)	3.0
Physical violence – direct threats: pupil to pupil	43.4
Physical violence – threats to pupils from third parties (usually parents; less frequently former pupils)	16.1
Bullying and harassment – pupil to pupil	32.2
Damage to teachers' property	26.8
Physical violence – threats from pupils to teachers	5.0
Unwanted physical contact – towards teachers (pushing, touching)	8.9

Source: Adapted from Neill, 2002, pp. 2–4.

to identify the really seriously problematic behaviour from that which is largely to do with adolescence, or adults who are ineffective in keeping order and/or making relationships with young people in schools. When it comes to investigating behaviour in schools, it should be remembered that there are numerous perspectives, although most of the research concentrates on pupils and teachers, as opposed to parents and surrounding communities.

Table 3.3 illustrates data from a survey carried out by the National Union of Teachers (NUT), based on 2,575 responses from 13 LEAs (Neill, 2002).

It is interesting to note how the language in relation to pupil behaviour is changing – 'disruption' and 'disaffection' were commonly used terms in relation to pupils until relatively recently. Increasingly we are seeing the use of terms like 'harassment', as in Neill's survey. Arguably using the term 'harassment' raises the stakes and presents pupil behaviour in a more serious light. Another teaching union survey conducted across 304 schools (primary, secondary and special) in the north-west of England revealed 964 incidents of abuse against teachers in a two-week period in January 2003. About one in eight of these (126 cases) involved what were termed 'physical assaults' (NAS/UWT, 2003). It is clear for teachers replying to these surveys that disruption in class, offensive language and damage to property are relatively common occurrences, as is witnessing threatening and abusive behaviour between pupils. Physical violence may be less common, but the threats are there and nearly one in ten (8.9 per cent) of the teachers responding reported weekly experiences of unwanted physical contact, such as pushing and shoving. While not wanting to undermine the importance of these experiences for those

Table 3.4 Violence and weapons in schools

Type of incident	% schools reporting incidents in previous school year
Physical violence – pupil to staff:	
Hitting, punching, kicking	18.7
Hitting with weapon or object, stabbing, slashing	2.9
Physical violence – pupil to pupil:	
Hitting, punching, kicking	50.7
Hitting with weapon or object, stabbing, slashing	6.9
Weapons – carried by pupils on school site	12.1

Source: Adapted from Gill and Hearnshaw, 1997, pp. 1–2. Based on 9 per cent of schools nationally; 2,303 responses.

responding, one does not know how representative these samples are; it may be that respondents with a bad experience were disproportionately motivated to respond. The latter concern is one that has frequently been raised by surveys carried out for or by teaching unions.

Another way of trying to get an idea of the extent of very problematic behaviour in school is to look at serious incidents at school level. Gill and Hearnshaw (1997) provide a picture of what a random sample of 3,986 schools experienced in one school year. Selected findings from this research are presented in Table 3.4.

This sort of survey presents a slightly different picture, with one in five *schools* experiencing physical attacks on a teacher in a school year, more than half experiencing physical violence between pupils and one in eight reporting that pupils have carried weapons on the school site. Again, it is important when looking at such surveys to consider the way the data was collected, and how it is presented may affect our perception of the issue. It is clear that from the perspective of teachers and whole-school surveys such as this, that violent and threatening behaviour is fairly common in schools. Teachers' feelings about violence on the school site are likely to be influenced by the fact that they are part of a community, in which particular events might be amplified and achieve significance because of their position as teachers and the fact that perpetrators within that community have to be faced on a daily basis. The same can clearly be said for pupils, of course.

Interestingly, the MORI (2004) self-report youth survey shows a higher level of young people carrying *potential* weapons than school-based surveys, where a teacher is reporting what is officially known or recorded. However, the MORI survey is not just about behaviour in school – it includes behaviour in the community. Over a quarter (28 per cent) of young people in mainstream schools reported carrying any kind of knife in a one-year period and over half

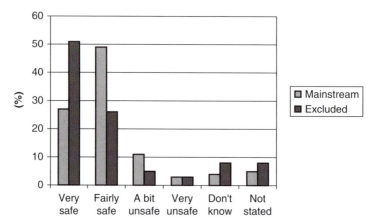

Figure 3.4 Pupil perceptions of safety at school or education projects
Source: Developed from figures in MORI, 2004

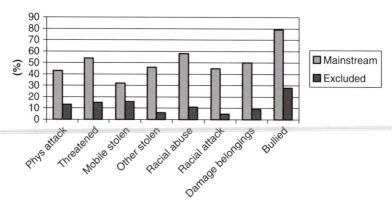

Figure 3.5 Proportion of victimisation offences occurring at school or education projects

(57 per cent) of excluded young people. It is important to emphasise, however, that the largest proportion of knives in each sample was penknives, which may not necessarily be carried as a weapon. Nearly a quarter (23 per cent) of mainstream pupils reported having carried a 'BB' gun[5] in a one-year period, and nearly half (45 per cent) of excluded pupils had done so.

We don't have equivalent data on the harassment of pupils by teachers. We do, however, have various types of evidence about the extent to which pupils are bullied at school by other pupils, as well as the extent to which they feel safe in school.

It is clear from the MORI (2004) evidence that most pupils feel 'very safe' or 'fairly safe' at their school or education project. It is interesting to note that excluded pupils in education projects are proportionately more likely to feel 'very safe' in comparison with pupils in mainstream schools. However, we should take note of the minority who feel 'very unsafe' or a 'bit unsafe' at their school or education project.

Perceptions of safety from pupils within their education setting are borne out by the levels of victimisation reported. In all types of victimisation in the MORI survey, a higher proportion is reported to occur in school for mainstream pupils. Victimisation was proportionately more likely to occur outside school in community settings, for young people attending education facilities for excluded pupils.

Pupil-based surveys, such as those on bullying, have come up with varying rates of prevalence of this specific type of behaviour. There are problems of definition and comparability across surveys. For example, 'physical violence, pupil to pupil' (as referred to in Tables 3.3 and 3.4) may be one-off acts of aggression; they may, on the other hand, be more sustained. According to Smith (2002), 'bullying is a subset of aggressive behaviours, characterised by repetition and power imbalance' (p. 117). Bullying takes various forms – physical, verbal and social exclusion, and indirect forms, such as spreading rumours (p. 118).

Bullying surveys produce fairly wide-ranging estimates, depending on the way questions are asked and the timescale involved. Overall, Smith and Myron-Wilson (1998) estimate that 'around 1 in 5 children are involved in bully–victim problems' (p. 406) in the UK, with similar incidences reported in other countries. What is clear from the data presented in Tables 3.2 to 3.4 is how widespread various forms of unwanted and problematic behaviour are in schools. Thus any strategy to improve behaviour has to involve the whole school system.

Much has been written about exclusion from school and its association with criminal activity. The evidence points to a complex association between offending behaviour and the type of behaviour that results in some exclusions from school. More generally, exclusion from school has become an important indicator or predictor of the likelihood of other problems in a young person's life, as well as poor prospects following exclusion. As we have seen, surveys such as those carried out for the YJB by MORI organise their sampling and comparison on the basis of excluded and non-excluded children. The Youth Cohort Study (see, for example, DfES, 2003c) has also produced comparative data on excluded and non-excluded children, as well as on regular truants; showing worse outcomes for excluded and truanting pupils in terms of qualifications achieved, likelihood of being in work, education or training at 17, and so on. Figure 3.6 presents the overall picture for permanent exclusion, for which national data has been available since 1992. The graph shows a rise from 1990 to 1997, followed by a fall and then fluctuation. While these figures represent large numbers of individuals, it is important to appreciate that they are a tiny proportion of all school pupils: the rate of permanent exclusion was 13 per 10,000 school population in England, or 0.13 per cent in 2003–4. However, some pupils are more vulnerable to permanent exclusion: pupils with special educational needs (46 in 10,000), travellers of Irish heritage (66 in 10,000), black pupils (29 in 10,000) and pupils of mixed ethic origin (25 in 10,000). Boys are four times more likely to be excluded than girls. This disparity is even more noticeable within particular ethnic groups: for example, the permanent exclusion rate of Asian boys is ten times that for Asian girls (DfES, 2005b).

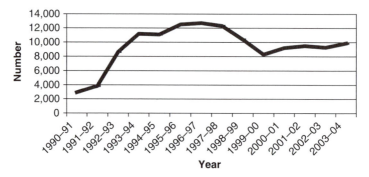

Figure 3.6 Trends in records of permanent exclusion from school (1990–2004)
Source: Developed from data within www.dfes.gov.uk.

On the other hand, permanently excluded pupils are the tip of the iceberg in terms of disaffected and other difficult-to-manage behaviour in school. Fixed-period exclusions (usually a matter of days) are much more numerous. Work conducted by the author for one urban education authority found records of exclusion for about 2 per cent of the whole school population in a one-year period; most of these were fixed-period exclusions, for a matter of a day or so (Hayden, 2000). More recently the DfES has published records of fixed-period exclusion as well, showing a similar rate nationally. For example, in 2003–04, 344,510 fixed-period exclusions (i.e. records, not individual pupils) were recorded. A total of 201,780 individual pupils (or 2.6 per cent of the school population) had one or more fixed-period exclusions – most lasted one week or less (DfES, 2005b). The most common reasons given for both fixed-period and permanent exclusions are: 'persistent disruptive behaviour' (30 per cent), 'verbal abuse/threatening behaviour against an adult' (20 per cent) and 'physical assault against a pupil' (20 per cent) (DfES, 2005b).

A larger proportion of children do not attend school for various reasons. These reasons are varied, but in some cases at least they represent disaffection or disinterest in schooling; avoidance of work pressures or bullying may explain some cases, and sometimes the non-attender is a young carer. Figure 3.7 shows

Table 3.5 Non-attendance (% half-days missed, 1995–2005)

Whether authorised	1995–96	2004–05
Authorised	6.9	5.66
Unauthorised	0.7	0.79
Total non-attendance	7.6	6.45

Source: From figures available at www.dfes.gov.uk.

that the proportion of children missing school because of authorised (e.g. by parent or carer) absence has improved, while unauthorised absence (where no reason is supplied and/or parents/carers do not supply a reason) has become slightly worse.

Other estimates for children not attending school include half a million engaged in illegal work, of whom 100,000 are believed to truant from school daily in order to work (TUC/MORI, 2001). The most commonly quoted figure in government announcements on children truanting from school on any school day is 50,000 (NAO, 2005). There is a complex set of circumstances in which and reasons why children are not benefiting from school. They all have their behavioural manifestations, although it tends to be the 'acting-out' child that causes most consternation among teachers, because such behaviour demands attention.

Children in Trouble at Home

The concept of children 'in trouble' at home can be applied on a number of levels. Children get into trouble with their parents and carers as a normal part of growing up and testing the boundaries. Parents and carers may or may not feel able to respond to children's behaviour appropriately and, indeed, there are major differences of opinion about approaches to discipline and behaviour management in the home. Since early concerns were expressed about child welfare (as opposed to punishment) there has also been a concern about parents who are abusive and/or cannot 'control' or 'look after' their children. An important part of the general concern about children's behaviour comes from the experiences and concerns of parents and carers.

Legislation dating back to 1860 in Britain allows parents to use 'reasonable chastisement' as defence against charges of assault against their children. However, it is against the law for schools and institutional care in the UK to use physical punishment on children. These changes are still relatively recent, with state schools ending these forms of punishment in 1986 and private schools ending such practices in 1998. Children's charities, such as the NSPCC, Barnardo's and the Children's Society, as well as the ADSS (Association of

Directors of Social Services), have for some time pushed for a total ban on any form of physical punishment of children (Leach, 1999).

There are various reasons why some individuals and organisations are concerned about the smacking and physical punishment of children. First, the use of physical punishment tends to be readily passed from one generation to the next – parents smack their children because they were smacked as a child. Secondly, there is evidence that harsh punishment in childhood is associated with anti-social behaviour in adolescence (Farrington, 1991), as well as increased rates of psychiatric disorder (MacMillan *et al.*, 1999). Thirdly, frequent smacking appears to teach children to respond to conflict with aggression (Thompson and Pearce, 2001). Also, drawing the line between physical punishment and child abuse is not straightforward. The views of some professionals and children's organisations appear to be at odds with what parents in the UK (and elsewhere) actually do. Available evidence tends to suggest that the great majority of children in the UK are smacked. For example, Nobes and Smith (1997) found that 99 per cent of the parents in their London-based study had smacked their children (aged 1–11) at some point in their lives. Leach (1999), in reviewing the evidence in the UK and the United States, concludes that over 90 per cent of children are hit by their parents, with the peak period being in the pre-school years. Earlier studies by Newsom and Newsom (1989) found, in their Nottingham-based research, that 75 per cent of parents of 4-year-olds reported smacking them at least once a week. More recent research in Nottingham found that 63 per cent of parents of 3–5-year-olds had smacked their child in the previous week, 22 per cent several times in the week and 11 per cent once a day (Thompson and Pearce, 2001). Indeed, it has been said that these studies might provide an underestimation of the frequency with which children are hit in two-parent households, because of the tendency of research to rely upon the report of one parent (Leach, 1999). Research by Nobes and Smith (1997) showed that the child who is hit once a week by one parent is also likely to be hit by the other parent. This latter study found that 20 per cent of children had been hit with implements. Although hitting is the most frequent type of punishment meted out by parents a range of other practices are common, such as shaking, being forced into a cold shower, hair-pulling, biting or pinching, washing a child's mouth out with soap or force-feeding.

How parents actually behave towards their children in terms of physical punishment has been described as comparable to the consumption of alcohol. Both behaviours are sanctioned culturally and both can be described as behaviours along a continuum with the potential for extreme behaviour. Writing about the United States, Whipple and Richey (1997) acknowledge that the desire for a total ban on physical punishment from professionals is understandable in that they see the consequences and severity of harm in some cases. However, they also highlight the fact that this is generally out of step with the American cultural context. The real issues for professionals left with trying to judge what is abuse is trying to find out about the frequency, severity and escalation of physical punishment.

Staying at home for some children can at times seem untenable. It is estimated that about one in nine (11 per cent) children will run away for at least one night before they reach the age of 16. Nationally about 100,000 children run away from home or care in a year (Whittle, 2004); of whom around 77,000 have run away for the first time (Safe on the Streets Research Team, 1999), and around 20,000 children who run away are under the age of 11. Research by the SEU (2002) emphasises that running away is a signal that something is seriously wrong in a young person's life. A key issue is conflict or abuse at home, and some young people are forced out of their home (even though the parent may still view the child as having run away). Some may be unhappy in a care placement and want to return to their birth parents. 'Looked-after' children are particularly likely to run away from care. Evidence suggests that nearly half of looked-after children will run away or 'abscond' from care at some point (Hansard, 2003). Ultimately, persistent 'absconding' from care can lead to secure accommodation for a time. Some runaways are being bullied at school and overall they are more likely to be truanting, have drug problems and be in trouble with the police (SEU, 2002). The SEU report highlights the fact that runaways may become involved in 'survival crimes' such as begging, stealing and prostitution: they estimate that one in 14 runaways or around 5,000 children a year survive in this way. One in five runaways say they were physically or sexually abused while away from home, although many are fleeing this situation.

Child Protection statistics present the official situation on the most vulnerable children. The children may not be 'in trouble' as such, but they are certainly in a difficult situation, where many of the risk factors identified by researchers like Farrington (1996) come into play. Referrals to Social Services Departments are in excess of half a million a year, of which about a quarter are re-referrals within 12 months of previous cases. Less than half of these referrals go as far as an initial assessment. Over a third of a million children (376,000) can be defined as 'in need' according to definitions based on the Children Act 1989. Within this overall figure are the more vulnerable categories of those who are 'looked after' by the local authority (61,100 on 31 March 2004) which overlap with those on the CPR (26,300 at the same date). Reasons why children are on the CPR are shown in Table 3.6. Overall, 23 per 10,000 children aged under 18 are on the CPR in England (DfES, 2005c).

The overall trend is a decline in the number of children on the CPR, from 38,600 in 1992 to 26,300 in 2004 (DH, 2002; DfES, 2005c).

Some children may be 'looked after' by the local authority for a time because of these Child Protection concerns or because parents cannot look after them (for example, because of illness or death). Looked-after children in England number around 60,000 at any one time (Harker *et al.*, 2004), although the total number of children who pass through the care system in a year is

Table 3.6 Reasons why children are on the Child
Protection Register

Reason	%
At risk of neglect	41
Physical abuse	19
Emotional abuse	18
Sexual abuse	9
Mixed categories	14

Source: DfES, 2005c.

higher (94,300 in 2002–03) (DfES 2004). A smaller number are looked after for at least a year (44,900) and about three-quarters of this latter group are of school age (35,100) (DfES 2004). The behaviour of some of these children is likely to be difficult because of their experiences with their birth parents, but also because of the disruption and upset associated with having to change where and with whom they live. Sadly, finding a care placement often involves children moving schools and thus difficulties in seeing friends, at the same time as they are moved out of their home. Not surprisingly, some looked-after children can be troublesome and are often troubled, but it is important to emphasise that they are looked after primarily because of what their parents have done, not done, or been able to do, rather than what they – as children – may have done. Nevertheless, there have long been strong associations between being 'looked after' and being in trouble. 'Looked-after' children are proportionately more likely to have poor outcomes, in comparison with the general population of school-age children. These outcomes add to the risk in their already vulnerable situation (Hayden, 2005a).

Despite the policy emphasis of keeping children with their birth parents wherever possible, the number and rate of 'looked-after' children has increased in recent years: from 58,100 in 2000 to 61,100 in 2004 (an increased rate of 52 to 55 children per 10,000 population); a 5 per cent increase (DfES, 2005c). Two-thirds of looked-after children are placed with foster-carers in the community and around one in ten still live with their parents but are subject to supervision from Social Services. The proportion of looked-after children in different types of placement is shown in Table 3.7.

Mental Health

Most evidence suggests that adults are more likely to suffer from diagnosable mental health problems than children and young people, with women being more susceptible than men. For example, the London Health Observatory found that one in six adults surveyed in England exhibited symptoms in the

Table 3.7 Types of placement for looked-after children

Placement type	%
Foster care	68
Children's homes	11
With parents	10
Freed for adoption	5
Other (residential schools, lodgings, other residential settings)	5

Source: DfES, 2005c.

week prior to interview sufficient to warrant a diagnosis of having a mental health problem (LHO, 2000). Patterns are slightly different with children and young people, but in general diagnosable problems increase with age. It is recognised that adolescence is a time of turbulence to different degrees for individual young people, some of whom certainly have a great deal more to deal with during this process than others. Young Minds (2005, para. 2) estimates that about 20 per cent of children and young people experience mental health *problems*. Mental health problems are defined as problems that interfere with a child's ability to learn, to enjoy friendships and relationships and deal with the difficulties and frustrations he or she faces. The Royal College of Psychiatrists (2004, p. 3) estimates that four in ten adolescents have felt so miserable that they have cried and wanted to get away from everything and that one in five have at some point felt that life was not worth living.

For the great majority of young people any difficult or turbulent behaviour passes, but for some a mental health *disorder* is apparent. Mental health disorders are associated with many of the issues to do with children in trouble already described in this chapter. Mental Health professionals use the term 'mental health disorder' when an individual's symptoms fulfil clinical criteria, as defined by ICD-10 (International Classification of Diseases, tenth revision). Such symptoms or behaviours are usually associated with 'considerable distress and substantial interference with personal functions' (Meltzer *et al.*, 2000, p. 1). Serious mental health problems are rare in children. However, mental health problems are known to disproportionately affect groups of children who are already disadvantaged or vulnerable, notably, looked-after children.

Meltzer *et al.* (2000) conducted a survey across England, Scotland and Wales to produce prevalence rates of the three most common childhood mental health disorders: conduct disorder, hyperactivity and emotional disorders. The overall prevalence of these disorders in the 5–15 age group was found to be 10 per cent: made up from conduct disorders (5 per cent); emotional disorders (4 per cent) and hyperactive disorders (1 per cent). The less common disorders (tics and autistic and eating disorders) affected less than 0.5 per cent of the sampled population. The overall rate of 10 per cent includes some children with more than one type of disorder. However, this latter rate varies greatly in connection with other issues and circumstances. One of the overall patterns is that children in the more disadvantaged socioeconomic circumstances are more likely to suffer from a mental health disorder, compared with children in more comfortable circumstances. Other patterns to do with gender and ethnicity are also apparent. The association between mental health problems and identified special educational need is also clear.

Studies of trends in the mental health of young people, such as that of Rutter and Smith (1995) referred to in Chapter 1 in relation to their cultural position, indicate that the mental health of young people in the UK and elsewhere in Europe has deteriorated in recent decades. In discussing the possible interpretations and explanations for these trends, they discount individual difference as the major factor because of the trends that are not only apparent at the level of an individual society, but also across European societies. Rutter and Smith argue that improved socioeconomic conditions, rather than a reduction in crime and anti-social behaviour, may also have increased the opportunities and possibilities for certain activities, such as theft. Increased inequality in some societies, alongside increased opportunity, is another explanation offered. The break-up of families and negative influences of some aspects of the media are also implicated, as are the pressures inherent in a state of 'perpetual adolescence' and the normalisation of drug and alcohol use among young people. In other words, there is no shortage of potentially negative influences on the mental health of young people – all of which can put them in danger of getting into trouble. Rutter *et al.* (1998, p. 110) conclude that epidemiological data indicate that alcoholism and drug addiction are the psychopathological disorders most strongly associated with crime, although some association is evident with a wide range of psychiatric conditions.

Reviewing the Evidence

The opening quotations to this chapter remind us of a number of important considerations when reviewing the needs, scale and impact of children in trouble. The great majority of children are not 'in trouble' but individual children can cause real consternation because of their behaviour. This has probably always been so – the issue is how we understand and respond to behaviour that is affecting the well-being of the individual and others. We need to be able to identify the underlying causes and motivations behind children's behaviour, as well as the particular family, school and community circumstances that may be sustaining or reinforcing it. All this needs to be understood in relation to wider social and structural conditions in order to develop appropriate responses.

This chapter has reviewed the various ways we might measure the proportion of 'children in trouble'. We have noted again the issue of mental health – or children who are 'troubled' – and outlined trends that would suggest that more children are 'troubled' now than in the past. Children who are troubled are a higher-risk category for getting into trouble both because of their behaviour, but also because of the wider circumstances of disadvantage associated with these problems. The various ways we measure behavioural problems tend to point to adults reporting greater difficulty in responding to the behaviour of young people, although there is an extent to which the issue of children and young people's behaviour is amplified by the media, as well as by political posturing. This latter observation is particularly evident in relation to 'anti-social behaviour', as we noted in Chapter 2. Despite the overall reduction in offending, there is a higher rate of violent juvenile offending. Although there will always be debates about recording and reporting, this is an issue that we should try to better understand. Explanations of the heightened anxiety and increased problems vary and include society-wide issues and processes, such as more family breakdown, longer periods of enforced dependence on parents, pressures and expectations from the educational system, greater polarisation in life chances and opportunities, and so on.

Reviewing the evidence, it is possible to create a typology of children *and* trouble (see Figure 3.7). This would remind us once again that some 'testing the boundaries' and experimentation is part of growing up for most children, although not all will break the law or even get a detention at school. A proportion are likely to 'temporarily lose their way' through more significant conflicts at home or school, perhaps through truanting and regular stealing or perhaps drug use. Those 'in trouble' are more likely to be on the receiving end of formal sanctions. Those 'in serious trouble' are often outside mainstream systems in various respects: either through permanent exclusion from school (nearly 10,000 children a year) and/or through conviction and detention in a YOI (around 6,000 children a year). However, it must be emphasised that there is a fluidity in time across these categories, so, for example, many children who have 'temporarily lost their way' will return to the majority, but some will move on to get into more trouble. Similarly, the increased potential for getting into more serious trouble once you are 'in trouble' is obvious.

Notes

1   As defined by Section 17 of the Children Act.
2   *Notifiable offences* cover a wide spectrum from homicide to minor thefts. They are offences serious enough to be recorded by the police.
3   A *serious offence* is classified in this survey as burglary, theft of a vehicle, robbery, theft from a person, assault with injury, or selling Class A drugs (Budd *et al.*, 2005, p. 7).
4   *Class A drugs* include opiates, cocaine, hallucinogens and Ecstasy.
5   A gun that fires small-bore projectiles called BBs.

> *The majority – testing the boundaries/experimentation and growing up*
> Nearly all will be in trouble with the their parents or carers at some point
> Many will have been involved in one or two minor offences – stealing from a shop, fare-dodging, and so on (e.g. 26% of 11–16-year-olds in school commit some offence in a year)
> Many will experience occasional instances of being formally 'told off' in school, the odd detention, sometimes being late for school, truanting once or twice
> Two-thirds (67%) will have drunk alcohol by the age of 16

> *Temporarily lost the way*
> A fixed-period exclusion at secondary-school level
> More frequent truanting at secondary-school level
> Likely to be underachieving at school
> Some conflict at home and/or school
> Experimentation with drugs such as cannabis (15% of 11–16-year-olds in school)
> Minor criminal acts which may include vandalism as well as stealing and fare-dodging; behaviour that is often seen as 'anti-social'

> *In trouble (up to 10%)*
> Multiple fixed-period exclusions and regular truanting, starting at primary-school level (2.6% of all school pupils had a record of one or more fixed periods of exclusion in 2003–04)
> Underachievement at school very apparent, academic qualifications highly unlikely
> More likely to associate with delinquent peers and have involvement in criminal activity; serious offences likely (assault leading to injury, theft, burglary, robbery, TWOC)
> More regular use of drugs and/or alcohol, use likely to be problematic
> Warnings and reprimands, community-based punishments
> Runaways (around 100,000 yps a year)
> Mental health problems likely

> *In serious trouble (up to 3%)*
> Not attending school/dropped out or 'disappeared' (e.g. around 10,000 between 15 and 16 years old)
> Some will attend a pupil referral unit (around 12,000 yps at a time)
> Very likely to have been permanently excluded from school (around 9,500 yps a year)
> Likely to have a long history of problematic behaviour, fixed-period exclusions and severe underachievement at school, likely to be no useful record of achievement
> Time spent in secure estate (around 6,000 yps a year)
> Frequent serious offending (assault leading to injury, theft, burglary, robbery, TWOC)
> Alcohol or drug use problematic; drug use more likely to include class A drugs
> Mental health problems very likely

Figure 3.7 Typologies of children *and* 'trouble'

Note: yps = young people; all statistics are used elsewhere in this chapter, and categories are derived from an interpretation of these statistics.

4

Families and Children
in Trouble

We have found no better way to raise a child than to reinforce the ability of his parents to do so.

> – Court Report, 1976, quoted in Pugh, 1998, p. 4

Time-poverty can be almost as grievous for children as the more ordinary kind ... In a family in which parents suffer from so many demands on them, the danger (we are saying) is that they will not have enough time for their children when the children need so much of it.

> – Young and Halsey, 1995, pp. 10–11

Inadequate or ineffective parenting, especially in early childhood, can aggravate bad behaviour, and parental stress is sometimes exacerbated by difficult social, family and/or economic conditions ... it is often families under stress who exhibit all the signs which, in the current unforgiving political climate, are translated into accusations of lack of respect for others, irresponsible or intimidating behaviour, and personal failure as a parent.

> – Payne, 2003, p. 322

The Importance of Families and Parenting

Children first learn what is seen as acceptable behaviour in their home environment. Children behave the way that they do partly due to the way they are brought up or socialised by their parents or carers. Home circumstances are crucial, but interrelate with school and community-based issues. Children who spend time living away from home – those who are 'looked after' – are more likely to be 'in trouble' in various ways than children who are not looked after. This chapter will review what is known about the extent to which families are both part of the problem and part of the solution for children in trouble. It will include an overview of what is known about children who cannot live with their families for a time and are 'looked after' in foster and residential care. The chapter includes a brief look at three pieces of original research: one on a local *Sure Start* initiative that investigated how an early programme was working 'on the ground'; another is a quasi-experimental design in which the impact of Family Group Conferences (FGCs) was evaluated; the third piece of research investigated the scale and type of need provided for in out-of-area placements for children living away from the family. These pieces of research explore different approaches to different levels of problem. Sure Start as a community-based initiative is located at the preventative end of the range (in the sense of very early in a child's life), starting with pregnancy, albeit in communities already identified as impoverished. FGCs are used in a range of circumstances where problems are already occurring. Out-of-area placements, on the other hand, only happen in the most problematic circumstances in which neither the family nor local foster and residential care can meet a child's needs.

The importance of families and parenting in relation to children in trouble may seem self-evident; it has certainly been long recognised. Chapter 1 highlights how particular aspects of family life and parenting styles are known to be risk factors for adverse outcomes, while families and parenting styles can also be protective factors against various types of risk.

The work of Bowlby (1951) is often seen as the landmark study in establishing the importance of 'bonding' between babies and their mothers. This bonding is seen as crucial in meeting a baby's emotional needs and in laying the foundations for a secure attachment, positive self-esteem, self-confidence and respect for others. When a baby's needs are not met in a predictable way or the baby is neglected, they may respond by becoming unsociably aggressive or withdrawn. The focus on 'the mother' has been criticised by feminists (the language now emphasises main 'carer'), and has been viewed as having an implicitly blaming inference. Bowlby's early work is also criticised for underestimating the extent to which developmental and behavioural problems can be reversed (Rutter, 1981). That said, there is increasing evidence about the importance of early parent–child relationships for establishing healthy patterns of functioning in childhood and adulthood. Secure attachments in the early years are known to be a basis for forming attachments later in life. The ability to empathise with and understand the feelings of others are also related to early parent–child relationships. Problems in these latter respects are associated with increased levels of violence and criminality later in life (Barlow *et al.*, 2002).

Interest in the early years extends to pregnancy. Known risk factors to the baby's later development include: low birth weight; delivery complications or birth trauma, as well as exposure to alcohol or drugs in the womb; mental illness or learning difficulty in the mother; teenage parenthood; violence in the family; and poverty. The potential physical consequences of many of the above risk factors are well known; however, there is also increasing evidence about the development of the human brain that further supports the case for the earliest support for parents. The pattern of growth and development

Table 4.1 Parenting – positive and negative qualities

Positive	Negative
Authoritative	Authoritarian or permissive
Warm and affectionate	Cold and hostile
Setting clear limits	Having inconsistent rules
Quick to recognise needs	Unresponsive to needs
Accepting of faults	Rejecting
Predictable and consistent	Unpredictable
Respectful of the individual	Disrespectful
Open and effective communication	Inadequate supervision
Recognising good qualities or behaviour	Punishing bad qualities or behaviour
Empathic	Inappropriate expectations

Source: Pugh, 1998, p. 11.

in a baby's brain is affected by the environment in which it is developing. In the first two years the 'wiring' of the brain, or physical connections between neurons, is being established. Children who experience violence in early life develop brains that are pre-tuned to danger. Understimulated children have been found to develop brains that are 30 per cent smaller than normal. Where a main carer is depressed and is disengaged, irritable or impatient with a baby, they have been found to develop brains in which the left frontal lobe area (which is the physical centre for light-hearted and joyful feelings) shows little activity (Rickford, 2000). More broadly, different parenting styles have been identified and these are associated with different outcomes for children.

The positive qualities shown in Table 4.1 are associated with well-adjusted children, who in turn tend to have better outcomes in adolescence and adulthood. At the more extreme end of negative parenting, it has been estimated that in any one year about 350,000 children are living in what has been described as 'low-warmth and high-criticism environments' (DH, 1995, p. 19). Half of the children in these types of environment are referred to the Child Protection process and around a third of these are then visited by a social worker. In other words, there is a sharp funnelling process from the relatively large numbers of children who experience poor-quality parenting and those whom the system intervenes with actively.

It is important to emphasise that the capacity of parents to offer 'positive parenting' depends in part on wider social and environmental circumstances, what Rutter has referred to as the 'permitted circumstances of parenting' (quoted in Pugh, 1998, p. 14); that is, adequate income and housing, good mental and physical health, and employment compatible with family life, as well as the availability of the support services needed – such as good quality child care. Negative parenting is associated with difficult and often aggressive behaviour from children. In both UK and US studies, aggressive behaviour in primary-school children has been linked to a harsh early upbringing provided by hostile, abusive or punitive parents (Utting *et al.*, 1993).

Becoming anti-social or conduct-disordered (often referred to as 'delinquency' in earlier studies) or being convicted of an offence are often used as important outcome measures in studies tracking aggressive and troublesome behaviour in childhood. In the Cambridge longitudinal study, nearly half those identified as 'troublesome' at primary school later became delinquent (Farrington and West, 1990). In the Newcastle longitudinal study, 70 per cent of children assessed as 'deprived and receiving poor domestic care' were eventually convicted of a criminal offence (Kolvin *et al.*, 1990). Indeed, official crime statistics and longitudinal research on cohorts of children tend to find that children from low-income households are more likely to present anti-social and offending behaviour than children from more comfortably off backgrounds. For example, another longitudinal study, the Child Health and Education Study of over 13,000 children born in 1970, has shown that anti-social and neurotic behaviour in pre-school children is consistently associated with social disadvantage (Utting *et al.*, 1993, p. 18). However, these kinds of findings have long been subject to criticism for their failure to acknowledge the way that the criminal justice and social care systems are more likely to focus on 'problem areas' in which poorer families live. That is, the problematisation of working-class youth is to a degree socially constructed. On the other hand, it is argued that evidence suggests that the issue may not be so much about poor families and the likelihood of offending, rather the focus should be on the type of offence committed. Self-report studies tend to show a reduced social class bias in terms of likelihood of offending per se, but a difference in terms of type of offence. Serious offences are more often committed by young people in relatively poor social circumstances (Utting *et al.*, 1993).

Family circumstances are dynamic; there have been a number of notable changes and reversals of longer-term trends in recent years, such as a reduction in workless households and children living in relative poverty; both of which still affect around one in six and one in five children, respectively. Other difficult family and living circumstances are experienced by a substantial minority of children and some relate to relationships; such as divorce, living in a house headed by a single parent and domestic violence. Experiences such as being a young carer or being 'looked after' are less common. Taken singly, these circumstances do not necessarily result in adverse outcomes; it is often the relationship between circumstances and other risk factors in the community or school, as well as individual temperament, that result in either adverse or positive outcomes. For example, poverty and single parenthood are connected; neither circumstance produces bad parents, but both circumstances make parenting more difficult, particularly as such parents often live in poor quality housing and within communities in difficult circumstances.

Sadly, such communities are also most often associated with the least popular schools, with academic results well below the national average.

Specifically, the consequences of disruption in the home through relationship breakdown or bereavement are much debated and there are some conflicting results. It is worth noting that a focus on divorce underestimates the issue of relationship breakdown, as around 40 per cent of all births are outside marriage and cohabiting is common (www.statistics.gov.uk/socialtrends35). Nevertheless, evidence about the impact of divorce on children may give us some indication of the impact of relationship breakdown on children. Divorce is relatively common: it is estimated that one in 25 children experience their parents' divorce before their fourth birthday; one in nine before their eighth birthday, and one in four by the time they are sixteen (Pugh, 1998, p. 7). Overall findings tend to indicate that deviant behaviour is more prevalent in children whose parents have split up. A meta-analysis (see Chapter 7 for an explanation of the methodology) of 50 US and European studies on marital breakdown and delinquency suggests that delinquent behaviour could be 10–15 per cent more prevalent in such homes, in comparison with those where both parents are living with a young person. Higher rates of truancy, running away from home, and underage smoking and drinking were found in young people whose parents had split up, in comparison with those who had not (Wells and Rankin, 1991). Interestingly the impact of bereavement is not as great as divorce and separation when it comes to patterns of offending. Marital conflict, on the other hand, is associated with behavioural and learning problems, whether or not the parents eventually separate (Cherlin *et al.*, 1991). Rutter (1985) states that although things frequently get worse after a divorce they do usually get better in the longer term, and he concludes that divorce is better for children than ongoing conflict. Utting *et al.* (1993) emphasise that the most important influence on children's behaviour in terms of family circumstances is the quality of the relationship between parents. Pugh (1998) agrees with Utting *et al.* in saying that there is no clear evidence that the needs of children are more likely to be met by families of a particular type or structure; she sees the key factor as the nature and quality of the parenting.

Domestic violence is known to happen to either sex and in same-sex relationships, although most of the evidence focuses on women and domestic violence and the effects on their children. Interpersonal violence is relatively common, with around 13 per cent of women and 9 per cent of men self-reporting either domestic violence, sexual assault or stalking in a year, according to a representative sample from the BCS (Walby and Allen, 2004). This latter study indicates a lower proportion of women suffering from domestic violence in a year at 4 per cent (in comparison with the Women's Aid estimate of 10 per cent shown in Table 4.2) and a relatively higher proportion of men (2 per cent). The difference in BCS and Women's Aid estimates may be explained by the different average number of incidents experienced by

Table 4.2 Families and living circumstances

Circumstance or indicator	% of all children
Parents divorced	25.0 (by the age of 16) (Pugh, 1998)
Live in a household headed by a single parent	24.0
Live in a stepfamily	10.0
Live in a 'workless' household	15.3 (Bradshaw, 2003)
Live in relative poverty	18.3 (Bradshaw, 2003)
Proportions of mothers working/ age of youngest child	55.0 (<5 yrs); 73 (5–10 yrs); 80 (11–15 yrs)
Domestic violence	10% of women a year; 25% in their lifetime;* BCS estimates are less: 4% women; 2% men (Walby and Allen, 2004)
Low-warmth, high-criticism environment	3.0 (350,000) (DH, 1995)
Young carers	1.3 (149,000 of 11.7 million dependent children)
Looked after in a year	0.5

Sources: *www.womensaid.org.uk; www.statistics.gov.uk/socialtrends35, 2005, where the source is not cited.

men and women: for women this was 20 and for men 7. Walby and Allen make clear that although interpersonal violence is widespread, it is also concentrated in multiple victimisations, particularly of women. Further, they note the increased risk of domestic violence in low-income households. It is known that many children either witness or overhear domestic violence and the manipulation of children may be part of a parent's strategy to maintain control in a relationship, both before and after a separation (O'Hara, 1995). Domestic violence is said to be the single most quoted route to homelessness. There are also strong associations between physical child abuse and domestic violence (Humphreys *et al.*, 2001).

The negative impact of poverty on child development and opportunities has long been established (see, for example, Coates and Silburn, 1971). Classic studies, such as that of Coates and Silburn, led to the 'rediscovery' of poverty in 1970s Britain. Using the same measure for relative poverty,[1] Bradshaw (2003, pp. 162–3) calculates that there was a 'huge surge' in child poverty during the 1980s: from 10 per cent of children in 1979 to 31 per cent in 1990–91, peaking in 1998–99 at 35 per cent. By 2001 figures had changed dramatically, with an estimated 18.3 per cent of all children living in relative poverty. From the late 1990s paid work was more actively encouraged as the route out of poverty for poor families. A commitment was made by the Blair government in 1999 to end child poverty in 20 years. The Work–Life Balance Challenge Fund was launched in 2000; offering employers encouragement and assistance to introduce more flexible working arrangements. As policy has developed, more flexibility at work has been more closely linked with addressing child-poverty targets (HM Treasury/DTI, 2003).

For those in work the dominant pattern is now 1.5 earners, typically a father in full-time work and a mother in part-time employment. The largest change in labour-market participation has come from mothers with a child under 5 working: an increase from 43 per cent in 1991 to 54 per cent of mothers in 2001. Weekend working for parents is common: nearly four in ten mothers and over half of fathers work at least one Saturday a month; and, a quarter of mothers and just under a third of fathers work at least one Sunday a month (La Valle *et al.*, 2002). Three in ten two-parent households have adopted 'shift parenting' where each parent works hours that do not overlap, in order to share child care (La Valle *et al.*, 2002). All this sets a context for stress and tiredness in many working families, with the kind of child-care support needed not being readily available at a price that is affordable or recognised by child-care subsidies. Informal arrangements from relatives, friends and neighbours are preferred by many parents; especially those in low-income households. Employment patterns and child care have an important bearing on children's well-being when young, as well as the level of supervision parents are able to put in place when they are older.

The term 'young carer' usually refers to a child or person who provides the care for a parent or other member of their household who is unwell, has a disability or needs help for another reason. A key experience of young carers is a lack of time and freedom to participate in the normal activities of childhood. They can have difficulties in their schooling, particularly in relation to punctuality and attendance and in coursework and homework completion. In addition some face the worry that they may inherit a parent's condition or feel the stigma of association when a parent has a mental health problem (Ames Reed, 1995). The 2001 Census indicated that there are around 149,000 young carers in Britain.

Children 'Looked After' by the State

Children 'looked after' by the state are a tiny proportion of all children, at around 0.5 per cent of children under 18. All the evidence suggests that looked-after children are the most vulnerable children in Britain, as many will have been the victims of abuse and neglect. However, the circumstances in which they come into care vary: some will have been remanded into care; others will have been considered beyond parental control; others will have been taken into care for their own welfare and protection. Despite these varied routes into care the association between being 'in care' and being 'in trouble' has a long history in terms of public perception, although the research evidence has been relatively sparse (Taylor, 2003).

Recent years have seen a period of unprecedented government policy attention focused on looked-after children. We now have data on looked-after children, compared with the general population of children as one of the outcome indicators of the *Quality Protects* programme (DH, 1998). One such indicator is offending rates. Figures show that the rate of looked-after children who are convicted or subject to a reprimand during a year is about three times that of children in the general population (9.5 per cent compared with 2.9 per cent; DfES, 2004).

There are also a number of estimates of the association between time in care and offending from studies conducted some time ago: for example Dodd and Hunter (1992) estimated that 23 per cent of adult prisoners and 38 per cent of young offenders had spent some time in care at some point in their lives. A more recent Office for National Statistics (2000) study found that for young offenders with a psychiatric condition, 29 per cent of sentenced males, 35 per cent of young women and 42 per cent of male remand prisoners had been in care. Thus, while it is clear that children who spend time in care are more likely to offend than their counterparts who have not spent time in care; it is not clear to what extent this is associated with the poorer and more stressful family and community circumstances from which they disproportionately come, as opposed to the care experience itself.

Evidence also shows a high rate of mental health problems in the looked-after population: conduct, depressive and anxiety orders seem to be particularly common, with children looked after in residential care being particularly likely to have these problems (McCann *et al.*, 1996). The poor educational outcomes of looked-after children have been noted for decades (Ferguson 1966). The main reasons have been well debated and documented and are interconnected with many of the problems associated with leaving care. Reasons have included: inadequate corporate parenting; the care environment; a failure to prioritise education; inappropriate expectations; placement instability and disrupted schooling as well as pre-care experiences (see, for example, Harker *et al.*, 2004). Martin and Jackson (2002) have researched care leavers who are high achievers in order to investigate what they can tell us about improving the care system so that it is more supportive of children's educational needs. They have noted the importance of supportive carers, of stability in home and school placement, and of the opportunities and facilities (such as a desk and books at home) available to help develop interests and encourage young people to benefit from education. Many of these factors could be summarised as what the 'good parent' would want to provide for their child.

In sum, children looked after by the state are proportionately more likely to be 'in trouble' than children in the general population. They are also more likely to be 'troubled'. They are a group of children subject to a range of risk factors that have often been compounded by the care experience itself, despite the best efforts of individuals within the system. The stark differences between being in care and being cared for within one's family of birth could be illustrated in all kinds of ways, but one important issue is who is viewed as responsible for a child's welfare. Taylor (2003) makes the interesting observation that while legislation has brought in sanctions against the parents of children who offend, in the form of Parenting Orders, the state is not held criminally responsible for the children in its care who offend.

A Local *Sure Start* Partnership – What Do the Parents Think?

A theme throughout this book and in many others on children and families in difficulty is the need for early intervention (see also Chapters 2, 5 and 7), as well as the need for agencies to co-operate in the support that they give families. *Sure Start* is a high-profile example of a national programme focused on pre-school children in deprived neighbourhoods. The focus of the first round of local programmes was on the poorest 20 per cent of wards in the country, a figure that has been much used in subsequent related policy developments. Almost 50 per cent of the children under three years of age in the first Sure Start zones lived in workless households. As a programme it was put forward by New Labour as key to the eradication of child poverty within 20 years (HM Treasury, 1998). Launched in 2000, there were 524 Sure Start local programmes (SSLPs) commissioned by 2002. Tunstill *et al.* (2005, p. 158) note how governments are often remembered for specific significant policy achievements and that for New Labour, Sure Start has been perceived as that achievement. The national evaluation was initially set to run for six years and report in 2008. However, as Tunstill *et al.* (2005, p. 168) comment, as part of the national evaluation team, 'it may be argued that in this case national policy has developed in advance of conclusive evaluation findings'. Following national headlines on 'Doubts about the value of £3 billion Sure Start', the head of the national evaluation team made the political pressures more explicit and is quoted as saying 'to some extent we are reporting these findings now because of the political pressure to do so' (Ward, 2005, p. 1). The changes to the original programme have been such that Glass (2005), one of the people involved in developing the original programme, has argued that, in essence, Sure Start has been abolished and is just a brand name.

The desire to adapt and change some aspects of the programme while also extending it to other areas might be interpreted as the enthusiasm of a reforming government, but was a reality that confounded the difficulties in evaluating the impact. Only two years into the programme the pre-school focus changed and the term 'Sure Start' was being used to cover all services for children up to 14 and their families. Programmes like *Sure Start Plus,*

focusing on teenage parents, began in 2001 and other specific developments such as *Children's Centres* rose into the ascendancy. This plethora of
programmes was influenced by a number of interconnecting strands of what
might be termed an area-based anti-poverty strategy.

The programme within which the research reported upon here was undertaken was established as part of the second wave of SSLPs. Comprising four
inner-city wards of a unitary authority, the catchment area has high levels of
multiple deprivation and economic disadvantage – indeed, one ward falls
within the worst-off 10 per cent of wards nationally. Many families live in
high-rise flats and have no access to safe outdoor space. The wider remit of
the research we will now look at was to investigate partnership working and
the factors within this specific programme that were promoting or imped-
ing it. Interviews with 33 staff working within the Sure Start partnership
(74 per cent of all staff involved at the time of the research) revealed many
practical difficulties and tensions in this early SSLP for staff, the manager
and the partnership. Most of these difficulties related to different professional
cultures and practical difficulties in terms of staff shortages and the lack of
support from the lead agency. There were additional and specific difficulties
with building refurbishment and suitability as well as the way certain members of staff had been redeployed to the programme, rather than actively
applied for the work. Many of these sorts of difficulties have been noted in
the national evaluation (Tunstill *et al.*, 2005), and it is clear that they were
resolved more satisfactorily in the SSLP with strong managers.

As part of the research 25 parents were interviewed about their experiences of Sure Start. Parents in the SSLP were aware of staff shortages and
some of the tension between staff, but this was of little concern to them.
Overall, interviews with parents illustrated how much they needed the services provided and benefited from what was on offer. Parents particularly
welcomed the variety of support services available. Services included groups
focused on babies: postnatal support, breastfeeding, weaning, baby massage,
and so on. Services for toddlers included a toy library, a music group and
various opportunity groups. Nursery, crèche and child-care facilities were
available for short periods, although none were attuned to working parents'
needs at the time of the research. There were general education sessions on
child nutrition and dental health as well as services such as 'Home Check'
that focus on safety checks and provision of equipment, such as stair gates.
Other well-established services such as Homestart and Portage were also
readily available within this SSLP. Thus many of the services already existed
prior to Sure Start through the former Social Services family centre that
used to occupy the building taken over by Sure Start, as well as the various
services and groups run by local voluntary agencies. There were initial problems with the fact that the main Sure Start Centre was located in a former
Social Services family centre, as it was perceived as stigmatising. A key difference soon became apparent to parents, however, in that the former family

centre did not offer services in the more integrated and convenient way appreciated by parents in the area. Here is a typical comment from a parent:

> '*It's the convenience factor … it is all under one roof … essentially, no appointment, just being able to go and have a chat and bring things up that you might be worried about or you might have some questions over.*'

For parents in more difficulty the co-ordination of various services around the individual's needs was important. In the case below of a parent of two young children, co-ordination within Sure Start helped bring together all those working with her and her children:

> '*Portage arranged a meeting with all the people working with me – like Homestart, my health visitor, my child development worker and my "Little Learners" teacher was there. She got them all together to see what else they could do, because I've had Portage for six months and his* [her older child's] *behaviour is getting worse …*'

Nearly all the parents interviewed had attended at least one of the many vocational and non-vocational adult education courses on offer because Sure Start had provided the child-care facilities. Some parents had attended several courses and their enthusiasm was obvious:

> '*The courses they do are really good because I've done a computer one and I'm starting the cookery one, and I've done the first-aid course which comes to an end on Thursday. And "Learning Through Play" … the first one my health visitor encouraged me to go to, that was the computer course …. we are doing the "Running Your Own Business" course which starts on Friday.*'

Two of the 25 parents interviewed had become involved in the planning and management of the programme, as was the aim of Sure Start. They had different experiences. One parent had been co-opted onto the Publicity Sub-Group but had withdrawn due to lack of child-care facilities for her older daughter when she was attending meetings. The other parent reported a much more positive experience:

> '*Sure Start now have got me* [into] *committees and everything else. I'm on "Noah's Ark" – I'm secretary for that one – and I'm also on the steering group for their new day nursery … Yeah, it does* [give parents more of a say in the services provided]. *I'm surprised that more parents aren't doing it. They* [Sure Start] *provide a crèche for everything and I think that is such a good thing. It makes me feel I'm more than just a mum.*'

The parents interviewed approved of the higher level of services and support they received and the shorter waiting times they experienced because they lived in a Sure Start area, although some did indicate that this situation had led to resentment and a perception of unequal treatment from those living nearby, but just outside the particular Sure Start catchment area. One group, for breastfeeding mothers, had been opened up to women outside the catchment area because the number from within the area was relatively small. Certain parents went as far to say that the support provided by Sure Start was part of the reason why they wanted to stay in the area, despite its obvious limitations in terms of lack of safe outdoor play space and the large number of high-rise flats. For mothers with a partner working shifts and needing to sleep during the day, the difficulties of living in a flat with small children were all too obvious, as was the need for somewhere to go.

> '*I don't want to tell my child "You have to be quiet because your father is sleeping", but I have to tell him, and after nine o'clock we go out. Which is all right if the weather is nice ... .that's why we are* [Sure Start] *regulars because there isn't anywhere else to take my child.*'

Although the specifics of how Sure Start programmes now operate has changed, there has been no loss of impetus in early intervention work with children and families, a theme we will return to in Chapter 7, when we will review the evidence base on 'what works'. This brief presentation of parents' perspectives is, however, a reminder about the relatively ordinary types of opportunities and support that may make a difference and are certainly needed and valued by families living in relative poverty in inner-city environments.

Families as the Solution? Family Group Conferences

In contrast to community-based initiatives like Sure Start, Family Group Conferences (FGCs) focus on individual families and the children in difficulty within them. FGCs were introduced into the UK in 1992, by the Family Rights Group. The practice originated in New Zealand as a response to concern about the over-representation of Maori children in the state childcare system. The UK was one of the first countries outside New Zealand to implement the FGC model (Sundell *et al.*, 2001). FGCs are family-led decision-making meetings. They are thus different in character from meetings with a similar purpose that are led by professionals. In FGCs 'family' is defined inclusively and broadly, to include the child/ren, parents, extended family and significant friends and neighbours to the family who may not actually be blood-related. The referrer is required to be committed to the process and attend the FGC. It should be emphasised that essentially FGCs are an approach to planning and decision-making that involves the wider family network in partnership with, and supported by, the statutory and other agencies. That is, an FGC is not an intervention as such.

One of the central aims of the FGC approach is to 'empower' the children and family members involved – both in terms of the process itself and the outcomes, over which they have more control (Lupton and Nixon, 1999). There is growing interest in children's participation in family decision-making. To date, research has tended to focus on divorce or care proceedings, although there is also a small body of research on the private aspect of everyday family life (Leach, 2003). Leach (2003) sees children's participation within everyday family decision-making as unequal and structured by the boundaries set by parents. He does not view children's inclusion in family decision-making as democratic, as has been argued by others (see for example, Giddens, 1998). In relation to FGCs, concern has also been voiced about the extent to which children can have an equal voice in the way the meeting is run and the FGC plan drawn up (Lupton and Stevens, 1998).

Despite some sustained research interest and a growing body of small-scale evaluations, it is probably fair to say that much of the FGC literature is explicitly promotional and based on a strong belief in the value of this way of working with families. Much of the research is essentially based on process and immediate outputs, rather than outcomes.

The study we will now look at in more depth employed a quasi-experimental design that included an intervention and a comparison group, for which key outcome data were compared. The outcome data were agreed on the basis that they were key performance indicators for the Education Department and they were also specified as issues that the FGCs aimed to address. The intervention group (n = 41) were referred for an FGC and the comparison group had the 'normal' service from the Educational Welfare Service (EWS) (n = 38). In the event, 11 FGC cases did not result in a conference (they were 'non-convened' conferences). Outcome data showed that the EWS had proportionately more impact on school attendance, in comparison with convening an FGC, although the difference was not great: a less than 10 per cent increase in attendance in the EWS group, with the convened FGC group having a similar rate of attendance before and after the intervention. This finding was disappointing for the service, but less surprising to the FGC co-ordinators who actually set up the conferences. They were keen to emphasise that the impact of an FGC could not and should not be measured by changes in school attendance or exclusion from school alone. Indeed, other data collected in this research tended to back up this view.

A standardised questionnaire was used: the Strengths and Difficulties Questionnaire (or SDQ; see Goodman, 1997). This measured any change in the level of perceived difficulties a child had before and after an FGC, as well as the perceived impact of the behaviour on others. In all respects modest improvements were found in terms of mean scores, as Figures 4.1 and 4.2 illustrate in relation to the total level of difficulty scores. Comparison with what might be expected in a total population of children in Figure 4.2 illustrates that this sample was proportionately more likely to be presenting

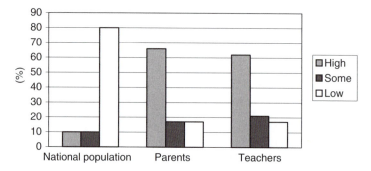

Figure 4.1 Comparing level of need at referral (SDQ total difficulties scores)

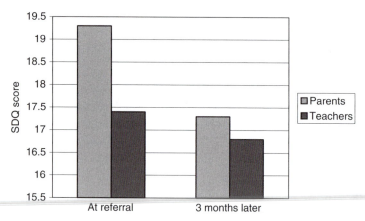

Figure 4.2 Comparing parents' and teachers' assessment of total difficulties (at referral and 3 months later)

behaviour in the 'high' level of need category (denoting 'abnormal' behaviour); 66 per cent of parents and 62 per cent of teachers put children into this category, in comparison with 10 per cent of the whole population of children. The 'abnormal' behaviour category indicated by the SDQ scoring system identifies 'caseness' for psychiatric purposes. What is interesting to note here is the children who apparently present normal behaviour in a context of an FGC referral. The referral itself is an indication of high levels of adult concern to what amounts to a scarce resource.

The modest level of change in the SDQ 'total difficulties' score in Figure 4.2 reminds us of the difficulty of bringing about positive improvements in circumstances where most children are already viewed as behaving in an out of the ordinary way in both home and school. Furthermore, the greatest changes were reported by parents, yet the FGC was centrally based on sorting

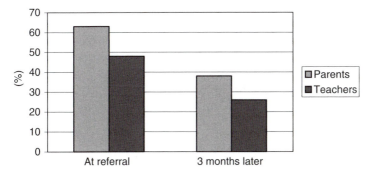

Figure 4.3 Comparing parents' and teachers' sense of 'great burden' (at referral and 3 months later)

out problems manifest in school through behaviour and attendance. There were, of course, bigger improvements in individual cases, as well as a worsening of circumstances in some cases. Overall the younger cases of primary-age children were more likely to show measurable improvements in terms of behaviour and attendance following an FGC. Both parents and teachers reported finding FGCs useful in a range of ways and also that they had a reduced sense of 'burden' in relation to coping with the child who was the focus of the FGC, in the months following the meeting (see Figure 4.3). Both the reduced SDQ total difficulties score and sense of burden for parents were statistically significant findings.

Feedback from children and young people who had an FGC was obtained in various ways in the research; through questionnaires in 20 cases (10 primary; 10 secondary) and via a group interview with 7 young people. Data from children and young people showed very varied experiences, as elsewhere in the research, although improvements were apparent in half of the secondary-school cases. A strong theme in the group interview, however, was self-consciousness and the need for peer support in the actual experience of the FGC. A typical response to a question about what didn't help was 'everyone looked at me', and in relation to 'other comments' that they would like 'less people there, especially adults from school'. Several young people said that they 'would have liked a friend there but it wasn't allowed in school time'. The latter issue pointed to the potential conflicts in terms of timing, participation and support for the children in planning meetings such as an FGC.

The evidence in the study overall was that FGCs, like many other ways of trying to work with families in problematic circumstances, worked for some but not for others. FGCs were clearly not the panacea hoped for by the service and often claimed by those who promote this way of working. Part of the issue here is about what the FGC is trying to achieve. We also have to consider how we measure this and whether the measure is valid (see Chapter 7 for more detailed discussions about methodological issues). In relation to FGCs, we already knew from existing research that families willing to commit to an FGC generally have positive experiences of the process, but there was no evidence that FGCs could set in motion the kind of support that would lead to changes that agencies working with families are expected to bring about (i.e. in this study, improved school attendance in particular). Furthermore, schools have to be able to cope with young people's behaviour; if they feel they cannot, they are likely to exclude them. It is important, then, when looking at interventions that try to harness the resources and support of the family for children and young people, to consider whether this can happen quickly enough and in a way that also meets the remit and performance targets of the agencies responsible for providing a service. Research on 'early intervention' in Chapter 5 also highlights these issues in relation to a Joint School and Family Support Team.

Living Away from Home and Locality: Why Are Some Children in 'Out-of-Area' Placements?

As we noted earlier, a minority of children (around 0.5 per cent) are looked after in any given year. An even smaller proportion are looked after away from the locality in which their families live. The general principle for children looked after by the state is to keep them as near to home as possible with a view to returning them to their parents when this is considered to be the right time. However, there are circumstances when the important principle of keeping children close to home is not met. It frequently happens when people are sent to the secure estate, although this is a much less frequent option (around 3,000 young people at any one time; see Chapter 3) than in the looked-after system and facilities are even more unevenly available. Sometimes children are sent 'out of area' primarily because it is felt that a young person needs to be away from their family or peer group for a period. Occasionally very severe mental health problems may mean that specialist facilities are required. Goldson (2002) highlights the irony of locked institutions being used as protection for one group of children and punishment for another. In reality these issues often overlap in particular cases. Residential establishments for children serve diverse and often complex needs (Sinclair and Gibbs, 1998). They operate in a difficult climate for a number of reasons. The general decline in the number of residential establishments has partly been brought about by concerns about institutionalisation as well as cost. Evidence of abuse of children in residential care has further hastened its decline and image problem. This means that children in residential care today tend to have more severe problems than in the past and display more extreme behaviour (Hayden *et al.*, 1999).

Therapeutic communities are a very particular type of residential establishment for children. They are based on creating a whole living environment and set of relationships in which the adults working with the children enter into a therapeutic relationship with them. Children live, attend school and spend their leisure time in the same setting. Such communities are changing and adapting with contemporary expectations for greater contact and work with parents and other relatives, as well as fostering greater integration with other services and groups that work with children and families in trouble (Little with Kelly, 1995).

As Little and Kelly (1995) point out, children living away from home tend to come from the extremes of the class system – those who are sent to elite residential boarding schools because of family tradition and parents working abroad and those who are in various forms of residential care or secure accommodation because of severe problems and needs, many of whom come from the poorest homes. Living in some form of residential establishment is a very atypical childhood, and where this has been initiated by the state it has often had very negative connotations. Little and Kelly (1995) present a picture of one of the well-known therapeutic communities. They show that staff were good at building a safe and supportive environment and the strong commitment to education produced good outcomes. However, Little and Kelly were critical of some of the 'treatment' aspects of the facility, describing them as ill-thought-out. They also found that contact with relatives was unsatisfactory. Beedell (1993) charts the types of backgrounds and experiences of children in nine therapeutic communities:

> The main treatment need for them is to provide a stable and reliable environment of care, comfort and control; to anticipate the circumstances in which they are liable to panic (i.e. to suffer unbearable anxiety) and become unable to manage themselves or allow others to do so. This will lessen the occasions in which their feeling is that the world has let them down. (p. 4)

Overall there is a relative lack of research into out-of-area placements of various types. We do not have accurate numbers and overall we are uncertain about the outcomes from these placements. The issue tends to become subsumed under the broader literature on residential care, although there is beginning to be more research and evidence about the secure estate (see, for example, YJB, 2001b).

The number of cases where a local authority can only provide for a child 'out of area' is very small. The study we will now look at involved an audit and analysis of Social Services 'out-of-area' placements of young people for social and behavioural reasons from a city (total population around 200,000) in a full calendar year in the late 1990s. The total number of cases was 20, not including 8 cases where disability was the main reason for the placement.

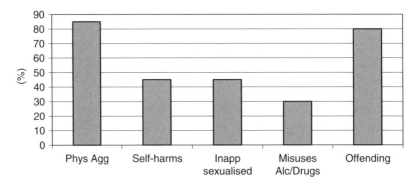

Figure 4.4 Children placed out of area – behaviour and offending
Key: Phys Agg = physically aggressive behaviour; Inapp sexualised =
inappropriate sexualised behaviour; Misuses Alc/Drugs = misuses alcohol
or drugs.

In the following section we will look at the kinds of needs identified for
these children and young people and why an out-of-area placement was
used to try and meet these needs. At the time these were all Social Services
cases: although some contribution was made from the Education Department
in certain cases, a financial contribution from mental health services was rare.
In the majority of cases (16, or 80 per cent) Social Services had been
involved with the child and family since the child was a baby or at primary
school. In the other four cases the children and their families came from
outside the local area and their Social Services history was not so clear. In all
but one case (19, or 95 per cent) there was clear evidence of abuse and in
ten cases there was evidence of more than one type of abuse. Most (15, or
75 per cent) of these children and young people had experienced multiple
placement moves. For the whole group the range in number of placements
was 2–12, with 6.25 as the mean. Out-of-area placements had broken down
in eight (40 per cent) cases and nine (45 per cent) children had spent time
in secure accommodation (in a LASCH) before going to a care-focused
placement.

Figure 4.4 illustrates that physically aggressive (17, or 85 per cent) and
offending behaviour (16, or 80 per cent) was particularly prevalent in this
group, but also that a number of children self-harmed (9, or 45 per cent)
and displayed inappropriately sexualised behaviour (9, or 45 per cent),
and a minority had clear evidence of drug and alcohol misuse (6, or 30
per cent).

Mental health problems were also strongly in evidence (and in this research
verified by a community psychiatric nurse). There was clear evidence of mental health problems in 12 families (60 per cent) and three-quarters of the
individual children (15, or 75 per cent). Violent relationships and behaviour

from adults within the family were in evidence in three-quarters (15, or 75 per cent) of cases. This included domestic violence, violence shown towards Social Services staff and excessive discipline and physical abuse of the children in the study. In one case the family was said to be part of a paedophile ring. Special educational needs (17, or 5 per cent) and exclusion (16, or 80 per cent) from school were common and a minority (6, or 30 per cent) also had records of school attendance problems.

Given this very wide-ranging array of needs and difficulties in the lives of these children it might seem obvious to ask why the Social Services was the organisation that had primary responsibility for accommodating them. The key issue was whether or not parents could look after the children and, failing that, whether the local authority could provide for them within foster or residential care. From the perspective of other departments (education and health in particular), this led to the argument that the primary responsibility lay with Social Services.

It was not that other services had no involvement with the children; indeed, involvement with the educational psychology service was evident in 14 cases (70 per cent) and with educational welfare in 6 cases (30 per cent). Families had been referred to the Family Resource Centre (Social Services run) in more than half the cases and to child and family therapy in nearly three-quarters of cases (14, or 70 per cent). The Family Resource Centre had great difficulty getting the families in this study to commit to the work they were trying to do with them; indeed, in many cases staff queried whether the families had the capacity (never mind the willingness) to change. Despite referral and the occasional attendance at Child and Family Therapy Services there were very few clear diagnoses: several children were referred to as having a 'conduct disorder' and/or an 'attachment disorder' and in one case 'post-traumatic stress disorder'. Five families had been involved in residential-based work and four had either psychotherapy or play therapy. Families and children were also well known to the police (16, or 80 per cent) either because of offending behaviour, or because the child was at risk. Half the families were also known to other areas of the criminal justice system, either the courts or YJB.

At the start of this research there was a belief in the local authority that a relatively small number of families were known to be in need of help from all the key statutory services. In a sense this was true; an internal document put the figure at around 80 families for a city of a little under 200,000 inhabitants. This snapshot of cases where Social Services had the main responsibility for provision out of area did reveal the involvement of all the key agencies, but not necessarily at the time the placement was made. That is, the situation was dynamic: for example, some families had residential support when their child was a few years old but had had very little or no involvement since then; there was no obvious sequence of events, rather a series of referrals to try and get help and support with whatever issue was most pressing at a particular time. Several case-holders expressed the view typified by the following quote:

> '*It feels like you have to watch children deteriorate over a considerable period of time before they can be considered* [for a specialist out-of-area placement].'

Others highlighted the in-fighting between departments over who should pay and where needs should be met. The children's needs were often assessed as one-to-one care, with the same level of support educationally. Yet sometimes the Education Department expected children to go to a local education facility when they were placed out of area. This was rarely realistic and led to long periods of time spent outside education. What social workers believed to be necessary for these children was

> '*Supersonic project carers, one at least would be employed as a carer and available to the child all the time.*'

Changes in Who Cares and Family Forms

The increasing 'professionalisation' of foster care and a growth in the use of remand foster care (Lipscombe, 2003) recognise the kind of need encapsulated in the last quotation. As an alternative to incarceration of young offenders specifically, it is a response to the recognition that being cared for by well-meaning substitute parents may not be enough to 'hold' the most damaged young people with the most difficult behaviour. However, placement breakdown is often associated with very difficult-to-manage behaviour and research indicates that many foster carers consider giving up due to the overall pressures of caring. Furthermore, there is a shortage of carers (Wilson *et al.*, 2000). More optimistically, Martin's (2002) study shows that local authorities are beginning to provide better training and support for carers, as well as recognition through a pay structure that rewards level of training and responsibilities.

Family forms are changing rapidly and the various pressures and expectations (in terms of self-actualisation, material comfort and dual careers, as well as care of the elderly) are competing with the time available for bringing up children. In one of the opening quotations, Young and Halsey (1995) characterise some families (working single parents and dual-income households especially) as 'time-poor' due to the amount of paid work they do alongside family responsibilities, while other households could be seen as 'time-rich' but economically poor. Young and Halsey view society as polarised in terms of time as well as money, and they argue for a redistribution of resources in favour of children. There has been some move in this direction since they presented this argument. Arguably children's services (see Chapter 8, 'The move to integrated services for children') may be more able to resolve some of the interdepartmental differences that were characterised in the research on out-of-area placements presented above. The various ways in which families are either supported or relieved of their immediate responsibilities for everyday care of their children are evolving in directions that have to take account of changing family forms and pressures.

Note

1   Relative poverty is calculated by Bradshaw (2003) as the proportion of children living in households with incomes less than 50 per cent of the average equivalent (after controlling for the needs of families of different sizes) income after housing costs. Other measures used include a calculation based on 60 per cent of the median (middle value) household income (see Hirsch and Miller, 2004).

5

Children in Trouble at School

The idea that social exclusion may result from dim future prospects makes one think pretty quickly about children. 'Exclusion' may offer a useful label for the fate that awaits some children who suffer from various disadvantages in childhood which threaten their capability in future … This includes disadvantages in traditional dimensions of 'child development': *education* and health.

– Micklewright, 2002, pp. 9–10; my emphasis

Every pupil has the right to learn without disruption; no teacher should be subject to abuse or disrespect. We have given head teachers the powers needed to maintain discipline and the highest standards of conduct. Violent behaviour, including the use of knives, will not be tolerated. We are working with schools and teaching organisations to implement a zero-tolerance approach to lower-level disruption. The number of places in out-of-school units has almost doubled.

– Labour Party Manifesto, 2005, p. 39

'In Trouble' at School

Schools for most children are the main public facility that they attend. It is the key place where they make friends and acquire much of the knowledge and skills they will need in life. Being excluded from this normal childhood environment is at the extreme end of adult sanctions against behaviour they do not want. The tension between individual needs (adults as well as children) and that of the group is apparent throughout the education system. At school children are expected to adjust to being in a large group, to respond to the expectations of adults other than their parents, and to spend much of their time in a classroom. Many children have some adjustment problems when they start school, or change schools – particularly when they enter secondary school. There are plenty of potential sources for these problems in school – such as difficult relationships with other children or particular teachers, as well as problems with academic learning and other activities. There are also problems that children bring into school – such as worries about parents or conflicts in the local community. Further, being in an organised environment with large groups of people simply does not suit some children. Adults in school, although they have chosen to do this form of work, are very variable in their capacity to understand children and young people and teach in a way that engages them. Exemplary and charismatic teachers do exist, but not in every classroom. Parents and carers are expected to ensure that their children attend school and, not unreasonably, are most concerned about their individual child; they expect schools to understand and cater for this. Parents have been encouraged to believe that they can chose their child's school and that the school will be able to cater for their individual child's needs and aptitudes, as well as keep them safe in school and on school trips.

The central most important thing to keep in mind when one thinks about schools is the fact that they are mass institutions – children are in the great majority and they often have to be moved around in large groups (as at break times and lunchtime, and the start and end of the school day). Some activities can be dangerous if they are not well structured. Clear rules and good organisation are essential in providing a framework to ensure order in schools. Adults in school are well aware that they are in the minority and that they rely on the goodwill of students to more or less keep within the rules. All in all this situation presents a rich mix of expectations, competing priorities and potential areas of conflict, even before we consider the wishes of parents and carers, children with more severe problems and disabilities, or the additional agenda of schools as the hub of child-care services (as in *Every Child Matters*, see Chapters 2 and 8).

Children can get into trouble in school in a number of ways. Some are in trouble because of failure to do their work; some because of their behaviour towards other pupils and/or teachers; some because they do not attend regularly or punctually. In one way or another the focus is usually upon children's behaviour, as failure to do work can be interpreted as 'disaffection', rather than inability to do the work set. The onus of responsibility in relation to behaviour and attendance at school differs in important respects. In relation to school attendance the onus rests on parents. Parents can be fined up to a maximum of £2,500 or imprisoned for up to three months for their child's non-attendance at school. The first parent to be imprisoned for their child's non-attendance was convicted in 2002 (Passmore, 2002). On the other hand, head teachers have the right to exclude children for a fixed period (or series of fixed periods) of up to 45 days in any one school year, or permanently from that school (subject to appeal). Schools should set and mark work for children to do while they are excluded from school. There is an expectation that parents can influence their children's behaviour in school, with home–school agreements and individual parenting contracts (in the most severe cases) making this explicit.

After setting the scene in relation to concerns about children's behaviour in school, this chapter will look at key findings from two original pieces of research. These studies are both evaluations: one is a piece of longitudinal research carried out over a three-year period as a formative evaluation of a new intervention with primary-school children; the other is a 'before' and 'after' evaluation of an established behaviour-management training programme for staff across children's services, although the research reported upon here is based on schools. Chapter 4 reported on another evaluation of an intervention that is used in schools – FGCs. This latter research could arguably be included in either Chapters 4 or 5, but it has been left in Chapter 4 as an example of an intervention that is used in a range of contexts with families (including child protection, family placement, youth justice and young carers) and because it is essentially about empowering families to come up with their own plans to help their children.

Behaviour in Schools

We already have a sense of the long-standing nature of adult concerns about children's behaviour in schools from earlier chapters. Whether or not pupil behaviour is actually getting worse is difficult to establish for a host of reasons, including changing behavioural norms over time, different school 'cultures' and a lack of reliable and comparable monitoring systems. From time to time government-initiated enquiries have tried to review the situation. At the time of writing, the Steer report (Steer, 2005) is the most recent enquiry. In many ways it reaches very similar conclusions to the Elton report (DES/WO, 1989), 16 years earlier:

> It is often the case that for pupils, school is a calm place in a disorderly world. We realise that this is not the case in every school, but in our experience, where unsatisfactory behaviour does occur, in the vast majority of cases it involves low-level disruption in lessons. Incidents of serious misbehaviour, and especially acts of extreme violence, remain exceptionally rare and are carried out by a very small proportion of pupils.
>
> (Steer, 2005, p. 5)

The Steer report also recognises the connection between pupil behaviour and the quality and appropriateness of teaching. Steer (2005) recognises, however, that certain problematic aspects of pupil behaviour in schools are new, such as the general availability of technology to pupils, e.g. mobile phones, which are then used in new forms of bullying and to record assaults and humiliations (such as 'happy slapping') or to summon angry parents into the school at the behest of a pupil who has been disciplined. Further, Steer notes the uncertainty about the meaning and application of *in loco parentis* (which gives teachers the same authority over their pupils as parents have over their children) for contemporary teachers. It is highlighted by Steer, as well as by the Elton Committee in 1989, that the legal judgements supporting this concept are very old and that the principle is based on an ancient doctrine of common law (2005, p. 79). This is seen as problematic in a context in which 'the trend for parents to challenge schools at law, noted in the Elton Report, has continued and intensified' (Steer, 2005, p. 80).

Although much of the focus is on 'managing' or 'improving' pupil behaviour, most of the strategies and training packages developed in this area require adults and institutions to include how they 'manage' or 'improve' their behaviour; in essence, how they build relationships and relate to pupils and their colleagues. Patterns of behaviour in school associated with pupil disaffection have both complex causes and highly individual expressions. At the school level, school ethos is recognised as important (Rutter *et al.*, 1979). At the level of the individual pupil, behaviour interpreted as disaffection may relate to a number of issues, including child abuse and poor parenting, disrupted and stressful living circumstances, the disruptions associated with being 'looked after'(being 'in care'), relative poverty, special educational needs (or learning needs not met), and so on. However, disaffection, whatever the various causes, is only one explanation for not attending school or behaving in a problematic way. Common issues relating to non-attendance are academic pressure and fear of failure, being bullied, being a young carer, and being part of a travelling family.

Teachers are left with interpreting a complex picture in responding to children's behaviour. Some children might be characterised as simply *'naughty'* or they present *'inappropriate' behaviour (at school)*: these children are unlikely to get into major difficulties at most schools. Most children will present this sort of behaviour at some time in school and often it will go unnoticed. The concept of *disaffection* is often used to characterise a broad group of children who to varying degrees don't like school. *Bullying* behaviour is also common and is often related to other issues and can lead to non-attendance and mental health problems.

At the school level there is widespread recognition that the school ethos and environment are crucial in promoting positive behaviour and a raft of policies, agreements and strategies are expected, such as behaviour management; anti-bullying, anti-harassment and equal opportunities policies; home–school agreements and particular strategies or approaches to realising these policies and agreements. The use of the curriculum both to promote pro-social values, for example through citizenship education, and through teaching and learning strategies, is yet another part of what all schools are expected to do. At the level of the individual pupil there are a range of strategies and approaches that are widely known and used to both promote positive behaviour, as well as to more broadly promote inclusion.

When the various types of support for behaviour in schools are reviewed in this way one could be led to believe that we had a national system of comprehensive support. However, as has already been intimated, in reality support is patchy and partly dependent on time-limited resources, rather than national services. We might conceptualise support in four tiers, with Level 4 being the apex and Level 1 the base of a pyramid (see Figure 5.1). Levels 1 and 4 are in place with varying degrees of efficacy nationally. Levels 2 and 3 are much more patchy and some types of provision are simply not available

Level 4 – Out-of-school provision
PRUs, home tuition, vocational and other provision in further education (FE) colleges. Include (and other independent and charitable organisations) programmes in some LEAs. Residential placements (see out-of-area residential placements in Chapter 6)

Level 3 – Combination and reintegration programmes and plans
Part-time at school, part-time at a PRU or FE college. Sometimes with a view to full reintegration. Include (a national charity) programmes in some LEAs (see FGCs in Chapter 4)

Level 2 – In-school and more intensive support
Withdrawal rooms or 'learning support units' (LSUs); group work and individual work – can come from core services such as EWS, educational psychology (EP), or from a wide variety of special and time-limited projects, such as BIPs and BESTs. Learning mentors. Connexions–Personal Advisers (see Joint School and Family Support Team (JSFST) in this chapter; FGCs in Chapter 4)

Level 1 – Whole-school
Policies and strategies: behaviour, bullying, harassment, equal opportunities, special educational needs provision, teaching and learning
Agreements: home–school agreements
Individual pupils: all have educational targets and expectations about behaviour set. Some individuals in need of further support may have individual behaviour plans (IBPs) and/or pastoral support plans (PSPs), and all 'looked-after' children should have personal education plans (PEPs)
The curriculum: personal social and health education (PSHE); citizenship education; teaching and learning strategies (see the Team-Teach approach in this chapter)

Figure 5.1 Levels of response to problematic behaviour in schools

in some areas. In general, cities and the poorer areas of England have gained additional resources under New Labour, albeit with strings attached. Thus vulnerable children in more affluent areas have fewer options between Levels 1 and 4. This raises important issues of equity in educational provision and support for vulnerable children.

Schools also have to consider risk and safety on a number of different levels: in terms of access to the school site from intruders, in terms of vetting the suitability of their staff and in terms of the everyday relations between children, as well as children and adults who attend, work or visit the school. Schools were awarded £10 million in 2002–03 to increase security measures through the Capital Modernisation Fund. Research intended to inform the development of policy and practice in this field was undertaken at the same time (Lloyd and Ching, 2003). Interestingly, this latter research identified external threats such as intruders, arson and burglary as greater concerns than internal threats from within the school community. The dynamic nature of school security concerns is highlighted by this research, with pupil behaviour issues emerging in relation to the impact on school security in its widest sense.

Although many of the more mainstream issues about parents and schools emphasise the positive support parents can provide, this is not always the case in relation to children in trouble. More coercive measures are being used towards parents in relation to ensuring their child attends school. Parenting contracts have been available to schools in England and Wales since early 2004 through the Anti-social Behaviour Act 2003. The Steer report (2005) also adds support to the use of parenting contracts and the possibility that schools can give parenting orders in highlighting the need for a 'more immediate and consistent response to schools dealing with violent or abusive parents' (p. 95).

Early Intervention: Working with Parents and Primary Schools

Early intervention is a concept that may be variously understood – it may mean early in a child's life or early in the development of a problem. It may also mean working preventatively in problematic situations or families. Intervening early is thought to have a better chance of addressing problem behaviour in children that may become more problematic with time. Further, approaches that attempt to make an impact in more than one setting, 'the ecosystem' of the child, are thought to have the most impact (Cooper and Upton, 1990). Early signs of difficulties in parenting, in pre-school facilities and at school are known to be powerful predictors of social maladaptation, particularly when behaviours are externalised. Behaviour problems tend to be particularly stable when established earlier on in a child's life (Fortin and Bigras, 1997).

The research we will now look at was based on a project that set out to develop a city-wide service for children aged 8–11 (Key Stage 2) using an ecosystemic model of intervention. The service was thus seen as intervening relatively early in the school life of children and while they still had only one or two class teachers working with them. The research was conducted in the late 1990s and followed through in depth the early planning stages and first two years of operation of the service, known as a Joint School and Family Support Team (JSFST). The Team was set up by a new unitary authority with the key focus of preventing exclusion from junior schools in a city. At the time of gaining unitary status this city was one of the highest excluding authorities in England (a situation which has since greatly improved), and reducing exclusion was high on local and national political agendas. The development of the Team depended upon the co-operation between the new Social Services and Education Departments in the city and a sense of shared vision and responsibility for vulnerable children and families.

The Team was located within the educational psychology service in the city and consisted of two part-time educational psychologists, a part-time social worker and four staff who were known as 'project workers'. The educational psychologists concentrated on overall management of the Team and the whole-school-based work and the social worker concentrated on work with the families. The 'project workers' focused on the direct work with children. The principles on which the Team was based were clearly informed by evidence about risk and protective factors, as identified by Farrington (1996), and upon promoting resilience, as advocated by Rutter *et al.* (1998). Overall, research on resilience underlines the central importance of relationships in childhood. Close attachments to one or two significant adults, not necessarily parents, appear to play a key protective role. The logic then of trying to work with parents as well as teachers is obvious. When considering the efficacy of the work of the Team we needed to acknowledge the difficulties in establishing an accurate identification of children 'at risk', particularly at risk from exclusion from school and thus 'prevention' of this eventuality. Although the risk factors related to behavioural difficulties are well known, research often focuses on particular factors in isolation rather than studying these factors in combination (Fortin and Bigras, 1997). It is clear from our research that the families in receipt of support from the Team generally had to contend with a number of very stressful situations, although parents and children did not always agree about how upsetting specific events were. In many cases families were in significant difficulty owing to, for example, domestic violence, loss of employment, rent arrears, moving home, and so on. Problems at school could not be seen in isolation from these other major intervening factors.

One way of estimating the scale of potential need for support from the JSFST was to look at evidence from official records of exclusion in the city. In the school year that saw the establishment of the JSFST there were 89 fixed-period exclusions (one day or more) and 11 permanent exclusions from over 50 primary schools in the city. These exclusions, however, were concentrated in the Key Stage 2 phase (31 schools) – 83 of the 89 fixed-period exclusions and all 11 permanent exclusions. In many ways these figures might seem quite reassuring, when it is considered that these children were part of a primary-school population of around 12,000. However, as we saw in Chapter 3, behaviour resulting in an exclusion is only part of the problem; it is usually a response to the 'acting-out' behaviour that often gets most adult attention. If the numbers of children known to have identified social, emotional and behavioural difficulties (SEBD) as a SEN are included in the estimate of children who are likely to need most support from the Team, the number rises to over 200 children at Key Stage 2 (or 1 in 60 children in the city in this age group). When the scale of need is compared against the number of staff available (2.5 full-time equivalent project workers; the equivalent of a full-time equivalent educational psychologist and a half-time social worker), the nature of the task they might be able to do needed careful planning.

The Team responded to the realities of the resources available against the likely need for support by offering different levels of service: in the first two years this involved individual work (34 children), consultations (31 children) and group work in five schools (over 500 children participated in a one-year period). The Team started its work focused upon individual referrals, around which work with home and school could be undertaken. One of the key principles in the operational policy was to have no waiting list – the Team was charged with the task of giving priority to children in greatest need. In practice this led to the development of a wider range of responses than just the individual cases, as described below. During the time of the evaluation the range of work of the Team developed from the individual casework to include consultations with schools, liaison and networking with other agencies and services on behalf of individual children, additional activities with children and school-based activities.

The intervention process with individual cases was intensive and aimed to produce long-term change by developing systemic change in the school and family, while maintaining a child-centred therapeutic approach; the welfare of the child was paramount. To this end, the aim of the Team was for children to actively participate in the assessment, intervention and evaluation process and attend all meetings, thus ensuring they played an integral role in the design and development of all programmes. Following an intervention period of six weeks, children were given the opportunity to participate in a peer-group support programme. This phase of the programme aimed to reduce the likelihood of a relapse.

Consultations were held with schools where children could not be taken on as individual cases but where permanent exclusion was still a possibility for a pupil. Consultations were held after school on the school site. Parents/carers, children and relevant staff and Team members were all invited. The consultation aimed to provide an opportunity to discuss the complex issues surrounding an individual child's situation, consider problem-solving processes and develop an 'emergency' Individual Behaviour Plan (IBP).

For cases not considered suitable for the intensive support of the Team, other forms of support were facilitated. This included other LEA or Social Services Department (SSD) services, such as Educational Welfare or EP, family centres or the family resource centre. Support also came from the Child and Family Therapy Service and related mental health services, as well as a range of voluntary organisations, specialist services (such as Victim Support or the Family Mediation Service) and more generic community-based services (such as mother and toddler groups, play-schemes, and so on).

Places on play schemes and other activities were accessed for individuals who were current cases over the summer period. By the second year, the Team was operating a weekly group for the children finishing a period of intensive support. Overnight camps and activity days were organised at a local outdoor centre. Using a 'Circle of Friends' approach (DfEE, 1999), social support was created around individuals in school when they had completed a period of intensive support.

School-based group activities got under way during the second year of operation and arose out of an approach from a group of five inner-city schools for earlier preventative work with groups. These schools all had experience of group work via the SSD or a previous school support project and were willing to pay for a service. It was agreed by the Advisory Group for the project that this work could go ahead as a pilot, although it breached the principles of a city-wide service and equal opportunities for support. All the four project workers in the JSFST had involvement in this work in at least one school. By year three of the Team this work extended to 12 schools.

The Evaluation

The evaluation showed that in the individual cases, the Team were working with children who were in difficulty at home, sufficient to have had the involvement of a social worker for home-based issues in nearly nine in ten cases (30, or 88 per cent). One in seven (5 of the 34) of these children already had records of concern held at the police station. More in-depth work in case studies of children and their families (14 in all) undertaken across individual, consultation and group-work interventions showed the prevalence of major stresses in their lives: 86 per cent (12) family breakdown; 79 per cent (11) unable to do the school work set; 50 per cent (7) bullied; 50 per cent (7) their family was a recent victim of a crime, and so on. In other words, these were cases where significant problems were already present, although case studies also demonstrated that there was very little difference in the range of needs and stresses in the lives of children accepted for individual work and those accepted for consultations.

The structure and range of the work of the Team were impressive. It was clearly evidence-based in its approach. In terms of measurable outcomes permanent exclusions at primary level did go down, from 13 in the year before the Team was established to 2 in the third year, and in recent years the LEA has all but eliminated permanent primary-school exclusions. The picture in relation to fixed-period exclusions was less positive, however. The trend here is upward, with over 200 individual pupils and over 500 records of fixed-period exclusion (i.e. some children have more than one record of exclusion a year) a few years after the Team was established. Anecdotal evidence suggested that instead of permanent exclusion schools were resorting to the use of fixed-period exclusions to give them respite from children's behaviour they felt they could not manage.

Further problems emerge in assigning the reduction in permanent exclusion to the work of the Team per se. The general policy direction in the later 1990s was to reduce school exclusion and, indeed, records of permanent school exclusion were reduced by a third nationally between 1997 and 2000 (see Chapter 3, Figure 3.6). Also the LEA quickly realised that there was a difference between the need to support children and families and the needs of schools. Changing behaviour is likely to take time and in the individual cases referred to and accepted by the Team, the issues likely to be affecting their behaviour were numerous and complex and mostly beyond the capacity or remit of individual primary schools. Thus the LEA provided additional classroom assistant support to individual children in danger of permanent exclusion: over four in ten (14, or 44 per cent) of the 34 children who started individual support programmes also had additional funding from the LEA for classroom assistant time.

What the evaluation really illustrated was the need for coherent, regular and focused support for managing behaviour in primary schools, which was supportive of children, their families and teachers. This is an ongoing and much bigger issue than that of permanent exclusion alone. The volume of children (over 500) involved in group work in just five schools, albeit those in some of the most stressful circumstances in the city, is illustrative of that. Properly managed, direct LEA 'emergency' funding of additional classroom support for individuals was probably the best way to keep children in school and thereby reduce permanent exclusions. The type of changes needed to keep children in school successfully and which may sometimes result from the work of a Team like the JSFST may take too long to avert a crisis. The research evidence did not support evidence of major changes in children's behaviour as a result of the intervention; indeed about half the children who had individual support or consultations continued to receive fixed-period exclusions. There were also key issues to do with appropriate curriculum, group sizes and resources in schools, as well as wider patterns of aspirations and opportunities in the community to contend with when considering the business of managing their behaviour in school. However, a major strength of the JSFST was that it was a city-wide and coherently organised service with a longer-term future (i.e. not a 'special', short-term project). This enabled its development, adaptation and expansion over a relatively short period of time. It has proved important as a service around which other related initiatives have since grown in this LEA.

Some key learning points from this evaluation related to the role of people in an interdisciplinary team (education and social work backgrounds). The educational psychologists were most clear about their role; the social worker, on the other hand, tended to get drawn into the very numerous family-based difficulties. These were so major in some cases that very little positive impact from the JSFST intervention on the child's behaviour was likely, and the parents' needs could easily exhaust the limited resources available. Some of these families already had a social worker who should have been ensuring the necessary support. It is clear that children and families' social workers in England are expected to focus more on the importance of a child's schooling as a potentially positive outcome from social work support, although there is continuing evidence that social workers are uncomfortable with the task (Hayden, 2005a). On the other hand, social work involvement in the parenting training in schools was a particularly appropriate use of social-work time and skills. It was crucial that the Team had expert advice and support from a social worker in Child Protection issues, as well as for official reports needed on the child and family circumstances, that arose in individual cases in contact with the Team. The project workers undertook most of the direct work with the individual children and ran the group sessions in schools. The skills necessary to do this were underestimated. Some individuals were more experienced and confident than others, whereas certain individuals could not credibly cope with the group work, leading to criticism from schools.

In short, this was a well thought-through and structured approach to a specific issue – young children in serious trouble in school – but in reality the issues underpinning the most needy cases were such that the intervention was not sufficiently resourced (nor appropriately staffed) to meet their need. In a sense a key problem was the focus on prioritising cases deemed to be most in need; this created a group of children who were more needy than the intervention envisaged. This prioritisation may have seemed logical at the time, but the idea that a six-week 'solution-focused' intervention could really meet their needs was misguided. What these children and families needed was much more intensive and longer-term support. The pragmatic approach of the local authority helped, however: keeping children in school through the provision of additional classroom support had a lot to commend it in terms of solving the immediate threat of exclusion. However, the hope that parents and schools might be more mutually supportive in helping this most needy group of children did not generally bear fruit. The parents usually had so many issues to deal with themselves that they found it hard to play their part in supporting their child in school. Many had very negative experiences of school themselves and did not want more of a relationship with the school. Teachers needed more practical and realistic advice about how to work with parents and the time to do so. Schools tended to prioritise the work that they saw as more truly preventative – that is, small-group work with children who needed help with their behaviour and who were expected to stay in mainstream schools. Schools clearly felt that the very problematic individual cases needed longer-term, more intensive and expert intervention from the LEA (now children's departments).

Behaviour Management Training in Schools: An Example

As we have just seen, most special projects or additional services to schools and families quickly demonstrate that the potential size and scale of need could overwhelm a service. Partly in response to this, there is great emphasis on behaviour management as a whole-school issue, for all schools. Schools are expected to provide an overall context (level 1 in Figure 5.1) that encourages positive behaviour, while also having strategies to respond to individual children that may present more of a challenge.

Some well-known strategies such as *Assertive Discipline* (Canter and Canter, 1992) and various forms of *Circle Time* (Mosley, 1993; Lucky Duck, 2002) have been widely used in schools. Overall, Assertive Discipline training does appear to train teachers to give more positive feedback and praise to pupils and teachers tend to perceive positive changes in pupil behaviour (Wood *et al.*, 1996). Circle Time is different philosophically from Assertive Discipline and is not generally used as a behaviour management intervention as such (Lucky Duck, 2002, p. 2) but is widely seen as a positive way of improving behaviour and relationships in schools. Increasingly, peer mediation schemes and other types of 'restorative' approaches are becoming more common in schools (see, for example, Hopkins, 2004). Such approaches are likely to be particularly useful at the whole-school level (level 1 in Figure 5.1) and also in more problematic cases (level 2 in Figure 5.1).

The research evidence we will now look at is based on an evaluation of *Team-Teach* as a whole-setting, holistic approach that addresses significant factors that can contribute to a critical incident involving children in social-care, education and health-care environments. That is, despite its name, this approach is used in environments outside schools and the education service. Team-Teach is thus informed by an interdisciplinary approach and its application includes residential child care, special schools and pupil referral units, as well as mainstream education. As an approach it could be used as a framework at all levels in Figure 5.1. The approach is distinct from most of the behaviour management strategies currently available in educational settings in that it includes both training in de-escalation skills and physical interventions, known as 'positive handling strategies'. Further, Team-Teach provides course members with reporting and recording skills; and equips them to rebuild relationships and manage their feelings. Policies and other documentation are part of the supportive framework provided by this approach. The emphasis of the approach is 'about the way people relate to each other' (Team-Teach, 2003, p. 11). Team-Teach views 'positive handling' as a concept confirming a commitment by organisations, and individuals within an organisation, to a framework of risk-reduction strategies (non-verbal, verbal and, where absolutely necessary, physical). These strategies are documented in the 'Individual Positive Handling Plans' and embedded within a whole-setting, holistic approach to behaviour supports and interventions. 'Positive Handling Plans' are the agreed strategies (non-verbal, verbal and physical) that aim to support the individual, providing them with a sense of security, safety and acceptance, allowing for recovery and repair, and facilitating learning and growth. Course documentation is at pains to stress that physical interventions are not the main focus of the approach, with preventative, diffusion and de-escalation techniques said to make up more than 95 per cent of responses to challenging behaviour (p. 11). Importantly, the approach clearly addresses the issue of feelings as well as procedures.

Team-Teach was devised in 1997 for use in special schools, mainstream schools and children's residential care settings. It is a whole-setting holistic approach to behaviour management that aims to provide a supportive infrastructure to ensure the well-being of all concerned. The need for staff to reflect on their own verbal, non-verbal and de-escalation skills is emphasised, as is the need for tight policies and documentation relating to challenging behaviour. Positive handling strategies (risk-reduced physical interventions that form part of the holistic response) are learned as 'last-resort' techniques.

There are five types of course in all. Some are designed for people who want to learn to manage behaviour effectively and others are for those who also hope to teach the skills. Each course builds on the knowledge gained from previous courses, while stressing the same basic principles and values. There is a clear framework for staff to refresh their skills and keep up to date with the latest advice on behaviour management through reaccreditation and refresher training. Video clips on the Team-Teach website are designed to enable participants to remind themselves of the positive handling techniques when necessary.

In keeping with most whole-school approaches, all staff in a school are recommended to have Team-Teach training – including classroom assistants, lunchtime staff, administrators, drivers and escorts. This is important in terms of consistency of approach from all adults in a setting, but also it is reasoned that those not usually involved with managing challenging behaviour on a day-to-day basis may act as 'critical friend' or witness in a crisis. Informing and involving children and young people, parents and governors about the approach is seen as essential, as is the active support of senior management. Officers from children's departments are also encouraged to do the training to enhance their chances of being able to offer appropriate support to schools.

A full range of strategies and support mechanisms are offered so that school staff are able to use a range of positive behaviours to encourage a culture where incidents involving challenging behaviours are less likely to happen and are routinely defused and de-escalated without the need for physical intervention. Trainees are taught to use all other de-escalation strategies before resorting to positive handling and are expected to reflect on their own behaviour and ensure their verbal or non-verbal behaviour does not exacerbate a situation. They are also taught to take full advantage of the support of other adults during a crisis, even if that means handing over responsibility to them to defuse a difficult situation.

Team-Teach views documentation as a key issue in the management of challenging behaviour. It believes schools and LEAs should ensure their policies clearly spell out what should be done to address all foreseeable risks and provide a supportive structure. Trainees are provided with information and advice to enable them to draw up positive handling plans to support individual children who experience behavioural difficulties and to effectively record, report, monitor and evaluate incidents involving positive handling. Finally, Team-Teach maintains that school management should ensure there is both a supportive and a reflective structure in place so everyone involved can take the opportunity to recover, learn and move on from a challenging incident.

The research reported upon here is part of a study that includes wide-ranging data. For example, the evaluation of over 500 courses conducted between 2000 and 2003 and observations of courses, as well as in-depth case studies of different types of institution (three schools and a behaviour support service operating through three pupil referral units in different areas of England and Wales), together with consultation with children and parents. This account focuses primarily on key evidence about the impact of the training on teachers from the different settings in the case studies. In these case studies, teachers completed a questionnaire directly before and directly after the Team-Teach training. About three months later a researcher visited the institutions to investigate in more depth the longer-term impact and issues arising out of training in this approach.

Evidence of Impact on Teachers

Many of the questions teachers were asked both before and after the Team-Teach course related to levels of confidence, knowledge and preparedness in relation to particular aspects of behaviour management. Improvements were seen in all aspects, as Table 5.1 illustrates.

The most positive aspects following training relate to staff confidence and increased knowledge of techniques perceived as effective in relation to safety, for themselves, aggressive children and other children. The biggest changes following training were found in relation to staff preparedness to respond to a physical challenge, confidence in being able to cope with children fighting, and, knowledge about the legal framework in relation to positive handling. Knowledge of the legal framework had the lowest proportion of staff reporting that they felt 'fairly knowledgeable' or better *before* the Team-Teach training. Least change was evident in whether staff felt 'confident' in providing physical or psychological support to children and preparedness to respond to deliberate manipulation from children.

There are interesting differences from this overall picture when individual institutions are compared. Overall the mainstream primary school showed very positive improvements in nearly all aspects monitored, although it was still concerned about keeping an aggressive child physically safe. In contrast, the mainstream secondary school showed the most positive 'after' rating for this latter issue, having started from a very low knowledge base. Both the mainstream and special secondary schools felt less confident with respect to giving psychological or physical support to children, or responding to deliberate manipulation, in comparison with colleagues in the primary institutions. Before the training a sizeable proportion of staff, particularly at the special school and PRUs, admitted that they physically intervened on a daily or weekly basis, despite not being trained to do so. However, following training one in five staff still voiced concerns about using positive handling strategies,

Table 5.1 Immediate impact of Team-Teach training

Type of impact	Before (%)	After (%)
Fairly 'confident', or better, that they can *keep themselves safe* from an aggressive child	44.1	79.3
Fairly 'confident', or better, that they can *keep an aggressive child physically safe*	27.0	77.8
Fairly 'confident', or better, that they can *keep other children safe* from an aggressive child	35.7	75.0
Fairly 'confident', or better, about coping with children *fighting*	20.0	71.7
Fairly 'knowledgeable', or better, about the *legal framework* and positive handling	15.9	71.1
Fairly 'confident', or better, in relation to *psychological support* to children	45.5	59.3
Fairly 'confident', or better, in relation to providing *physical support* to children	33.7	57.7
Fairly well 'prepared', or better, to respond to deliberate *manipulation*	29.9	55.2
Numbers in all 4 case studies combined	*187* (6 teachers did not complete the first questionnaire)	*193*

reminding us that even with training this is likely to remain a worrying issue for staff. Worries centred on knowing how to do the positive handling correctly and recalling techniques when needed.

Three months after the training, follow-up interviews were held with 39 staff and the four head teachers across the case-study schools. All schools reported positive benefits from the Team-Teach training, particularly in relation to consistency of approach, reporting and recording, as well as increased confidence, as noted immediately after the training. However, none of the 19 staff interviewed at the two mainstream schools had used the positive handling strategies in this three-month period, although there was a record of one incident at the secondary school. Nearly half the staff at the special school and primary PRU, on the other hand, had used positive handling strategies. Staff in these types of setting were upbeat about the whole Team-Teach approach. For example:

> *'I think I've got more empathy with them possibly than before. Possibly I would be riled by some of the things they said in the past and now I think "they are the children and I am the adult and this is my job".'*

Two of the four head teachers described their staff as more confident and aware of their rights, responsibilities and roles as a result of the Team-Teach training. The training also had the effect of encouraging staff to reflect on how their own behaviour may influence situations; their right to protect themselves in situations where they may not have the physical prerequisites to cope effectively; and the advantages of using a team approach when managing difficult behaviour. All four head teachers planned to train new members of staff and to organise refresher sessions to maintain their staff's competence in the Team-Teach techniques. The timing of the planned refresher sessions ranged from once a month in the pupil referral unit to half-yearly in the mainstream primary and yearly in the mainstream secondary school.

Children's Perceptions of How They Can Be Helped to Behave Well in School

Eighteen young people whose behaviour was seen as high profile in the four case-study schools gave their views about what would help them behave better in school. An important theme was being treated fairly and with respect, as the following quotes illustrate:

> *'She treats us like adults and I think you can learn more when it is like that because they respect you and you have more respect for them.'*

And

> *'I don't misbehave in her lesson because I respect her.'*

The need to be helped individually and listened to also came across:

> *'Listen to us more – about what we think.'*

> *'Spend individual time with people – well, explain it to the whole class but then individually as well.'*

Seven of the eighteen children had been physically stopped from doing something by a teacher. These children reported a mixture of emotions: three felt angry, others felt frightened, safe and secure, and sad, with one child saying he didn't like himself. Parents generally believed that these interventions were probably necessary and based on common-sense reactions to an incident in time.

We'll leave the last word to one young person who simply said in relation to teachers:

'They don't understand us – they're adults, aren't they?'

Managing and promoting positive behaviour and relationships is an important part of what schools do. It is a role that is recognised as central to future citizenship. This is not an easy task and the indicators of unhappy situations and very difficult behaviour in schools are all too apparent. On a more positive note, however, schools do offer tremendous opportunities for improving the way people relate to each other and take their place in society. If this is within an inclusive agenda, the behaviour presented in schools may on occasion necessitate physical intervention, if teachers are going to be able to exercise their 'duty of care' towards pupils. Equally schools have a 'duty of care' towards their staff, which includes appropriate training. Allen (2002) reminds us that 'emergencies occur in all walks of life' (p. 8) and that 'as with other types of crisis management, plans need to cover situations of varying severity' (p. 9). Allen (2002) is writing about people with learning disabilities; however, the warning is clearly relevant to mainstream schools that include children with behaviours that may warrant physical intervention, if staff are going to be able to exercise their 'duty of care' towards pupils.

The case studies in this research were of very different types of educational setting, with different levels of need for support with behaviour, and inevitably they present a complex picture at the level of individual institution. However, the overall trend following training is one of increased confidence and comfort for staff in relation to managing very difficult behaviour; staff feeling better informed about the legal framework to physical interventions and more prepared to respond to such situations. Nevertheless, directly after the course, one in five of the trainees still did express various concerns about the positive handling strategies – particularly in relation to knowing how to do this correctly, as well as general recall. This latter situation is an important reminder that even strategies that are seen as relatively successful will not be experienced as such by all staff. Three months later these concerns about positive handling strategies were still pertinent, especially in the mainstream primary and secondary schools; there were no incidents of physical intervention directly experienced by these interviewees. More broadly, however, a range of positive associations with the Team-Teach approach were reported, particularly to do with de-escalation skills, consistency, communication and confidence. The need for refresher training is built into the Team-Teach approach and follow-up interviews clearly demonstrated that this was needed.

Overall the evaluation provided a positive endorsement of the Team-Teach approach, especially in relation to staff confidence, as well as knowledge of the legal framework for physical interventions. The impact of the training was more pronounced in the special school and pupil referral units, as they also experienced more empathy with the children and were more likely to use risk assessment. Importantly Team-Teach provides a clear framework for staff to refresh their skills and keep up to date with the latest advice on behaviour management – through refresher training and reaccreditation and also through the extensive resources, including video clips (introduced after we conducted our case studies) on the Team-Teach website.

Children remind us about what is important to them – being fair and being shown respect came over strongly, as did the desire to be listened to and given individual time. These are reasonable requests, but ones that are not always met.

Schools and Their Role in Preventing, Reducing and Responding to Troublesome Behaviour

There is no doubt that schools at their best can provide a safe haven for some children; they can identify and develop talents and help to provide a route out of poverty. Schools can also be a place where problems are confirmed and in some cases made worse, because the school does not have good systems for identifying and supporting children in difficulty and/or their wider social circumstances are so chaotic and other external support services are ineffective or lacking. There is no doubt that very difficult behaviour is a real and practical concern in schools and that some mainstream schools are better at responding to such behaviour.

Schools are environments that can do a great deal to actively promote pro-social behaviour. They are the normal place for children to spend much of their time. Their potential to address, rather than entrench, problems for children cannot be overestimated. However, as our examples show, this does not lead to straightforward solutions and the gains from adopting a particular approach or strategy are as much about having a different attitude or style of relationship with children, or between schools and families as children's behaviour per se. At the time of writing it is clear that schools are seen as central to enhancing the life chances of vulnerable children. However, there are some major tensions in this, as outlined in Figure 5.2.

None of the competing priorities shown in Figure 5.2 are necessarily mutually exclusive; indeed the issues identified may more usefully be seen as part of a continuum, or overlapping relationships in some cases. For example, it is well known that some bullies are victims and vice versa. For schools in

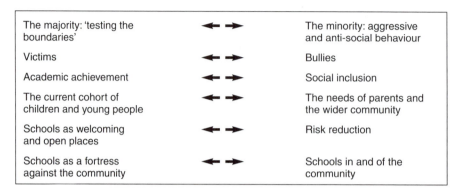

Figure 5.2 Competing priorities for schools

general (rather than only schools in the most deprived areas), to achieve a better balance in relation to these priorities we would need a fundamental rethink about the funding, staffing and evaluation of schools. The role and potential of schools in relation to promoting positive behaviour is a relatively easy case to make. The bigger questions remain, such as the extent to which social inclusion is prioritised over academic achievement. In relation to very disruptive and aggressive behaviour we have to balance the needs of the individual child in relation to the majority of children. These are especially pertinent questions when we consider the reality of differential access to the most popular schools (which are also those that are well ordered and in better-off areas); there is also the issue of private education that further complicates the issue of school access and intake. These issues tend to result in the pattern of access to schooling (and its advantages and disadvantages), mirroring existing socioeconomic inequalities.

6

Children in Trouble in the
Community (*with M. Johns*)

The human landscape can be read as a landscape of exclusion ... power is
expressed in the monopolization of space and the relegation of weaker groups in
society to less desirable environments.

– Sibley, 1995, p. ix

Anti-social behaviour destroys lives and shatters communities. It is a widespread
problem but its effects are often most damaging in communities that are already
fragile. If left unchecked it can lead to neighbourhood decline with people moving away and tenants abandoning housing.

– SEU, 2000, p. 5

Community, Neighbourhood and Social Exclusion

Throughout this book we have frequently mentioned the extent to which
children in a lot of trouble are often in difficulty in more than one area of their
life. For many young people, where their problems can come to a head is the
locality in which they live. Although greater emphasis is now given to processes
of globalisation and the interconnections between people and places made
possible by technology, it is also still true that many young people – particularly
those who are in the least advantaged socioeconomic groups – tend to live out
their lives in limited geographical areas. These latter areas are often linked
by family of origin and school.

'Community' is used in this chapter as shorthand for the setting or place
outside the home and school in which children and young people encounter
other sorts of influence and get into particular sorts of trouble. Debates about
'community' or 'neighbourhood' show that these concepts are variously
interpreted; they are both intuitively meaningful but also hard to pin down.
The concept of community is almost always used to invoke a positive picture
of what might be, or what once was. As Hall *et al.* (1991, p. 46) have argued,
for adults, 'community was just always in the childhood you left behind'.
Etzioni's (1995) ideas have been influential; he assumes the existence of
community in putting forward the concept of civic renewal as a means of

reasserting moral order and controlling behaviours. He has argued that increasing levels of crime might be addressed by strengthening civic institutions, building neighbourhood values and imposing high standards of conduct. A crucial principle is the balancing of rights against responsibilities. These concepts have been a feature of numerous policy discussions since the mid-1990s (see, for example, Blunkett, 2003). However, the collective efficacy of communities in exercising control over behavioural norms can be hardest to establish in areas where fear of crime and high levels of social disorder are most apparent (Crawford, 1998).

The community or neighbourhood is regarded as a key setting for many of the processes that shape life chances, including aspirations, quality of public services; and, for young people, the peer group with whom they associate and social norms that may influence their expectations and aspirations. Concepts of 'community' and 'neighbourhood' underpin many contemporary initiatives designed to promote what are often seen as desirable goals – social inclusion, community safety and neighbourhood renewal. It is also within the frame of reference that includes geographic or defined communities that 'actuarial justice' is most apparent; that is, the form of justice that is based on the refocusing of enforcement towards categories of persons or localities that are seen as socially excluded and in need of improved safety. Like 'community' and 'neighbourhood', 'social exclusion' is a term that has become widely used by academics, as well as politicians, policy-makers and the media. 'Socially excluded' is often used to describe particular places and the people in them; although as we noted in Chapter 2 the concept has been used to describe quite diverse problems and experiences. Despite being critical of the concept, MacDonald and Marsh (2001) believe that it has some use when applied to the study of young people in that it recognises process and change as well as locality. It offers the potential of trying to map how the multifaceted aspects of disadvantage tend to cluster together in particular areas; a process that makes a response more containable. In practice, Stephen and Squires (2003) note that these particular notions have increasingly solidified around concerns about anti-social behaviour and young people.

'Social capital' is another concept that has currency in this debate. Whiting and Harper (2003) have measured it based on five dimensions: social participation, civic participation, reciprocity and trust, social networks and social support, and views of the local area. They argue that the standard quantitative measures on young people tend to show that in comparison with adults they are less likely to participate in social and civic activities; less likely to vote; less likely to be involved in their community and less likely to undertake formal voluntary work (2003, p. 1). However, more in-depth research questions the validity of these observations, both in terms of the relevance of the questions asked and concepts used. For example, Whiting and Harper (2003) found that young people define community differently – they focus more on school, parents and friends' homes and particular localities (such as town centres or other meeting places). Reciprocity and trust were more often based on close friendships, rather than neighbours, and so on. Brent (2001), in concentrating on young people in a stigmatised area, provides another alternative in the concept of 'neo-tribes' inventing their own communities in 'wild zones', where other resources are thin on the ground.

The opening quotations highlight contrasting perspectives about how patterns of opportunity and ideas about what is viewed as anti-social behaviour are intertwined and particularly pertinent in some localities. In this volume we are most concerned about how this impacts on children and how we respond when they are in trouble. Later in this chapter we will explore some of the key themes that relate to children and young people with three examples of original research. Each piece of research focuses on different levels and perspectives on children in the same area of southern England. The first piece of research is based upon a small-scale survey of 'ordinary' 15-year-old schoolchildren in a city comprehensive, and investigates their perception of anti-social behaviour and safe and unsafe space within their locality in a city. The second study is based on the documentary analysis of all records of police concern about younger children, aged 10 and younger, in one central-city police station over a one-year-period. The third study focuses on persistent young offenders from one youth court in a one-year period: it investigates their circumstances and creates four typologies in relation to the development of their offending behaviour.

Communities That Care?

There are numerous community- and area-based initiatives in the UK and else-where that aim to 'regenerate' an area, 'build capacity', 'promote social inclu-sion', and so on. All are relevant to the 'community' element of the response to children in trouble. We will focus briefly on one approach here – Communities that Care (CtC), which is an approach developed in the United States, based specifically on the concept of risk factors, already outlined in Chapter 1 (see also Chapter 7 for further discussion of CtC). Crow *et al.* (2004) would argue that CtC is more of a process than a programme, in that 'CtC does not deliver services by itself but facilitates and activates change in a local area' (p. 3). CtC is based on a social development model in which child development is influ-enced by the quality of interaction between children and adults. The focus is upon developing pro-social behaviour and ensuring that positive behaviour is recognised; such an approach fits well with the behaviour policies of most well-ordered schools. In recent years this sort of approach has become popular in that research has provided evidence of certain types of risk factor in child-hood, which in effect are problem attitudes and behaviours, and are predictive of further problems in adulthood.

CtC is based on early intervention, in the sense of trying to prevent prob-lems developing or getting worse in risky areas. It is evidence-based in the sense that it starts with identifying and measuring the levels of risk and protection within geographical areas. It puts forward youth crime and anti-social behaviour, drug abuse, school failure and school-age pregnancy as key issues that it sets out to tackle and reduce (www.communitiesthatcare.org.uk). Crow *et al.* (2004) note that the first part of the CtC process should be to assess community readiness. There are fairly obvious ways in which this might be done – such as identifying key stakeholders, recruiting a community leader to champion the initiative and assessing the factors that could inhibit the process (Hawkins *et al.*, 2002, p. 959).

Reporting on a three-year period of three CtC projects set up by the Joseph Rowntree Foundation, Crow *et al.* (2004) present useful pointers to consider in the setting up of such programmes, although the results on the impact of the projects are unclear. The key issues could be summarised under the heading of implementation problems: in fact, two of the three areas did not implement the CtC programme in the way intended. Specific problems included primary schools in two of the areas being described as 'difficult to bring into the programme', resulting in problems with implementing CtC services targeted at schools; also plans devised by staff and local people were not implemented because of lack of resources. Nevertheless the CtC programme has expanded and by 2005 there were over thirty areas around the UK with CtC projects. Crow *et al.* (2004) concluded that their evaluation was too early to really make an assessment of the potential and impact of CtC and that there is a tendency to want quick results in the UK, which shows a 'distinct lack of understanding of the ways communities operate' (p. 79). They note that in the United States, full-scale evaluations have only just started, yet they have been running CtC since the early 1990s.

Communities and Risk

We have already noted that not all communities have their equal share of 'trouble' and not all trouble is associated with young people. The spatial concentration of poverty and wealth in Britain has become more acute since the early 1980s, as a consequence of a range of social policies, including the sale of council housing, the promotion of owner-occupation, as well as the competition between schools brought about by league tables and encouraging parents to believe that they can 'choose' their child's school (although in law they only have the right to state a preference). In combination, these policies have further emphasised the tendency of people able to have most control over where they live and/or send their child to school moving away from certain communities and/or schools. We have known for some time that the result is that the differences in life chances between localities have polarised (Bentley, 1997). The connection between poverty, social problems and access to social housing means that particularly disadvantaged communities are concentrated in social housing estates (Coles *et al.*, 2000). The recognition of this connection by New Labour has led to a number of area-based approaches, such as Sure Start (referred to in both Chapters 5 and 7 in this volume). In relation to crime control it can be argued that social housing has become a site of crime control *because* it has become a residual tenure for marginalised groups (Brown, 2004, p. 1).

The concentration of disadvantage and environmental decay in specific localities has allowed underclass theorists and the media to demonise particular estates and even families within them, characterising them as 'anti-social' and as 'neighbours from hell' (Hunter and Nixon, 2001). Within this discourse young people, particularly males, are often singled out as a specific part of 'the problem'. In some ways it is not surprising that there is a perception of more problematic behaviour from young people in areas of social housing. Children and young people are proportionately more numerous in social hous-ing estates, as a result of social housing policies that have progressively prioritised families. Coles *et al.* (2000) estimate that around 28 per cent of people on social housing estates are under the age of 16; in comparison with 21 per cent in owner-occupied housing and 18 per cent in privately rented properties. This situation, in combination with lack of money and facilities, helps to create the public concern and even fear about teenagers 'hanging around' that is more prevalent in areas of social housing.

We noted in Chapter 2 how unspecified fears about and in relation to young people are common – they are often seen as 'at risk' or vulnerable, as well as a risk to others. Negotiating risk is often seen as a salient feature of contemporary society, a situation in which risks are both differentially distrib-uted and experienced, with those most 'at risk' not necessarily perceiving this evaluation of their circumstances. For young people, there is indeed less certainty both in the world of employment and in terms of family structures. There are increasing expectations about extending education and thus the period of dependency on family support. The level of uncertainty experienced in this context is to a great degree mediated by economic resources available to the individual. Green *et al.* (2000, p. 10) point out that there is a system-atic relationship between extreme poverty and extreme risk and Stephen and Squires (2003, p. 9) argue that fear of crime and victimisation should not be seen as separate from other material and social insecurities faced by people living in poverty.

Communities and Anti-Social Behaviour

Reducing anti-social behaviour (ASB) has become a popular target in the fight against crime and what is seen as the disintegration of poorer communities, as we noted in Chapter 2. Reasons for the introduction and application of the term 'anti-social behaviour' are various. One reason offered relates to concerns about witness intimidation and the difficulties of gathering evidence of a sufficient standard for criminal conviction (Burney, 2002). The latter view is apparent in relation to Anti-Social Behaviour Orders (ASBOs); the official view from the Home Office is that they were introduced to deal with persistent behaviour that cannot be dealt with by criminal law, because individual instances are considered too trivial (Campbell, 2002). Local authority pressure is said to have been behind the introduction of the ASBO. Local authorities were lobbied by councillors and housing managers, who were on the receiving end of a rising number of complaints about problematic behaviour from residents of poor council estates in areas of high unemployment (Burney, 2002). Brown (2004) sees the use of the ASBO concept as 'part of a confluence of interests of social housing and policing'; although she sees social housing as 'always having been about social control' (p. 204).

There are differences of opinion about the use and meaning of the term ASB, as we highlighted in Chapter 1. Critics of the use and application of the term 'anti-social behaviour' make the important point that ASB encompasses a range of behaviours, some of which break the criminal law, and some of which break civil law, and some behaviour that may ultimately be a matter of opinion (Brown, 2004). More generally, Brown (2004) views ASB as a social construction, indicating 'a new domain of professional power and control' (p. 203). Payne (2003) lists the more obvious behaviours associated with what many people might intuitively see as 'anti-social behaviour' as: noisy neighbours, drug dealing, drunk and disorderly groups, litter and graffiti, joyriding, cyclists on the pavement, swearing in the street, and so on. Significantly, she also notes that anti-social behaviour 'tends to be committed by somebody else' (Payne, 2003, p. 321). Brown (2004) argues that the term blurs a fundamental boundary; that between civil and criminal law. Added to this the standard of proof required for an ASBO is less than that under the criminal law, although breach of the conditions of an ASBO is a criminal offence. The potential for net-widening is obvious. Indeed, another tier has been added to the system with the advent of Acceptable Behaviour Contracts (ABCs) designed for 10–18-year-olds, or young people over 18 if they live with their parents. ABCs are individual written agreements between a young person and a partner agency and the police. Parental Responsibility Contracts are in operation for children under 10. In the latter contracts, parents accept full responsibility for their child's behaviour (Stephen and Squires, 2003).

Some commentators believe that a focus on anti-social behaviour risks dividing, rather than rebuilding communities (Payne, 2003). Hunter and Nixon (2001) note the increased vulnerability of female-headed households and households with children to anti-social behaviour orders, despite the fact that in the majority of the cases the behaviour complained about was committed by men. They argue that despite the impossibility of the women being able to control the behaviour of teenage sons and boyfriends, they were seen as 'responsible' for it and evicted from their homes. 'Communities' can become involved in the preparation of strategies to tackle ASB and may be

Table 6.1 British Crime Survey – anti-social behaviour indicators

Indicator	*% of interviews held 2003–04 reporting behaviour to be a very/fairly big problem in their area*
Speeding traffic	43
Cars parked inconveniently or illegally	31
Rubbish or litter lying around	29
Fireworks not part of an organised display	29
Teenagers hanging around on the streets	*28*
Vandalism, graffiti and other deliberate damage to property	28
People using or dealing drugs	25
Uncontrolled dogs and dog mess	24
People being drunk or rowdy in public places	20
Abandoned or burnt-out cars	14
People being insulted, pestered or intimidated	11
Noisy neighbours or loud parties	9

Source: Wood, 2004; my emphasis.

involved in setting up agreements about acceptable behaviour in a locality. 'Neighbours' become the catalyst for investigation and the primary source of evidence. Cases go to court to sanction individuals who are already viewed as perpetrators; they are guilty until proven innocent (a reversal of the criminal justice process in the UK).

There are various ways in which indicators of the prevalence of behaviour that may be judged 'anti-social' have been provided. One source of evidence is the British Crime Survey (BCS), which includes questions on anti-social behaviour indicators, as illustrated in Table 6.1.

Of particular interest to the focus of this book is 'teenagers hanging around on the streets'; which is seen as a 'very' or 'fairly big' problem by over a quarter of respondents to the BCS. Of course young people may be involved in the other issues, but the specific identification of 'hanging around' as anti-social does illustrate more generally the problem of adult perceptions of young people. It also illustrates the reality that the street is the main social space outside direct adult supervision and authority for most young people.

The connection between relative disadvantage and perceptions of high levels of ASB are made obvious in Table 6.2.

Other indicators of the level and type of behaviour or problem that may be seen as 'anti-social' can be found from snapshot surveys, like the one shown in Table 6.3. The data in this table are based on an analysis of reports from Crime and Disorder Partnerships in England and Wales by the Anti-Social

Table 6.2 British Crime Survey – perceptions of high levels of anti-social behaviour and type of neighbourhood

Type of neighbourhood	% reporting high levels of ASB
Inner-city areas	34
Areas where respondents did not feel neighbours 'looked out' for one another	33
Those in 'hard-pressed' ACORN[1] areas	31
Living in social rented accommodation	30
Victims of crime	29
People in 'very bad' health	28
National average	*16[2]*

Source: Wood, 2004.

Table 6.3 Problems in public – one-day count of reports from Crime and Disorder Partnerships (10 September 2003)

Indicator	Number of reports	% of all reports
Litter/rubbish	10,686	16.2
Criminal damage/vandalism	7,855	11.9
Vehicle-related nuisance	7,782	11.8
Nuisance behaviour	7,660	11.6
Intimidation/harassment	5,415	8.2
Noise	5,374	8.1
Rowdy behaviour	5,339	8.1
Abandoned vehicles	4,994	7.5
Street drinking and begging	3,239	4.9
Drug/substance misuse and drug dealing	2,920	4.4
Animal related problems	2,549	3.8
Hoax calls	1,286	1.9
Prostitution, kerb-crawling, sexual acts	1,011	1.5
Total	*66,107*	*100*

Source: ASBU, 2003.

Behaviour Unit (ASBU) (ASBU, 2003). While it is acknowledged that these reports are not the same as anti-social behaviour, they also give an indication of the types of issues reported as problematic by the general public and the relative frequency of different types of occurrence.

While the data in Tables 6.1 to 6.3 can be criticised as proxy measures for a contested concept, they do point to real difficulties: a common perception nationally that there are a number of problems to do with how people relate to their neighbours and use public space, and that these problems are perceived to be greater in poorer areas. Further, they are issues that people are willing to report to public bodies in great volume, suggesting that they want something done about them. However, what is also striking is the sheer range of problems and behaviours that can be grouped under the broad category of 'anti-social behaviour'. It is also apparent that how questions are asked (as in the British Crime Survey) or how data are collected (as in the one-day ASBU count) provide a different perspective about what the priorities might be and what needs to be done. Of note is the fact that car-related problems and litter/rubbish are top of the list in both types of data collection, rather than issues to do with the behaviour of young people in public.

Young People and Perceptions of Anti-social Behaviour

Originally ASBOs were to be focused on adults: on the 'neighbours from hell' of tabloid headlines. In fact draft guidance (Home Office, 1998) specifically discouraged orders being made on young people under 18. However, strong representation from local authorities that children should be included as recipients of ASBOs has led to the shift in emphasis towards children and young people.

Campbell (2002) reviewed 466 ASBOs, of which nearly three-quarters were for people under 21. Indeed 58 per cent of ASBOs were for children under 18. The great majority (84 per cent) of orders were for males. Where breaches of ASBOs occurred in this latter study, nearly half of those in breach were sentenced to a custodial sentence. The average length of time served was much greater for juveniles (139 days) compared with adults (79 days) in breach of an order. The practice of 'naming and shaming' young people, complete with photographs in the local press, has helped to reinforce the popular image of Britain at the mercy of 'young thugs'.

A different perspective is presented in a small-scale study that investigated families' accounts of ABCs, in which it is revealed that in half the cases both the parents and the children themselves felt they had little control over the behaviour that led to the contract. The lack of control tended to relate to learning difficulties and/or mental health problems. Further, a strong sense of injustice was evident in young people's accounts, in which they felt singled out for behaviour that was little different from their peers in the locality (Stephen and Squires, 2003). The research concluded that:

> Not one of those families came close to the populist stereotype of 'neighbours from hell' often depicted in the media. Indeed, while the young people's behaviour cannot be condoned in the light of its effects on local residents, the roots of that behaviour ... [are] far more complex than the Community Safety rhetoric suggests. We were also continuously disturbed by the number of young people with mental health problems and learning difficulties subject to ABCs. (Stephen and Squires, 2003, p. 95)

We will now look at another small-scale piece of research that investigated 'ordinary' (in the sense that they attended a mainstream mixed-sex

Table 6.4 Young people's perceptions of
what constitutes anti-social behaviour

Type of behaviour	% reporting
Verbal abuse/intimidation	71
Public order	62
Criminal damage	55
Substance misuse	24
Theft	20
Bullying	18
Noise	16

(n = 76)

comprehensive school) young people's perceptions of anti-social behaviour. The research was based on 76 15-year-olds attending a city school in 2004. The young people came from three different ability-group classes studying geography. Part of the research was designed to explore their perceptions of public space in the city. We will only briefly refer to this aspect of the research. Our main focus will be to look at what they perceived to be 'anti-social behaviour'. Nearly all the young people (73, or 96 per cent) were aware of the term ASB, with most reporting that they had heard the term in the media (70 per cent) or through school (67 per cent). They were provided with a Home Office definition of anti-social behaviour and asked to name three types of behaviour that they believed were anti-social. That is, the question was open-ended – they could name any activity they liked. Not surprisingly, different priorities emerged compared with adults who are the respondents to the British Crime Survey.

Litter and car-related problems hardly featured at all in young people's perception of ASB: only 5 per cent named joyriding or speeding and 3 per cent litter. Top of their list were verbal abuse and intimidation, followed by behaviour in public that could be categorised as public order issues. When they were asked to rate the extent to which specific issues or behaviours were a problem, 'violence, intimidation and verbal abuse' were ranked highest.

BCS questions were adjusted for meaning for this age group in order to make possible a comparison with national data from adults. When asked how much of a problem they thought young people were 'hanging around on the street'; they were very divided: 44 per cent thought it was a very big or fairly big problem; 43 per cent thought it was not a very big problem. Girls were more likely to be in the former category (47 per cent) and boys were more likely to see such behaviour as 'not a problem' (16 per cent of boys compared with 3 per cent of girls). Thus, overall, 15-year-olds were more likely than the adults in the BCS to view young people hanging around the street as a problem: 44 per cent of the young people, compared with the BCS figure of 28 per cent. This could, of course, be a peculiarity of the area or indeed the city, although it may also relate to age group.

Around three in ten young people (29 per cent) were 'very' or 'fairly worried' about being insulted or pestered while on the street or other public place, although six in ten (60 per cent) were not very worried. Girls were twice as likely to be worried as boys. Interestingly, they were more likely to be most worried about being insulted or pestered by their own age group: 56 per cent reported that 13–17-year-olds worried them most, with boys emphasising this more than girls.

Eight in ten young people (79 per cent) thought there were not enough public spaces and facilities for them to use, with boys and girls being in general agreement about this. Most reported that they believed adults thought they were a nuisance in public spaces: often (21 per cent) or sometimes (68 per cent), with boys being more likely to believe this was the case 'often'. Young people believed that noise was the most frequent reason why they were perceived as a nuisance: 50 per cent of boys and 28 per cent of the girls believed this to be the case. Beliefs about adult perceptions of young people as intimidating were also apparent from one in five young people.

Interestingly, when asked to specify a place in the city where they felt 'unsafe', about two-thirds specified the poorest areas of high-rise flats and social housing; the rest tended to indicate public parks and areas near nightclubs as 'unsafe'. Explanations indicative of this picture follow.

"X because it is very rough and lots of people get beaten up." (female)

"… because there are lots of teenagers who hang about shouting abuse to people, because they have nothing else to do." (female)

"I feel unsafe there at night because it's big and I know people who got attacked there." (male)

"Lots of flats, lots of gangs, druggies are there." (male)

The resonance with local folklore about areas of the city in these explanations for perceiving an area as 'unsafe' were obvious. However, these perceptions could be informed by indirect experience through stories from contemporaries and they could influence behaviour, enhancing the separation between young people occupying different areas of the city.

Early Intervention – Records of Concern about Young Children

One of the recurring themes in this book is early intervention. In relation to offending behaviour it is important to make best use of the extent to which

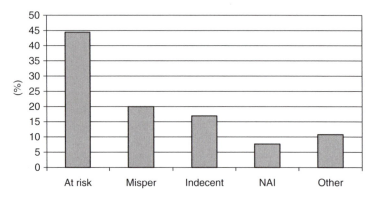

Figure 6.1 Police welfare concerns (children aged 10 and younger) (n = 65) *Key:* Misper = child reported as a missing person; Indecent = indecent assault on the child; NAI = non-accidental injury.

some children come to the attention of the police at an early age: either because of their behaviour, concern about their vulnerability and welfare, or both. The early onset of criminal behaviour is, not surprisingly, associated with later involvement in such behaviour as well as more serious offending patterns (Lauritsen and Quinet, 1995). Abuse or neglect have also been shown to be associated with criminal behaviour (Fergusson and Lynskey, 1997). Others have shown that the more extensive the maltreatment, the higher the level of anti-social and criminal behaviour (Zingraff *et al.*, 1994).

Until the late 1990s, children and young person's records were one way the police had of alerting welfare agencies to children in trouble. Increasingly, multi-agency partnerships such as YISPs (Youth Inclusion Support Panels) use actuarial instruments such as ONSET developed for the YJB. ONSET calculates the level of risk of offending and helps target responses and support for a child. Research conducted in one central-city police station in the 1990s revealed 963 children and young person's records of which 167 (17 per cent) were for children aged 10 or younger. Further analysis showed that these 167 records referred to 109 children (or around 0.9 per cent of primary-age children in the city at the time), although seven records were for a whole family. Analysis of the content of these records revealed three distinct groups: the first group were primarily vulnerable; the second were primarily behaving in an anti-social way in the community; the third group were of concern to the police for both reasons. Concern about the welfare of the child was apparent in six in ten cases (65, or 59.6 per cent) and concern about their behaviour and its impact on others was apparent in a slightly higher proportion of cases (71, or 65.1 per cent). Although such records almost certainly underestimate the scale of the problem, discussions with police officers revealed that getting as far as filling out a record on a child of this age was some indication of the severity of concern.

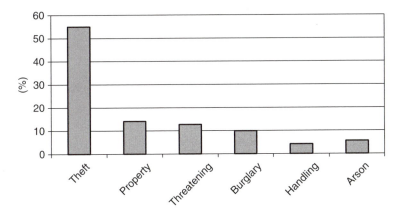

Figure 6.2 Main type of police concern about offending behaviour
(children aged 10 and younger)
(n = 71) *Key:* Property = damage to property; Threatening = threatening
behaviour; Handling = handling stolen goods.

The most common welfare concern for police officers was young children
who appeared to be at risk because they were out late at night, or in the early
hours of the morning, unsupervised and sometimes alone. Young children
reported missing by their parents accounted for one in five welfare concerns.
Indecent assault was also a relatively frequent concern (around one in six
records), considering the age group; followed by a range of issues including
sexual and physical abuse and alleged abductions.

Theft was the most common reason for police concern about offending
behaviour, accounting for over half of all records. This was followed by damage
to property, threatening behaviour in public and burglary. Handling stolen
goods and arson were the issues in a minority of cases.

Another important distinction across the 109 cases was between the majority (83, or 76 per cent) who had only one record of concern and those who had
two or more records (26, or 24 per cent). Indeed, only six children in the city
had four or more records in a one-year period, with 16 being the highest number in the group. In this most extreme case on record at the time; a 9-year-old
boy was variously recorded as a missing person, and as at risk; he was also
involved in numerous thefts, as well as burglary, criminal damage and attempted
arson. One of the records describes the situation in the following way:

> Kevin was found wandering around the railway station at 7a.m. … by the railway
> staff. He was crying and refused to speak to them.

Another said:

> Kevin went into Boots in […] selected two food items and left the shop. Kevin lives
> with his mother and stepfather and is described by his mother as 'out of control' …

His mother is constantly in touch with social services asking that they take him off their hands. He is not in school during the day and is frequently making a nuisance of himself.

Kevin went on to be a persistent young offender in his early teens; he spent time in care but went missing for long periods, during which time he survived as a 'rent boy'. Another young boy was eventually to become a headline in his own right as a 'one-person crime wave', accounting for over one hundred incidences of theft and assault, usually of other children, elderly or disabled people. He was small in stature and only 14 years old when he achieved this great notoriety. Cases such as these are often used by the media to create sensationalist stories about the nature of youth crime. However, we should remember that they are very unusual and to a degree both identifiable and predictable, if good use is made of existing recording systems that can flag up concern. This should be increasingly possible as the 'information hubs' envisaged under *Every Child Matters* are fully established.

Persistent Young Offenders

As we noted in Chapter 3, it has been known for some time that a relatively small group of young offenders are responsible for a disproportionate amount of criminal activity (West and Farrington, 1973). Persistent young offenders (PYOs) are of most concern to policy-makers and practitioners trying to reduce youth crime. PYOs can have a major impact on the community in which they live, as their own community is more often subject to victimisation than places further afield. Persistent young offenders are a small minority of all young offenders, although research has indicated that they are not necessarily a fixed group of individuals (Hagell and Newburn, 1994). The inclusion of young people within a definition of 'persistence' depends in part on the recording of offences, the number decided upon to denote 'persistence', as well as the time period chosen. For example, although Hagell and Newburn (1994) found that 6 per cent of the 193 offenders aged 12–16 in their study accounted for 23 per cent of offences in a one-year period, the individuals who committed 30 or more offences were different in each quarter of the year.

The study we will now focus upon is based on the identification of a group of young people who might be seen as persistent young offenders and an analysis of their home and school circumstances, as well as their offending patterns. This section goes on to develop four main typologies in relation to their circumstances. Persistent Young Offenders in this study were defined as 10–17-year-olds who had been sentenced by a UK court on three or more separate occasions for one or more recordable offences. The study started with reviewing all records of young offenders who went through a case-study youth court in a one-year period (495 cases in all); of these 44 (9 per cent) were

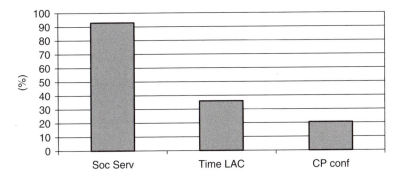

Figure 6.3 Persistent young offenders – problems at home
(n = 44) *Key:* Soc Serv = social services involved with family; Time LAC = time spent as a looked after child; CP conf = child protection conference held on individual.

identified as PYOs. The total number of offences ranged from 4 to 101, with a mean of 28.4 recorded offences per individual. The mean age of the sample was 14.6 years, with an age range of 11–17 years.

Figure 6.3 illustrates how the great majority (41, or 93 per cent) of the young offenders had Social Services involvement with their family in recent years and over a third (16, or 36 per cent) had spent time looked after by the local authority; nine had been the subject of a Child Protection conference. These distinctions were important in terms of patterns of offending: a higher proportion of persistent young offenders who had been looked after were in the medium/high offending group, compared with those who had not been looked after. All the young people who had been the subject of a Child Protection conference were in the medium/high offending groups. That is, those young people in most difficulty with their home circumstances were also more likely to show higher rates of offending in this study.

The pattern in relation to offending, exclusion and school attendance was less clear. In the lower and medium levels of offending groups there was very little difference in the proportions of individuals having a record of exclusion or not. This pattern held true when all records of exclusion were looked at as a whole and for fixed-period exclusions only. Interestingly, the proportion of individuals in the higher offending group was greater for individuals without a record of permanent exclusion. The proportions of individuals across the different levels of offending were similar, whether individuals were viewed as having an attendance problem or not. A stronger pattern of association was found in relation to special educational needs: eight in ten individuals with SEN were in the medium/high-offending group. Interestingly, this appeared to be partly explained by the patterns of association found between certain individuals all of whom attended a single special school for pupils with emotional and behavioural difficulties (EBD).

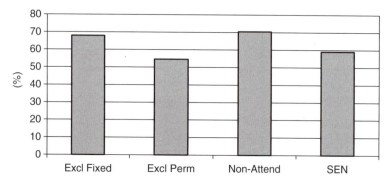

Figure 6.4 Persistent young offenders – educational problems (n = 44) *Key:* Excl Fixed = fixed-period exclusion record (a matter of days); Excl Perm = permanent exclusion; Non-Attend = non-attender; SEN = special educational needs.

Further analysis of cases showed that in terms of patterns of offending there were two broad groups: one where records of criminal behaviour followed major life events and another where records of criminal behaviour were present before major life events. All of these young people had some level of difficulty in their lives one way or another, most frequently because of family relationships and difficulties at school; but the second group tended to start their offending behaviour very early on. For example, one of the two young women in the study had records of concern at the police station from the age of 9, mostly because of stealing food from shops. She was not excluded from school until early in her secondary-school career, after which a spate of offending is evident. However, this young person also had an eating disorder and had begun to drink in a problematic way, following the split between her parents and moving in with her mother and stepfather. In other words, there were numerous risk and stress factors for the young woman.

In-depth case studies revealed four main typologies among these persistent young offenders. We will now explain and exemplify these typologies in a little more detail.

Young People from Offending Families

These young people had a parent who had spent time in prison; this parent was usually known for extreme and anti-social behaviour in the community, and violence within the family was common. Welfare agencies could have difficulty in working with such families because of threats of violence and/or a complete lack of co-operation. In some cases these were known 'families' in the sense that the family name was well known to the police and local people were aware of their reputation and activities.

For example, Martin's father had spent time in prison. He was described as violent and the mother and children had spent time living in a refuge. Martin and his father were involved in a firearms incident when Martin was 15 years old. On another occasion, Martin's father drove a motorbike (with Martin on the back) through a primary-school playground during break-time when it was full of children. In other words, there were no real boundaries to the behaviour of father and son. Indeed, the father appeared to actively endorse and take part in very anti-social and sometimes criminal behaviour with his son.

Young People 'Out of Control'

These young people were outside the control and supervision of their parents. They did what they wanted when they wanted. Often such young people were living with a single mother who felt unable to set limits for one reason or another. Sometimes there were two parents who were preoccupied by their own problems and/or collectively could not agree or felt unable to set limits.

For example, Robert and Philip were twins born prematurely. There were two other children in the family, although the focus of concern was on the twins. The father was unemployed and the mother worked part-time. There was evidence of abusive behaviour within the home and at one point one of the twins was accommodated in a children's home. It was also clear that the twins were seen as a major problem by their community. There is evidence that the brothers set out as a pair to intimidate other children, both at school and within the community. Their profile in the local community was such that there was a petition, resulting in around 450 signatures from parents and local residents, against their return to a primary school that had excluded them. The case and the residents' petition was reported in the local newspaper. By the age of 14, neither of them attended school, but they were both working illegally but regularly in the same workplace. Neither Robert nor Philip would comply with attempts to get them to have regular home tuition, even as a pair.

Official Neglect

Some young people and their families could be seen to have been the subject of official neglect. These families often had multiple problems, many of them severe enough to come to the attention of a range of agencies, but none of them received enough support to make a difference to the young person. Typically, families had substance misuse and/or mental health problems and the children did not attend school regularly. Often nobody within the household was in full time work.

For example, Sean came from a large family in which all children attended school irregularly and both parents were out of work. His mother had alcohol misuse problems and was hospitalised for depression for a time when Sean was in the last year of primary school. Sean began to present serious behaviour problems at this time and was permanently excluded from school. By the age of 12 he was glue-sniffing and using alcohol. There was evidence of some attempt to get him a place in a special school locally but this never came about. In the event he was out of school for nearly two years. Although he was eventually found a school place he attended very rarely (for example, 20 days in one school year). Sean had made it plain that he was unhappy about attending this school because it meant a long bus journey and boarding at the school during the week; he wanted to come home every night. No local school place was available for him, although he lived in a city. Things drifted, until he reached school-leaving age. He spent time in and out of care and became more and more aggressive, with frequent bouts of offending behaviour – mostly to do with vandalism and stealing.

Voted With Their Feet

In some cases young people could only get out of a situation that was bothering them through voting with their feet. This was particularly apparent when professionals were focused on a particular desired outcome that was not in accord with what was important or wanted by the young person. There are also elements of this situation in the last case: in Sean's response to the special school place allocated to him, although this was some two years after he was permanently excluded from school. 'Voting with his feet' came after the 'official neglect'.

For example, Jack went to a school that served a large and notorious area of social housing. He had difficulties coping there. He was 15 and some way into Year 10 when his very low school attendance became a major issue with the authorities. This followed an allegation made in the previous school year that he was being bullied, but this was not followed up at the time. Jack made it plain that he wanted to move school and away from the bullies, but there were no places available in the nearest school. His attendance deteriorated and his parents began to support his decision not to go to school. His parents were then threatened with prosecution. As a consequence Jack went into school more often. Jack did not want to be there, so behaved very badly, and then, ironically, received a fixed-period exclusion because of his behaviour: he was sent home for five days! Following this a case planning meeting was finally held in the November of the last year (Year 11) of his schooling, 2 years and 2 months after he first alleged bullying. At this meeting a reduced timetable with work experience was agreed, as well as an investigation into the bullying. One could also see this case as an example of official neglect.

These different typologies, although they share many things in common, have different levels of impact on a community and have different implications for the professionals working with them. Some of this depends on the types of offending with which the young person is involved. Nevertheless, they could all be seen as 'persistent' young offenders in terms of their offending behaviour. Different types of risk combination are apparent, as are the different types of opportunity to intervene and enhance protective factors.

Communities as Both the Problem and the Solution?

Locality or place, whether or not it is perceived as a community, is important in terms of patterns of opportunity and vulnerability. Identifiable localities share concentrations of risk factors in terms of the setting they provide for bringing up children and for young people making the transition to adulthood. Burney (2002) sees the common root in poverty, structural weakness and lack of social cohesion. While the development of opportunities and some improvement in public services and support systems, especially in poorer communities, has been an important and ongoing contemporary policy imperative, there is also a strong focus on enhancing social control in these areas. Education and training provide the most obvious routes out of poverty and this has been one of the more difficult issues to address in a meaningful way for young people in the poorest areas, particularly when they present very difficult behaviour. Indeed, the increased expectation of 'staying on' in school for the majority as well as the increased levels of participation in higher education can add further distance between the 'haves' and 'have-nots' in this respect. An improved quality of life through better public services and enhanced opportunities to participate as a citizen, as well as feeling safe where one lives are crucially important, but it will be very hard to achieve without real economic opportunity for residents in poorer areas. In this context Burney (2002) argues that 'it becomes increasingly hard for government rhetoric to blame individual nastiness for the destruction of communities' (p. 473).

One of the research examples presented in this chapter illustrates the way that 'ordinary' young people themselves may share some of the popular concerns of adults. Indeed, because they are the most common victims of anti-social behaviour and criminal acts, it is important that we know more about what life in the community is like for them. The extent to which these perceptions are related to experience, as opposed to the influence of adults and the media, is difficult to assess. The research on persistent young offenders shows that children in trouble in the community are usually in trouble elsewhere in their lives and that in part at least other agencies have failed them – particularly the education system, but also family support services. The work on younger children who are of concern to the police reminds us that the numbers are not very great and that some are primarily vulnerable, rather than troublesome.

Behaviour in public and between neighbours can clearly be very problematic and might be viewed as 'anti-social'. Some of the behaviour is also criminal, and evidence suggests that in many cases ASBOs are preceded by a long history of criminality (Campbell, 2002). At the same time, as one study concludes about the majority of ASBO cases; the perpetrators were part of a situation that was a problem in and of itself, rather than simply a neighbour dispute. Thus issues such as child protection, mental health, learning disability, substance misuse and drug-dealing were often the 'key problems', problems that other aspects of the system had failed to deal with effectively. Thus it could be argued that ASBOs have often become the response to problems that have not been effectively confined, primarily within the provision of social housing and/or the welfare and support agencies given the job of supporting and sanctioning families and individuals. Young people are only part of this picture, yet they feature strongly in the public imagination and, indeed, in the enactment of ASBOs. One of the reasons is because the spaces and places where they are legitimately allowed to be are very limited; that is, they are more likely to be in public spaces, especially when space at home is at a premium or relationships are not conducive to staying at home. Indeed the most important task for policy is how to balance the need for a meaningful response to public concern about anti-social behaviour, while attempting to prevent young people from becoming involved in crime, unnecessarily embroiled in the criminal justice system or reoffending, after conviction.

Notes

1   ACORN is a classification of residential neighbourhoods based on Census and other data. 'Hard-pressed' areas include areas characterised by low-income families, residents in council areas and people living in high-rise, inner-city council estates.

2   Overall percentages in this table are based on a measure derived from seven types of problem.

7

'What Works' with
Children in Trouble?

If [Number] 10 says bloody evidence-based policy to me once more I'll deck
them one.

> – Bowcott, 2005, quoting Louise Casey, government
> advisor and former head of the Anti-Social
> Behaviour Unit, para. 18

Despite an increased emphasis on the importance of using research in practice, a
number of barriers exist at both an individual and organisational level. At an
individual level, some practitioners may not feel sure where to start in relation to
acquiring, assessing, adapting and applying research in practice. Difficulties with
finding, and a lack of time or skills to search for, relevant research are some of
the obstacles encountered. Even when research information is found, practitioners may not have the skills to judge its quality or whether it could apply to them
and their service.

> – Frost and Liabo, 2003, p. 1

Social science should be at the heart of policy-making. We need a revolution in
relations between government and the social research community – we need
social scientists to help determine what works and why, and what types of policy
initiatives are likely to be most effective.

> – Blunkett, 2000, p. 12

Research Evidence and Children in Trouble

The questions of how and why society should respond to children who are 'in
trouble' are complex. The 'why' question means we need to understand and
agree upon the responsibilities of different agencies in relation to children
and the potential consequences of actions taken. We need to agree upon the
balance between individual and family responsibility and that of the state.
We also need an understanding of why children and adults behave the way
they do. These are both philosophical and political questions about which we

do not agree. The 'how' question would ideally follow the 'why' question and would be predicated upon some agreed understanding of why, as well as the best evidence about how. The apparent tensions and inconsistencies often noted in social policy in relation to children in trouble might be viewed as a result of the different perspectives from which we view the evidence, as well as how different groups see the role of adults and social institutions in relation to the issue. For some, the child is the private responsibility of the family unless there is evidence that a family is not able to exercise this responsibility to an acceptable standard of 'good-enough parenting'. For others, the state should take a stronger role in relation to social interventions that maximise children's life chances, rather than waiting for things to 'go wrong' or become 'unacceptable'. From the latter viewpoint a range of universal and targeted services should be available to children and families; children are a community responsibility.

Earlier chapters have presented evidence about 'why', as well as some discussion and case studies about 'how', along with different perspectives on children's behaviour. This chapter will outline the nature and quality of research evidence available on how to respond to children in trouble, while maintaining an awareness of the political realities in which decisions are made. The tendency towards punishment and control is strong in society in general, as is the common belief that adults have somehow lost the ability to 'control' children and young people. The knowledge that many of these children are also 'troubled' makes the task even more multi-faceted. The pace of social change adds a further difficulty in how we respond rationally, appropriately and effectively. In the preceding chapters we have established that many children in trouble are in circumstances where they need help with more than one aspect of their lives. We have established the enduring nature of the debate about how to respond to children in trouble. The competing priorities of care and control, punishment and welfare are ever present in any debate about what to do about children in trouble, with varying degrees of blame apportioned either to families, schools or the community and society at large. There is a continuity and predictability in the general tenor of these debates with shifts between the care/welfare, control/punishment continuums.

McGuire (1995, p. xi) writes that 'highly stereotypical, partly mystical, minimally logical and not even remotely scientific thinking' is apparent in relation to the issues of crime and punishment; a comment that could be equally applied to children in trouble. While there has been a shift towards a more evidence-based approach to developing responses across policy sectors since McGuire's comments, the muddled thinking he identifies is still very apparent in much public and political discourse about children in trouble. Thus a common popular response to children 'in trouble' displays an impulse to punish or control. In contrast, tolerance is promoted by behaviour-management programmes aimed at professionals working with children. It is a common belief that children with problem behaviour are somehow different from other children and should be sent somewhere else, where there is some-body qualified to help. These popular responses, by their nature, are not based on research evidence, but they may be based on experience and are often sustained by belief.

'What Works' and the Policy Process

'What works' has become a commonplace catchphrase or slogan in debates across public services and academic disciplines. 'What works' could be seen as based on an assumption that there is something that can be identified as 'not working' and which needs fixing by something that is proven to work. As a slogan this is appealing in its simplicity, but needs careful analysis of the premises upon which it is made. The phrase 'what works' is not new: for example, it appeared decades ago in an article by Martinson (1974) in relation to strategies to reduce offending behaviour. This was unusual at a time when many criminologists had become used to the idea that 'nothing works' to reduce offending behaviour. The concept of 'what works' underpins the notion of evidence-based policy and practice in public services, an idea that has been gaining ground for some time and which first became apparent in medicine. However, it should be emphasised at the outset that 'what works' is not the only research question in relation to children in trouble; we also need to understand why and how children get into trouble; what proportion of children are viewed as problematic, in what way and why, and so on.

A great deal of research has been undertaken on programmes designed to help children and their parents develop more 'pro-social' and 'acceptable' behaviour. The latter concepts are often contested as not agreed and essentially social constructions. It is important to maintain an awareness of different perceptions of what might constitute pro-social behaviour, as well as the differences in what is acceptable in particular circumstances and social groups. However, it can be argued that there are some very basic agreed social norms in relation to how children and young people behave that are important to establish for their own sake as well as those of others, such as reducing physically aggressive and impulsive behaviour, encouraging empathy for others, sharing and taking turns, and so on.

The desire to try and base programmes of intervention on good-quality evidence about 'what works' has been gaining ground in Britain, particularly since the post-1997 Labour administration was elected with the philosophy of 'what matters is what works' (Davies *et al.*, 2000, p. 1). The 1999 White Paper, *Modernising Government*, made it clear that policy decisions should be based on sound evidence. A number of cross-cutting reviews helped to establish the evidence base in certain key areas and led to developments such as Sure Start, as an early intervention programme focused on particular communities. However, this analysis presents a rationalist view of government that tends to underplay the complexity and compromise in policy-making and in the translation of policy to practice. As Nutley and Webb (2000, p. 13) point out, there are many examples of policy initiatives that appear to come about *despite* the evidence, or where there is very limited evidence. Some initiatives are popular, expedient, or seem to be based on 'common sense'.

Critiques of the assumptions behind evidence-based policy point to the fact that there are different types of policy knowledge and that research knowledge is only one of them. Knowledge sources include immediate experience; accepted, taken-for-granted realities; intelligence from the field; trusted informants; professional consensus; as well as social science research. There are, similarly, a number of different possible ways in which research knowledge informs the policy process. The process may be knowledge-driven; this is very much the natural-science model in which the expert knowledge of respected research evidence is used to lead policy. On the other hand, a problem-solving approach would see the focus of research as shaped by the concerns of policy issues. An iterative model would have research and policy as mutually influential, with some more influential researchers able to shape the agenda. A political/tactical model would view policy as an outcome of political processes in which research is politically driven and commissioned to support particular positions. In the latter model research is vulnerable to political attack. The enlightenment model is the traditional role of university 'blue skies' research, in which research shapes rather than serves policy agendas. Such research is illuminative, with indirect rather than direct benefits to policy-makers.

The state of readiness of the different service sectors in relation to an evidence-based approach also varies. In health care, especially NHS clinical services, the evidence base is extensive and available via the Cochrane Collaboration,[1] as well as local clinical effectiveness strategies. There is greater agreement in the field of health care about what constitutes 'good' research methodology in determining 'what works'. Nevertheless, it is acknowledged that even in medicine the complexities of implementing evidence-based approaches have been underestimated (Dopson *et al.*, 2003). Dopson *et al.* illustrate the fact that problems in translating evidence into practice are not new, citing the early example of using lemon juice to prevent scurvy. The effectiveness of this was demonstrated in 1601, but a repeat experiment was not undertaken until 1747 and the British Navy took until 1795 to act on it. While new evidence travels faster in contemporary society it still takes a surprising amount of time for some of it to reach practice.

In the fields of education, crime and social care the evidence comes from a variety of organisations such as the SCIE (Social Care Institute for Excellence) and RIP (Research in Practice) in the field of social care; and the EPPI-Centre (Evidence for Policy and Practice Information and Co-ordinating Centre), focusing on educational research. A cross-sector Economic and Social Research Council (ESRC)-funded Co-ordinating Centre for Evidence-Based Policy and Practice incorporates the more specific 'What Works for Children'. The Campbell Collaboration, based in the United States, is an international resource that has reviewed over 10,000 randomised and quasi-randomised trials in the fields of education, social care and criminology. Furthermore, the Cochrane Collaboration has also initiated a cross-sectoral database, SPECTR (the social, psychological, educational and criminological-controlled trials register). So all in all there is no shortage of initiatives to establish evidence about what works across the public sector. However, it is also increasingly recognised that the practicalities of implementation of 'effective' programmes may be more of a barrier than initially envisaged.

Professional Responses, Uses and Misuses of 'Evidence'

The opening quotation from Frost and Liabo highlights some of the barriers to professionals and services basing what they do on evidence. The underlying assumption is that this is partly due to access to information and capability in assessing the quality of information once identified. Based on this kind of assumption, the ESRC-funded *What Works for Children* project was set up to promote research-*informed* practice among Children's Fund Programmes. The move to research-informed (rather than research-based, or evidence-based) practice represents an important shift in thinking in itself; it recognises the realities that contribute to decision-making, other than research evidence. Frost and Liabo (2003) highlight a number of factors that contribute to decision-making about how a service is designed: national and local policy, local context issues, resources and economics, existing practice, experience, views of service users, colleagues, and time and planning constraints.

'Understanding time' was seen as the most common obstacle to the transfer of 'good practice' in a DfES-funded study based on schools. The study concludes that 'teachers are used to making judgements about pieces of good practice they observe. Their criteria for whether or not it is "good" usually depend heavily on relevance to their own context and the students they teach' (Fielding *et al.*, 2005, p. 4). It could be argued, in relation to any profession, that 'good practice' needs to incorporate ways of working that contribute to the core role of the work of a particular profession. So, for example, behaviour-management programmes in schools need to be clearly related to the business of teaching and learning, as well as the processes of inspection and performance management. Appeals to bigger ideals about the advantages of promoting more socially inclusive schools may not be convincing, or difficult to build into the existing work roles for ordinary teachers. Although this might also be seen as a question of vision and values, there should always be a proper consideration of practical possibilities.

'Evidence' is potentially a source of power, particularly the ability to interpret and manipulate evidence to one's own ends. Dopson *et al.* (2003)

note that in medicine, 'evidence' is used to support decisions, particularly about practices that may improve the quality of patient care, even when the evidence is not particularly strong. 'Evidence' is also used to prevent unwanted change. Yet at the same time, Dopson *et al.* report that many clinicians in their studies argued that evidence-based medicine stripped them of the right to make medical decisions without challenge, reducing clinical practice to following a set of codified instructions and protocols that might be inappropriate for the individual patient. It can be argued that evidence-based policy and practice tend to be associated with increasing technicality (actuarial scales, and so on) at the expense of the indeterminacy often associated with being a professional. For example, the insistence on 'programme integrity', ensuring that programmes are run according to a clear format, has been seen as a demand for a partial surrender of professional autonomy. It was observed by the late 1990s that 'what works' principles represent the knowledge base probation officers are expected to espouse if they wish to progress within the organisation, although newer entrants to the profession were more positive about these principles. However, as Newman and Nutley (2003) note, there still remains the question of *effective for whom?* In relation to the focus of this book, what might be effective for young people in trouble might not be effective for other young people who have to share facilities and social space with them. What might be effective for a child may not be effective (or as effective) for a teacher, parent or carer. Although it might be argued that adults should be able to put children first, this conflict of interests is sometimes at the heart of relationships between adults and children.

Methodological Debates

An important feature of using research evidence is how to evaluate it and particularly, how to assess it in relation to practical considerations. This section is an attempt to make sense of some of the debates about this important issue. There are various types of reviews of research literature that set out to summarise what is known in any area and various centres mentioned earlier in this chapter that publish reviews, as well as other research. The big academic research funders (such as the ESRC and the Joseph Rowntree and Nuffield foundations), government departments (such as the DfES and Home Office research departments), as well as children's charities (such as the Children's Society, Barnardo's and the NSPCC), all publish research reviews and summaries on the internet. Campaigning organisations such as CRAE, NACRO (the National Association for the Care and Resettlement of Offenders) and bodies like the YJB also publish research. This is without mentioning the organisational and management information data that has become a requirement of public services and short-term projects in recent years. The problem is not lack of evidence, but too much of it, and particularly evidence that may be of doubtful quality and generalisability, or evidence that masquerades as research but is not based on sound principles.

Traditionally literature reviews in the social sciences have been what is termed 'narrative reviews'; they tell a story about what is known from a review of accessible literature. How it is established that this is a competent review of the literature is not made explicit. For students, 'accessible literature' can often be heavily influenced by supervisor and staff publications in an institution, and for academic staff and other researchers it can be influenced by who they know and the languages they can read. The increasing availability of bibliographic databases, online journals, and so on has opened up all sorts of possibilities for both wider searches and more systematic and explicit ways of establishing what is known, including findings that may be uncomfortable, contradictory and against the argument or case that a researcher or organisations wants to make. Oakley (2000) illustrates why narrative reviews can be a problem in the field of assessing whether a way of working produces positive or negative effects: she cites work by Smith and Glass (1977) in which they show that although they could identify 475 studies of the effects of psychotherapy, most reviews used less than 40 studies and so hardly surprisingly reached conflicting conclusions.

Systematic reviews are one way of trying to make the content and nature of literature reviews transparent and quality-controlled (by some specific criteria on whether a study is included or not), as in this way they assure the reader that they can take some notice of the findings. Like the whole evidence-based approach, systematic reviews are most common in medical research, but there is an increasing use of this form of review across other policy and service sectors. For example, the influential American report on crime prevention by Sherman *et al.* (1997) – *Preventing Crime: What Works, What Doesn't, What's Promising*, used a 'scientific methods scale' to assess the quality of the evaluations reviewed. Sherman *et al.* used several different dimensions in rating the studies reviewed from 1 to 5 (as Table 7.1). Three factors were the most important in judging the methodological rigour of the studies: the study's ability to control extraneous variables, the minimization of measurement error, and the statistical power to detect meaningful differences. Simply put, these three factors are important because they all relate to assurances that a research study is presenting an accurate picture of what we want to know about. In the 'what works' debate this usually means that we want to know whether an intervention has an effect on a population greater that the alternatives or doing nothing. We want to avoid wrongly detecting an effect or *not* detecting an effect from an intervention, because our research design and sample size are not up to the task. The RCT (randomised controlled trial) is conventionally top of the hierarchy in systematic reviews. Random assignment to either the new 'treatment' (or intervention) and the existing service or way of dealing with an issue is a way of trying to achieve fair-comparison groups to see if something 'works' or has an effect. The removal of choice,

Table 7.1 Scientific methods scale (using crime prevention as the example)

Level 1 (lowest): Correlation – crime-prevention programme and a measure of crime or crime-risk factor

Level 2: Temporal sequence – between the programme and the crime or crime-risk outcome; or a comparison group present without demonstrated comparability to the treatment group

Level 3: Comparison – for two or more units of analysis, one with and one without the programme

Level 4: Comparison – for multiple units within and without the programme, controlling for other variables that influence crime

Level 5 (highest): Random Assignment – of comparable units to programme and control groups (RCT)

Source: Adapted from Nuttall *et al.*, 1998, pp. 139–40.

by randomisation, is a way of trying to ensure that the groups are comparable and have not been affected by practitioners or some other circumstance.

A Home Office report by Nuttall *et al.* (1998) also used a scientific methods scale, although not as the sole basis for judging effectiveness or strength of evidence (see Table 7.1).

According to Nuttall *et al.*, in deciding 'what works' at least two level-3 evaluations are required, as well as tests of statistical significance, and the finding should be supported by other available evidence. 'What's promising' is identified by at least one level-3 evaluation, and tests of statistical significance, but the generalisability is in question. 'What doesn't work' is established by at least two level-3 evaluations supporting ineffectiveness and statistical tests, and the finding should be supported by available evidence. 'What's unknown' includes programmes not in the above categories (Nuttall *et al.*, 1998, p. 140). A scientific methods scale is argued to be particularly useful when research sets out to determine the relative effectiveness of an intervention. The hierarchy of evidence is explicit and is based on experimental research as the cornerstone of evidence-based medicine.

Systematic reviews of completed research on a topic are increasingly used in order to establish what is already known and inform the best way of setting up an intervention or programme. Because systematic reviews are based on whether or not a study meets the explicit criteria specified, it is argued that systematic reviews set out to reduce the bias that can occur in traditional narrative reviews, where the author is not explicit about why certain literature has been included and other literature ignored or discarded. The systematic review in this sense is clear about why a study is or is not included in a review, and this decision is usually based on methodology.

The focus on methodology as a key criterion for inclusion or exclusion from a review can be a threatening procedure for some researchers. Further, some critics of the systematic review are unhappy about the level of support for the RCT made clear by the hierarchy of evidence used in the Sherman *et al.* (1997) and Nuttall *et al.* (1998) reviews. Hammersley (2001) traces the emergence of the systematic review as aligned to those about the advantages and disadvantages of meta-analysis, as an alternative to traditional or 'narrative reviews', which are often presented as essentially subjective. A key criticism of the systematic review and the associated ideas of 'evidence-based practice' is the assumptions made within an essentially positivist model of research and the belief that findings can somehow be accumulated or aggregated. An alternative view, based on Popper (see, for example, Popper, 1959), would be to view the growth of scientific knowledge as through the overthrow of theories and their replacement with more satisfactory ones. Hammersley (2001) argues that the terms 'systematic' and 'evidence-based practice' are presented in a way that tends to disqualify alternatives: 'unsystematic' reviews and practice *not* based on evidence are hard to defend. A further criticism of the 'what works'/'evidence-based' approach is that it tends to ignore the political realities in which decisions are made and the different sources of evidence used to make these decisions, as highlighted above. Hammersley (2001) would go further in his criticism of systematic reviews in writing that 'perhaps the most serious charge to be laid against the systematic review movement is that it extends the myth of the audit society to research' (p. 551). The latter comment makes explicit the belief that political and administrative imperatives are behind the choice of systematic reviews over other types of review.

Techniques like meta-analysis are another way of using existing research in order to establish whether particular types of intervention 'work' or have a positive effect. Meta-analysis is a technique for statistically combining the results of studies in order to obtain an overall effect. In this way the results of small studies can be combined to create a much bigger study that should provide a more reliable estimate of what particular types of intervention appear to be doing (Oakley, 2000). Like the systematic review, meta-analytic techniques focus on quantifiable results and experimental designs. There are also different types of literature review that start from other types of research paradigm, such as meta-ethnography and critical realist synthesis (Forbes and Griffiths, 2002), although these are not as commonly cited as justifications for changing policy and practice. A more useful approach might be to acknowledge that, in combination, these various ways of bringing research knowledge together should bring useful insights and a wider acceptance of different types of review methodology and may avoid time-consuming 'paradigm wars' (Oakley, 2000). For example, Edwards *et al.* (1998) suggest examining the 'signal' versus the 'noise' of studies, arguing that interesting and valuable insights (the signal) can be gained from some methodologically 'weaker' studies (the noise). Such approaches are more obviously subjective, although clarity about inclusion criteria in any review helps to make the rationale for the review more explicit. Importantly, the research review is a way of making sense of large

Table 7.2 A meta-ethnographic approach to research synthesis of qualitative data

Getting started – identify whether meta-ethnography is the preferred approach for what you want to know. Especially useful when 'how' or 'why' questions are being asked; when the investigator has very little control over events; when the focus is on contemporary phenomena in a real-life context

Deciding relevance – defining the parameters for the studies to be reviewed, with some rationale for these decisions

Reading the studies – and rereading the studies; meta-ethnography sets out to synthesise texts, which requires extensive attention to detail in the accounts and what they tell you about your substantive concerns

Determining how the studies are related – a synthesis requires that the relationships between studies must be determined; this might be done through metaphors, phrases, ideas and/or concepts (and their relations) used in each account and their juxtaposition

Translating the studies into one another – accounts can be treated as analogies, e.g. 'one program is like the other, except …'. At the same time translations are synthesised

Synthesising translations – compare translations: can some translations encompass other accounts? Analyse competing translations and translate them into each other

Expressing the synthesis – the results of the synthesis should be made intelligible for the intended audience

Source: Based on Noblit and Hare, 1988, pp. 26–9.

amounts of literature in a field that, from the point of view of policy-makers and practitioners, is simply overwhelming. A focus on what evidence there is to support what is perceived as 'known' is in itself illuminating.

Meta-ethnography is a way of synthesising the findings of studies based on qualitative data. It is argued that 'synthesis', when it involves qualitative data, goes beyond the summarising function of the traditional narrative analysis. Synthesis of qualitative data is likely to involve reinterpretation. In a synthesis studies may be analysed in three main ways: as directly reciprocal or comparable translations, as in opposition to each other as refutational translations, or, taken together, they may represent a line of argument (Britten *et al.*, 2002). Noblit and Hare (1988) developed a seven-step approach to this form of analysis, summarised in Table 7.2.

Realist evaluations go beyond the simple question of 'what works' and ask what works for whom, in what circumstances, in what respects and how (Pawson and Tilley, 1997). This view is 'panacea-phobic' and seeks instead to look more specifically at the conditions in which we might make a difference. Approaches, ways of working or programmes aimed at working with children in trouble are ultimately based on *theories* about what gives rise to their behaviour or predicament (see Chapter 1). Realists see programmes as embedded in social systems. From this perspective an intervention that sets out to work on aggressive behaviour would be influenced by the individual capacities of teachers, parents and children, as well as their interpersonal relationships, the institution(s) or place(s) in which an intervention occurs, and the wider infrastructural setting that may undermine or support change.

Realist evaluation puts forward four linked concepts for explaining and understanding programmes: mechanism, context, outcome pattern and context-outcome pattern configuration. This last unwieldy term is based on a commonplace social explanation in which outcomes are viewed as following a particular alignment within a case, with a specific combination of attributes. Pawson and Tilley (1997) use the recipe analogy, in which recipes 'work' through assembling the right ingredients in the correct proportion to suit the tastes of the diner. They advise asking the question 'would it work here?' before a service implements a programme that has been shown to be effective. Bearing in mind the methodological and other arguments about the nature and use of evidence, we will now consider some of the key research evidence available in relation to children in trouble.

Early Intervention

As we have noted at various points, early intervention has a number of meanings: early in a child's life, early in problem development or in a timely way in a given situation. Intervening early in the lives of children believed to be 'at risk' of adverse outcomes is generally recognised to be a good idea (Sutton *et al.*, 2004), as long as the intervention itself is not stigmatising. There is a considerable body of research in the UK, as well as Europe and the United States, which examines early interventions in the lives of children. On the other hand very few interventions have been rigorously evaluated. Birth cohort and other longitudinal research studies in the UK provide useful information about life-course trajectories, adding to our understanding of risk and protective factors, from the early years through to adulthood. Such studies also provide evidence about outcomes from time spent in day care, for example. The focus of most early intervention programmes is on children and families in need and high-risk circumstances; and, usually, pre-school children or children in the first years of primary school. There are also prevention programmes targeted at pregnancy. Research has established associations between low birth weight, maternal smoking or alcohol consumption during pregnancy and later health, education and behaviour problems (Sutton *et al.*, 2004). The risk to children in adverse circumstances are numerous and varied, ranging from the likelihood of low achievement at school, poor employment prospects and welfare dependency, to drug misuse and involvement in criminal activity. As we saw in earlier chapters, the evidence shows that there are a group of children who from an early age behave in ways that are different from those who might be seen as the 'adolescent onset' offenders, who will 'grow out' of their behaviour. The distinction between groups becomes more obvious with age and also the argument for more individual targeting becomes stronger.

We noted in Chapter 1 that 'conduct disorder' is a frequent diagnosis for children in trouble. One longitudinal research study in England has focused specifically on the potential financial benefit of intervening early by estimating the costs of not intervening with conduct-disordered children. This study, published in the *British Medical Journal* in 2001, followed 142 10-year-old children into adulthood, grouping them into three categories: 'no problems', 'conduct problems' and 'conduct disorder'. Data were gathered on six key areas of their lives: the provision of special education; foster and residential care; relationship breakdown, health and crime; and state benefits in adulthood. The mean comparative costs by the age of 28 were £7,423 for those with 'no problems'; £24,324 for those with 'conduct problems'; and £70,019 for those with 'conduct disorders' (Scott *et al.*, 2001). Scott *et al.* estimated the specific costs in relation to offending at £1,200 for the police to identify a young offender, and £2,500 for a successful prosecution, with the *weekly* cost of a place in a secure unit at £3,450.

The *Perry Pre-School, High/Scope* approach is well known. It is based on an approach developed from a project run between 1962 and 1967 in Ypsilanti, Michigan, in the United States. The research began in 1962 with the selection of 123 children born between 1958 and 1962. They were randomly assigned to a group that did attend pre-school and a group that did not. They were from poor socioeconomic backgrounds: around half the families were on welfare and a similar proportion were households headed by a single parent. The original project set the foundations for research into both short-term and long-term effects. In 1970 David Weikart founded the High/Scope Educational Research Foundation, which undertook the subsequent longitudinal research. The principles behind this intervention were based on a pre-school programme that emphasised active learning, a child-centred approach in which children learn through a sequence of activities (plan–do–review) guided by adults in a play environment. The longitudinal research showed positive benefits in the lives of children in a range of ways, the most striking of which related to achievement, motivation and social behaviour. Longer-term benefits included higher levels of educational attainment, a lower rate of teenage pregnancy, a reduced need for special education, lower welfare payments and more tax paid because of higher rates of employment, as well as lower rates of crime and drug misuse. The 'savings' to the public purse have been calculated to be in the region of $7 for every $1 of expenditure, with the largest proportion (65 per cent) of this saving coming from savings in the criminal justice system (Schweinhart and Weikart, 1980). The latter finding reminds us that the savings from an intervention may come about in different service sectors from the initial provider and/or funding agency.

While the financial arguments for early intervention are persuasive, we should remember that not everything can be given a cost: for example, children may be happier as a result of particular help, or adults may feel better able to work with or look after a child with very difficult behaviour. There are also potentially three key problems with targeting early intervention too explicitly and too narrowly: one is ethical, with the potential for labelling young children as potential delinquents; a second is the fact that there is movement in and out of the group of children with conduct problems; a third is the need to provide services that will gain the trust and participation of parents. Both McCarthy *et al.* (2004) and Sutton *et al.* (2004) highlight the different types of risk present and responses needed in relation to children of different ages, as well as the way particular risk and protective factors fluctuate over time.

We have already seen that some outcome measures, such as longer-term cost-benefit analyses, as in High/Scope, can take some time to establish. Other interventions, such as *Head Start*, were seen as a disappointing in the early stages (Westinghouse Learning Corporation, 1969), then later pronounced effective, because of what might be termed 'sleeper effects' (McKey *et al.*, 1985). That is, the benefits of some interventions might not be immediately apparent, emerging some years after a programme was experienced. Head Start was a pre-school programme for disadvantaged children which began as a summer programme in the United States in 1965 with over half a million predominantly African-American children. It quickly expanded and included white children in the following year. It was designed to close the gap between these children and their more advantaged peers. Head Start encompassed a variety of initiatives, including High/Scope. Early evidence suggested that short-term gains in test scores for Head Start children faded out after a few years in primary school, although Head Start has wider objectives than raising test scores. The later positive outcomes from Head Start were found in relation to educational attainment anti-social behaviour, use of special education services and track records in relation to employment and offending behaviour (McKey *et al.*, 1985). Research by Garces *et al.* (2002) examined a Panel Survey of Income Dynamics that included a question about participation in Head Start. They found that participation in Head Start is associated with a significantly increased probability of completing high school and attending college as well as higher earnings in one's early twenties, for white participants. The most significant difference for African-Americans who participated in Head Start was that they are less likely to have been booked for or charged with a crime. Differences in achievement levels between ethnic groups attending Head Start have been explained by structural factors in that African-American children attended lower-quality schools than white children (Currie and Thomas, 2000).

The influence of High/Scope and Head Start can be seen in the development of *Sure Start* in the UK. Sure Start emerged from the Comprehensive Spending Review (CSR) set up shortly after the Labour Government came into power in May 1997. In a departure from normal procedures, the government decided that in formulating its policy it would call upon the expertise of the wider policy community through a series of seminars. These seminars considered papers from practitioners and academics on the multiple causes of the social exclusion of children, the shortcomings of existing service provision, and the effectiveness of early intervention programmes implemented in the United States, the UK and in other European countries (HM Treasury, 1998). While there was substantial agreement on *what works,* several of those who submitted evidence to the cross-cutting review (e.g. Oliver *et al.,* 1998; Pugh, 1998; Richards, 1998; Utting, 1998) highlighted that the delivery mechanisms for comprehensive and integrated services were of equal importance. In other words, the question of effectiveness 'cannot be divorced from *how* an intervention is delivered and *by whom*' (Oliver *et al.,* 1998, p. 12; original emphasis). Evidence was presented on how comprehensive community-based programmes could present real challenges to service agencies, all of which tended to view children and parents differently, and operate under different legislative frameworks and within their own professional cultures (Richards, 1998).

The working model agreed for early Sure Start programmes was one in which interventions should be 'locally driven', rather than relying upon a single blueprint. This approach raises some of the key problems in the implementation of programmes based on 'evidence'. That is, although it can be demonstrated that *the ideas behind* Sure Start were clearly evidence-based, it was not actually implemented as an evidenced programme (such as High/Scope). Indeed, the emphasis on a locally driven agenda precluded the possibility. In this context it is difficult to establish whether any changes shown in Sure Start areas are due to simply more resources, rather than the implementation of an 'effective' programme. Indeed, as we saw in Chapter 4, the eagerness of government, both to reform but also to claim success, overrode many of the needs of a properly evidence-based development.

Cognitive-Behavioural Methods

Problematic behaviour is the common immediate issue for adults working with troublesome children. Although problematic behaviour may, in some cases, result from parenting, a child's behaviour can be poorly handled and even be made worse by schools; further, in some cases, there may be a genetic component to the behaviour viewed as problematic. Cognitive-behavioural methods overall show promising outcomes when working across a range of circumstances and particular problem behaviours with adults as well as children; including aggressive and violent behaviours, problem drinking, sex offences, arson, and so on. Cognitive-behavioural methods are a range of interventions drawn from behavioural and cognitive psychology. These methods focus on tackling the way an individual thinks and reasons and their associated behaviour. The specific focus may vary but the methods are based on the same principles; they include behaviourally based methods, relaxation and systematic desensitisation, social skills training, self-instructional training, training in moral reasoning and multi-modal programmes. Multi-modal programmes have shown the most promising results in reducing reoffending (McGuire, 1995), particularly with high-risk young offenders (Vennard *et al.*, 1997).

The importance of programme integrity and other factors in the process of implementation of what are generally seen as 'effective interventions' has been highlighted by a number of Home Office studies. For example, a study focused on reviewing existing evidence and a survey of the probation ser-vices' use of programmes concluded that 'cognitive-behavioural methods are generally more successful in modifying patterns of thinking and behaviour than more traditional counselling and therapy' (Vennard *et al.*, 1997). An evaluation of cognitive-behavioural treatment for prisoners, using a treat-ment and comparison group design, confirmed its effectiveness, concluding that 'reconviction fell considerably after cognitive skills treatment' and 'based on the number of prisoners expected to complete the cognitive skills pro-gramme in 2002–2003, this reduction represents almost 21,000 crimes pre-vented' (Friendship *et al.*, 2002, p. 1). However, a year later another Home Office study found no difference in the two-year reconviction rates in a study of a sample of male adult prisoners who had participated in a cognitive-behavioural programme, in comparison with those who had not (Falshaw *et al.*, 2003). The possible reasons for this included expected variation in any programme; differences in skill, motivation and resources for the pro-gramme; differences in the treatment and comparison group; and differences in the risks presented by offenders on the programmes. In other words, methods of intervention put forward as 'effective' are very dependent on context and human resource issues. This might seem an obvious point to make, but it is a crucial one for those in policy and practice who are strongly wedded to the concept of 'effective practice' and the 'what works' agenda. It is also important to note that even 'effective' interventions do not lead to posi-tive outcomes for all programme participants. Outcome measures vary according to the programme. For example, a reduction in recidivism of around 10 per cent would be seen as an effective programme with offenders.

Family-Based Initiatives

Family-based initiatives often mean parenting programmes of one sort or another. There is consistent evidence that family functioning, rather than family structure, has the greatest impact upon outcomes for children (Utting, 1995). Research in the United States shows that three broad categories of family-based interventions have been found to be effective in leading to improved outcomes for children and young people: early home-visiting

schemes and pre-school education (such as High/Scope); parenting programmes and structured family work (Sherman *et al.*, 1997).

Parenting programmes are focused, short-term interventions aimed at
helping parents improve their relationship with their children; they also aim
to prevent or treat emotional and behavioural problems in children. Parents
began to be actively used as modifiers of their children's behaviours in the
1960s, when early work with individual parents was shown to have an impact
on a range of problems from aggression to speech problems (Barlow *et al.*,
2002). Group work with parents did not begin until the 1970s and is now
offered in a range of settings and can be found in a number of countries.

Studies evaluating parenting programmes are numerous but most would
not meet the scientific methods scale criteria outlined earlier in Table 7.1.
Barlow's systematic review (1999) focuses on the effectiveness of parent-
training programmes in improving the behaviour of children aged 3–10.
Studies conducted prior to 1970 were excluded from this review and all
were published studies. All programmes included at least one 'group-based'
parent-training programme, and one standardised child behaviour outcome
measure. All are 'parent-only' training programmes, although it is acknowledged that many contemporary programmes include work with children.
Barlow wanted to focus specifically on work with parents. In all, 255 studies
were identified, but only 18 met all the specified inclusion criteria for this
review. Two of the 18 studies were follow-up studies. Only 6 of the 16 primary
studies included in the review used rigorous methods of randomisation.
This sort of review exemplifies the strict criteria used in systematic reviews, as
discussed earlier in this chapter.

Although Barlow (1999) is critical of aspects of the methodology of the
studies she reviews she concludes overall that 'they point to the effectiveness of
behaviourally orientated parent-training programmes in improving behaviour problems in children' (p. 49). Further, community-based programmes
are thought to be particularly worthwhile in terms of being 'cost-effective' and
'user-friendly', in comparison with clinic-based programmes. Barlow highlights the need for more research into longer-term outcomes from parenting
programmes; the extent to which improvements in behaviour are carried
into different settings (such as the school); and which parents benefit from
which type of programme.

The Webster-Stratton programme (see for example Webster-Stratton,
1999) is particularly well documented and researched – this was the only
programme in Barlow's (1999) review to have been systematically evaluated
in a number of trials (p. 44). The Webster-Stratton programme was developed
at the University of Washington's Parenting Clinic in Seattle, in the United
States. There are a number of different elements to the programme; the 'basic'
programme teaches parenting techniques, and the 'advance' programme
works on parental relationships; other programmes include direct work with
the child and with partners, also developing parent–teacher relationships.

The most marked improvements in behaviour were found when the programmes were applied together (WWFC, 2003). The programme combines behavioural, cognitive and affective components and is based on the use of videotape modelling in which parents watch numerous vignettes of interactions between parents and children. This programme works with children who have conduct or oppositional-type problems and parents who are both self-referrals, as well as professional referrals. The Webster-Stratton programmes are becoming widespread in the UK, either in their original form or using adapted approaches (WWFC, 2003). A multi-centre trial of the basic programme in the UK showed significant improvements in the children's behaviour. It worked well with families from poor backgrounds, attendance levels were good and the programme cost no more than comparable conventional interventions, at approximately £600 per child (Scott *et al.*, 2001).

School-Based Initiatives

Head Start and High/Scope, referred to above as 'early interventions', are both essentially pre-school educational programmes. Children from these interventions arrive in school more able to benefit from what is on offer. School-based initiatives in the primary school generally involve work with parents, as it has been long established that such work is likely to produce more benefits for the child. The early years of primary school offer another chance to intervene for the better, with multiple-focus programmes like FAST Track, Families and Schools Together (CPPRG, 1992). FAST Track integrates five intervention components designed together to focus on child conduct problems in early primary school. The programme involves parent training, home visiting and case management, social skills training, academic tutoring and teacher-based classroom intervention. Full-service schools are of growing interest in the UK and are a logical development from the principles underpinning *Every Child Matters*. Full-services schools are based on the premise that, as children's behavioural difficulties are multifaceted, they need addressing by means of a comprehensive, integrated model of intervention. Further, they are based on the premise that schools are *the* main community resource for most children. Early models of full-service schools have acted as facilitators of all other services that children, young people and their families need (Dryfoos, 1994, p. 12). Services include general as well as mental health, child care and parent education, recreation and cultural events, employment services and community policing.

As Fitz-Gibbon (2000) points out, 'education is a universal, compulsory treatment' (p. 83). Children, especially young children, spend a large part of their waking hours in school. Education itself is an important determinant of future life chances and choices and is connected to a range of positive or negative outcomes. Landmark studies, such as that of Rutter *et al.* (1979), have established that schools can make a difference, irrespective of social background. A number of assessment instruments exist to measure children's behaviour, and to assess their readiness to learn and commitment to school. This could mean that targeting support for children in school is more cost-effective than in-depth assessments of individual children (McCarthy *et al.*, 2004). However, overall, the research evidence base for what is actually done in schools in the UK is lacking and there is a tendency to over-interpret the politically popular findings on school effectiveness and school improvement and confuse the extent to which one can make generalisations on the basis of extreme cases (Fitz-Gibbon, 2000). While evidence about the academic curriculum is not a focus of this book, it is still relevant in that the lack of attachment, level of disaffection and disengagement with school that arises in the current system are part of an array of accumulating 'risk factors' that disproportionately affect children already experiencing adversity in other ways.

As in other policy sectors, much of the available evidence is from the United States. For example, a meta-analysis of 165 studies of school-based prevention activities analysed the evidence available about the impact of activities ranging from individual counselling or behaviour-modification programmes through efforts to change the way schools are managed. The analysis shows that school-based practices appear to be effective in relation to certain behaviours: reducing drug and alcohol use, school drop-out and attendance problems. In common with findings from research in other sectors, cognitive behavioural programmes were found to be consistently positive in effect. Non-cognitive behavioural counselling, social work and other therapeutic interventions showed consistently negative effects (Wilson *et al.*, 2001). Research in the United States consistently finds that school-based programmes can produce sustained positive changes in behaviour when they are carefully implemented, developmentally appropriate, sustained over time and build social competence (Derzon *et al.*, 1999; Mendel, 2000). Yet Derzon *et al.* (1999) found only relatively small effect sizes of between 1 and 5 per cent (i.e. change attributable to the programme) in their meta-analysis of 83 'school-based programs to reduce violence'. The most positive results were found in the reduction of verbal aggression, but negative effects were found for weapon-carrying. Wilson *et al.* (2003) also note that most school-based evaluations are 'research-orientated demonstration projects', rather than routine practice programmes; the latter generally show even smaller effect sizes. Wilson and Lipsey (2006) found bigger effect sizes (than Derzon *et al.*, 1999) in some parts of their meta-analysis of 219 experimental and quasi-experimental studies of 'school-based violence prevention programmes'. For example, they found a 9 per cent reduction in fighting. Overall they found that some programmes were effective in reducing the most common types of aggressive behaviour in schools – such as fighting, name-calling, intimidation, and other negative interpersonal behaviours. This was especially the case with the higher-risk students.

The conclusions from these studies may not seem especially encouraging. However, because of the mass nature of the school system it is potentially an important opportunity for informed interventions, which even with a relatively small 'effect size' could make a difference to a large number of children. For example, early aggressive behaviour is strongly associated with later anti-social and criminal behaviour, and schools are well placed to detect such behaviour and help improve it. Furthermore, schools have to do something when presented with aggressive behaviour and it is important that what they do is founded on the best evidence and at the very least does no harm.

Community-Based Initiatives

Before considering the evidence about community-based initiatives, it is worth briefly reminding ourselves of the relative lack of positive outcome data from various forms of institutional containment of children and young people. It is recognised that there are young people who present sufficient risk to themselves and/or others that they need to be taken out of the community. Most published studies show high rates of reoffending following release from institutions. For example Mendel (2000) found that at least 50–70 per cent of young people sent to training schools over a 30-year period in the United States were arrested within one or two years of their release. From time to time alternatives such as 'boot camps' are advocated instead of what are often seen as 'softer', community-based options. Boot camps were originally reported to be ineffective in terms of reducing reoffending but a later systematic review concludes that they 'are neither as good as the advocates expect nor as bad as the critics hypothesize', with an overall conclusion that they made 'no difference' (Wilson *et al.*, 2005, p. 16). Programmes such as 'Scared Straight' and other juvenile awareness programmes for preventing delinquency in the United States have involved visits to prison by young offenders and those considered 'at risk'. A systematic review concludes that they are 'more harmful than doing nothing' (Petrosino *et al.*, 2002, p. 2). In other words, there is little evidence that initiatives that take young people *out* of the community are effective in preventing and reducing reoffending, nor are initiatives that involve contact with prisons and inmates effective in acting as a deterrent.

McGuire (1995) focuses on reducing reoffending, but the guidelines produced for more effective programmes can also be a useful way of looking at what we do in response to problem behaviour from children and young people more generally.

A number of broad types of intervention in the community are common with young people at risk, such as counselling, individual support and mentoring schemes, sports and activity programmes and restorative justice. Many such programmes are also used in schools, sometimes in conjunction with community-based agencies. However, the evidence base for these forms of

Table 7.3 Guidelines for more effective programmes to reduce offending behaviour

---

Risk classification – matching risk classification to degree of intervention

Criminogenic needs – distinguishing between criminogenic and non-criminogenic need; focusing on individual features or problems that are supportive of offending if reducing offending is the purpose of the programme

Responsivity – staff being able to match their style of working with the learning style of the client

Community base – programmes located near to the young person's home environment have a greater chance of facilitating real-life learning

Treatment modality – more effective programmes have been found to be multi-modal (recognise the variety of offenders' problems); their contents and methods are skills-orientated; they utilise methods drawn from a behavioural, cognitive, cognitive-behavioural source

Programme integrity – stated aims are linked to the methods being used; there is adequate resourcing, staff training, and so on

---

Source: Adapted from McGuire, 1995, pp. 14–15.

intervention is complex and suggests that some may be harmful. Indeed, Lipsey's (1992) review of youth interventions found that 30 per cent of the programmes showed an overall counterproductive effect. Unstructured models of counselling or support were often found to be ineffective, and in some cases were counterproductive in terms of offending behaviour. However, counselling methods appear to be more effective when they are part of a multi-method approach. In a meta-analysis of 397 control or comparison group studies of the effectiveness of treatment for delinquency, representing over 40,000 young people aged 12–21, Lipsey (1995) found a 10 per cent reduction overall in recidivism in the treatment group. Other effects were more pronounced, but based on a smaller group of studies: a 28 per cent improvement on psychological measures; a 12 per cent improvement on interpersonal adjustment; a 12 per cent improvement in school participation. Greater differences were noted when aspects of treatment and treatment circumstances were investigated further, with modest differences also found in relation to characteristics of the young people. The three main pieces of practical advice for services and practitioners are shown in Table 7.4.

Little *et al.* (2004) report on the early pilot of the Intensive Supervision and Support Programme (ISSP), a variant of which has now been adopted across England and Wales. The focus is on children viewed as persistently anti-social. ISSP is a multi-systemic intervention, which in this research comprised seven main components, including better assessment and individual treatment, FGCs, mediation, reparation, mentoring, and so on. The study is one of very few RCTs in the UK. Part of the practical problem with this research

Table 7.4 Effectiveness of delinquency treatment

Treatment focus – behavioural, training or skills issues, appropriate to the client group. Use of concrete, structured approaches. Develop appropriate multi-modal packages, possibly including psychologically orientated treatment element

Monitoring, supervision and implementation – have a plan and remain faithful to it, so the intended treatment is actually delivered to each intended client

'Dose' or amount of service – preferably 100 or more total contact hours, delivered at two or more contacts per week over a period of 26 weeks or more

---

Source: Adapted from Lipsey, 1995, pp. 77–8.

design was practitioner resistance to random allocation. The authors note that in two cases, practitioners managed to bypass the agreed research protocol by re-referring young people allocated to the control group (these cases were excluded from the evaluation). Numbers were smaller than expected; 50 cases a year were expected at the outset, but it took over three years to reach that number. In the event the evaluation is based on 79 young people (an intervention group of 24 and two control groups). The evaluation showed that although reconviction rates were not affected, the volume of crime committed by ISSP participants was reduced by between 30 per cent and 50 per cent (on several measures).

Mentoring programmes have become very popular in the UK. Mentoring involves a trusting relationship in which a more experienced person helps, and provides a role model for, someone who is less experienced (St James-Roberts *et al.*, 2005). A national evaluation of 80 community mentoring projects in England and Wales found some modest progress in terms of young people re-entering education or training (a third did so), but about half the programmes ended earlier than planned. The study concludes that

> The reluctance of young offenders to take part in mentoring or other community intervention programmes is now amply documented, raising questions about their appropriateness as a stand alone intervention, and highlighting issues about service value and cost. (p. 6)

A review by Roberts *et al.* (2004) concluded that the benefits of mentoring are not clear, nor are the relationships between mentoring and offending behaviour, school attendance and anti-social behaviour. Indeed they found evidence of harm in some studies. In a context in which practitioners were attempting to improve mentoring schemes, Roberts *et al.* (2004) advise that directive mentoring and elements of cognitive behavioural therapy had the best chances of success.

Sport, leisure and outdoor activities have also been frequently used in both preventative and diversionary programmes. There is evidence that these sorts of activities contribute to positive personal attributes such as self-esteem, self-efficacy and social skills. However, Lipsey and Wilson's (1998) meta-analysis of wilderness and outdoor challenge programmes found them to be among the least effective types of programme for young people involved in serious and violent offending; although a later review found moderately positive results for delinquent youth (Wilson and Lipsey, 2000). This latter finding is a reminder about matching interventions with level of need. Overall, evidence on the impact of schemes involving sport, leisure and outdoor activities suggests that they should be combined with other interventions in order to ensure effective outcomes.

Restorative approaches are popular with some practitioners and are used in a range of circumstances, including for school- and family-based issues, as we saw in Chapter 4, as well as in youth justice contexts. Overall, evidence suggests promising, though modest, outcomes in general but limited results when applied to specific measurable outcomes in children and young people (Whyte, 2002). Furthermore, concerns have been raised about the extent to which restorative approaches can result in net-widening, and Whyte (2002) concludes that it is *un*likely that such approaches are sufficient on their own to turn around the lives of young people in major difficulty.

Communities that Care (CtC) was mentioned in Chapter 6. This is an interesting example of a process, rather than a programme, based on assessing and acting upon risk factors identified in a community. Crow *et al.* (2004) note wide interest in the process in a number of countries, including the Netherlands and Australia. They conclude that the evaluative evidence may be some time coming as 'it takes quite some time for CtC to be established in one country' (p. 79). Nevertheless, the process has spread from pilot projects in England in the mid-1990s to over thirty projects in 2005.

Evidence and Practice

The debates about 'what works' are common across the policy sectors and programmes working with children in trouble, although there are some important criticisms of this approach. The recognition that the evidence base is often inadequate or ambiguous, or that what is effective requires more resources than is available has led to the recognition that evidence-*informed* practice may be a more realistic and achievable goal. Most of the original research we reported upon in Chapters 4, 5 and 6 is relatively small-scale – concentrating on a particular service or local authority. This is the kind of research that most services are likely to experience or afford. Such research does have the advantage of increasing the responsivity of services and practitioners to findings – because it was about their local authority or service. A problem apparent in being part of large-scale national evaluations (as in the Sure Start local programme reported upon in Chapter 4) can be the perception from managers and practitioners that the research is remote and does not really relate to the particular needs of their programme, although the demands for data are onerous. We have seen in this chapter that the realities of the policy process and of practice mean that the implementation of 'effective' programmes still presents a major challenge. However, overall there is a move towards a greater use of evidence in developing and monitoring services working with children and young people. This is generally a sensible approach, especially when it is done in a thoughtful and sensitive way that fits with the everyday efforts of adults working with young people.

We do have a number of key positive indications about the kinds of programme that are likely to make a difference with children and families in trouble and those that do not. We know that early intervention is a good idea, but there are the political and practical realities to consider when trying to do this in a way that does not stigmatise children and families. We also have strong indications about what is likely to be most effective in developing programmes for delinquent young people (see Tables 7.3 and 7.4). The applicability of certain approaches across policy sectors is well demonstrated – as with cognitive behavioural therapy. Yet here, also, we have evidence of implementation problems. The evidence in relation to some programmes, such as mentoring, on the other hand, suggests that we need to look harder at the small print and note that mentoring programmes come in different forms, some of which may be harmful.

Some of the better known approaches to working with children and families, such as High/Scope and the Webster-Stratton programme (both of US origin), are more widely known and used partly *because* the evidence base for their effectiveness is well established. We know that schools that encourage a sense of 'connectedness' and that have positive reward programmes for pro-social behaviour act as a protective factor against the development of criminality, although there is a relative lack of good quality in-depth data about how particular interventions are actually implemented and operate in practice. We still need to know more about where to focus our efforts most, which elements of a programme are most important and for which children and families. We need to know more about the transferability of programmes across different cultures. At times we also need to be clearer about the kinds of changes we want to effect for children in trouble. The bottom line often relates to preventing or reducing offending behaviour, but it is obvious that we also want more socially integrated young people who are able to sustain relationships and responsibilities and take their part as full citizens in a democracy.

Note

1   The UK-based Cochrane Collaboration produced the Cochrane Database of Systemic Reviews of health-care interventions.

8

Reviewing the Evidence and Looking to the Future

When government talks about a 'culture of respect' it really wants to say 'respect for authority', which means it is talking a different language from that of the poor, excluded people who demand respect on the streets. They want respect *from* authority.

> – Richard Sennett, professor of sociology at the London School of Economics, quoted in Behr, 2005, *Observer*, 22 May, p. 17

This young man has caused absolute misery for the people he has terrorised in this neighbourhood, and is out of control. He should be absolutely clear we will not tolerate this kind of behaviour and unless he radically changes that behaviour, he faces a long period in custody.

> – Eddy Newman, Manchester City Council's executive member for housing, quoted in Bright, 2005b, *Guardian*, 27 May, p. 23

Who Is Responsible?

The previous chapters in this book have illustrated the development of thinking about and response to children in trouble in the UK, as well as the evidence about how many children are 'in trouble' and to what extent. We have reviewed the arguments about 'what works' and the use of evidence in developing a response to children in trouble, and we have considered the role of families, schools and communities in these respects. It is clear that all the aforementioned environments bear a responsibility to respond to children in trouble in ways that reduce rather than entrench or increase harm, but that the capacity to do so varies a great deal. Families have to be the first focus in any attempt to reduce the number of children in serious trouble. Families are where children first learn how to behave towards others. Families are fundamental in setting the boundaries of acceptable behaviour in different contexts, and many need support at some point in doing so. Many parents and carers are helped by relatives and friends when they are in difficulty, some consult written guidance, and so on. Some parents and carers may lack support and need the help of services – some will find that the response of universal services such as GPs and schools are all they need, whereas others need more specialist and intensive support. It follows that easily accessible parenting support and skills development, throughout childhood and the teenage years, are central to reducing the potential for difficulties becoming entrenched and harmful.

Schools are crucial as the only universal public service explicitly concerned with the socialisation of children and in contact with children on a daily basis for at least forty weeks a year. They have a crucial role in setting standards for appropriate behaviour in a group setting and in detecting children who are in need of more targeted support. Recognising this role fully does, however, highlight some of the tensions noted at the end of Chapter 5. Although a broader role is now recognised in school inspections, pupil achievement and league tables are likely to carry the most weight with parents able to exercise choice. Furthermore, the problem of overload both in terms of initiatives and in terms of workload has been continually highlighted by teaching unions. The latter comment may well be dismissed as whingeing, but there is plenty of evidence that would suggest that we should take this seriously. Schools need to be secure in the operation of their core role of teaching and learning if they are really going to be the hub of services to children more broadly; particularly those in trouble. It is notable how often preventative or more intensive work with children in trouble bemoans either the education service in general, or particular schools, for not being able to come up with the goods wanted by the programme, e.g. the CtC research (Crow *et al.*, 2004), the ISSP research (Little *et al.*, 2004) or research on PYOs (Arnull *et al.*, 2005).

The role of 'the community' in relation to children in trouble is much more difficult to pin down – not least because the concept of community is much contested. However, in relation to *where* children might get into trouble, the public sphere of the community offers different and often more serious possibilities than the school or home. A key underlying issue, in relation to communities as places or locations in which children get into trouble, is structured inequality. Simply, children in the poorest circumstances tend to go to the worst schools in neighbourhoods where peer-group influences are more likely to be an important risk factor. These areas are often under more surveillance, and so problematic behaviour from young people in the community may more often be noted and elicit a response. Indeed, as noted earlier in the book, people like Muncie (2004) query the relationship between social class and offending, as reflected in official statistics, noting that self-report studies are less conclusive. Nevertheless, targeted interventions tend to go where the official statistics indicate a problem. Further, there are real issues of opportunity for legitimate and law-abiding lifestyles in the worst areas. Any attempt to 'renew' such neighbourhoods must lead to real opportunities for employment on a living wage (a key recommendation of the research into the disturbances of the early 1990s; see Power and Tunstall, 1997). The differences in opportunity that underlie many of the situations in which children get into serious trouble are well recognised by the various area-based programmes that have characterised New Labour social policy. However, research also illustrates greater complexity in the patterns of opportunity and achievement than that found by poverty indicators alone (Hayden *et al.*, 2006), and not all poor children live in deprived neighbourhoods (Glass, 2005). This recognition means that we do need to look at how society in general balances its responsibilities of care and control for the next generation. This is ultimately a question of how the balance is drawn between the private and public spheres and responsibilities of the family and the state.

Problem behaviour from children is to an extent in the eye of the beholder and is likely to be related to the context in which it occurs. This is especially apparent in the more generalised adult perception that young people 'hanging around' in public places *is* a problem. Often problem behaviour is a developmental issue that ultimately settles down and goes away. There will always be differences of opinion about what constitutes more problematic behaviour, why it is manifest and what we should do about it in different contexts. However, it is important to recognise that many children who present the most extreme behaviour have been subjected to adults behaving badly and/or the indifference or ineffective response to their plight from the wider community.

It has been argued that at the start of the twentieth century there was a general assumption that teachers, doctors, police officers and other professionals were experts whose judgement could be trusted. There is less certainty about this in the early twenty-first century (Davies *et al.*, 2000). We are much more aware of professional self-interest, the power of teachers and schools to label and exclude, of residential care workers to abuse and of institutional racism and corruption in the police force. There is no overall consensus about what we want or expect from professionals, nor is respect for their status automatic. Moreover, the ready access to education, information and misinformation means that adults and children are more ready to question assumptions about what is appropriate behaviour in particular circumstances, while at the same time wanting assurances that they or their children are safe and free from risk, as well as protected from behaviour they see as a problem.

Thus, although the focus of this book has been about children in trouble it should be clear that a large part of the issue is the context created by adults. If we want children to behave better, then adults must be prepared to behave better as well. Adults and professionals have to be clear about their roles and responsibilities for children in trouble. The opening quotation from Richard Sennett reminds us that respect goes both ways.

Paying Attention to Evidence

Davies *et al.* (2000) note the massive rise during the twentieth century of organisations seeking to influence or advise governments on their actions. They view evidence as likely to play a central role in policy-making in the twenty-first century. Children's charities, professional organisations, statutory bodies, independent think tanks, as well as university researchers all try to present the evidence for a particular direction of action or change. The sheer volume of evidence available, never mind opinion and conviction about what needs to be done, means that it is imperative to consider how evidence is evaluated and presented. Chapter 7 outlined the methodological debates in relation to research evidence.

We have enormous amounts of monitoring data of various kinds in the UK that enable us to track what is happening to children in trouble – at least in terms of what is officially recorded. Certain basic principles and indicators of effective ways of responding to children in trouble are also well known. For example, it is well established that early behavioural problems in pre-school children are indicative of the likelihood of developing more problematic and entrenched difficulties later in life. The costs of intervening early are known to outweigh those of responding later. However, there are important ethical reasons for holding back and considering just how good the evidence is about continuity and change in the behaviour of young children; and, more importantly, whether we know how to intervene effectively in any case. Increasing sophistication in evaluative research is beginning to indicate that there is the potential for causing harm through intervening too early or inappropriately (Chitty, 2005). The latter is a crucial point to keep in mind, taking into account the very large numbers of children who do not develop major problems despite having the early signs; we need to bear in mind the intrusiveness of some interventions (DSRU, 2004, p. 10). DSRU (2004) also cautions against 'net-widening', or drawing families into services when they could sort things out for themselves. Furthermore, the resources needed to implement well-evidenced programmes with properly trained and supported staff have to be available. We need to consider carefully what outcomes we want from the services provided. The Dartington Social Research Unit (DSRU) (2004) advocates the use of validated instruments, such as the SDQ (reported upon in Chapters 1 and 4), in order to undertake accurate assessments related to level of need or concern. This is important and basic advice, as the FGC research in Chapter 4 illustrated. If measured (by the SDQ) in terms of reduced 'burden' and improvements in social adjustment, FGCs could claim some modest success. However, when compared on the outcome indicators used by the education service (attendance and exclusion figures) as a mainstream service, the indication was that FGCs did worse than the EWS as the mainstream service. Deciding upon achievable and relevant outcome indicators for a service is critical and an important part of focusing on what a service is trying to do, whether this is what it should be doing, and, if so whether it can do it.

Chapter 7 showed that we do have some good evidence about the kinds of programme that produce positive effects: early education programmes such as High/Scope and Head Start have been well evaluated and demonstrate clear gains for disadvantaged children. Structured parenting programmes, such as that developed by Webster-Stratton, have also been found to be effective in improving parenting skills and, in turn, children's behaviour. Cognitive behavioural methods have generally been shown to be effective in a wide range of circumstances (although not so in one Home Office study; see Falshaw *et al.*, 2003). The latter finding highlights the crucial issue of programme implementation. In short, for an intervention to be effective staff have to be prepared to support the way of working and be appropriately trained and resourced to do so. There is also the important issue of cultural transfer – because a programme 'works' in the United States does not necessarily mean that it will work in another cultural context. These words of caution about the 'what works' debate are made alongside a reminder that the best quality evidence is often not available to inform development. Further, even if there is, the evidence may not suit political and economic realities (an issue particularly in evidence in medicine).

In reality, most UK-based evaluations of interventions for children in trouble are relatively small-scale and do not meet the scientific standards criteria outlined in Chapter 7. Most evaluations are too short-term to follow through the longer-term impact (if any) of an intervention. It is impossible to conclude in some instances whether or not any improvements indicated may simply be due to more resources and attention paid to an issue. RCTs do offer more assurances on the impact of one intervention over another (or compared with doing nothing), but they are expensive and time-consuming to set up and conduct. Also, as medical trials and the Home Office research on cognitive behavioural methods illustrate, they too can produce contradictory results. Therefore, it is important in practical terms to take a sensible approach and accumulate 'best evidence' to inform programmes – this should include front-line staff perception and perceived 'workability' on an intervention, as well as the evidence from research. It is likely that a wider range of interventions with children in trouble will be more positive than we have good evidence for. It is also likely that we are doing harm with some interventions, or having no effect whilst utilising scarce resources.

The DSRU (2004) reminds us of the issues of sustainability and cost analysis. Many initiatives working with children in trouble are based on the assumption of sustainability. That is, it is assumed that after a period of funding the lessons learned from a project can become part of mainstream practice. This also assumes that mainstream practice can either change or accommodate the work (vis-à-vis other pressures), and that the new ways of working are compatible with performance management targets). It also assumes that staff are willing and able to change. This may well be the case in behaviour-management and parenting programmes (as a particular way of doing something that a practitioner already has to do); but some initiatives set out to add value to existing services through the provision of more individual or small-group opportunities for children, such as the JSFST reported upon in Chapter 5. Furthermore, projects aimed at the prevention end of the continuum may well uncover more need for services. For example, the Fort Bragg Demonstration in the United States was an attempt to deliver mental health services through a continuum of care (from outpatient therapies to residential treatment centres). Children in the intervention group were placed in the least restrictive, most normative environments possible. However, the project did not save costs. Indeed, the demonstration project expenditure was double that of the comparison group (DSRU, 2004, p. 26). On the other hand, projects in other fields have shown major cost savings, as in preventative services targeted at abuse and neglect, teenage pregnancies and youth crime (Hogan and Murphey, 2000).

The possibility that some 'preventative' services might actually uncover unmet need is a particularly pertinent issue to consider in relation to children in trouble. Behaviour problems, special educational needs and mental health problems are best seen as part of a continuum and at least one in five children will experience one or more of these problems in the course of growing up. Further, this level of need is very unevenly spread in communities, with higher levels of need being apparent in poorer areas. For example, it is not uncommon to find that half the children in the poorer schools in inner-city areas are assessed as having some level of special educational need. Thus the potential scale of the need for more help, particularly in poorer areas, alongside the widespread level of anxiety and concern from parents, schools, politicians and the media means that additional support for universal services has to be the focus for the majority of children when they are in some level of trouble.

We have already noted that when we do have good evidence about programmes that 'work' we need to be extremely careful about implementation – in terms of programme integrity, we also need to consider *who works*. The latter evidence may be the most complex and controversial area that we need to consider in that it is likely to lead us to the conclusion that some professionals working with children are not up to the task, and that some may be causing harm. While a moment's thought may cause us to recognise that this is an unsurprising observation, it does have major political and practical consequences. For example, it has been argued for some time that male role models may be particularly important for boys in female-headed, single-parent households. Newburn and Shiner (2005) found that the most positive impact of *Mentoring Plus* programmes with disaffected 15–19-year-olds was for young men mentored by men. They found very little impact in relation to social class or race. This sort of finding has important implications for mentoring programmes and possibly similar interventions working with disaffected young men.

Universal and Targeted Services

There is now much wider recognition of the need to advise and support parents in general on how to respond to and manage their children's behaviour. Indeed, there have been a number of television programmes focusing on the issue. There are also numerous media images of out-of-control and anti-social 'youths' and stories about very disruptive and aggressive behaviour in school. These images and concerns can be influential in constructing common perceptions and explanations of the issues to be addressed. It is common for various organisations, interest groups and the media to call for some issue to do with children's behaviour to be addressed by 'parenting programmes' or schools. Sometimes the behavioural expectations that are presented as the norm are at odds with subcultural differences and realities. So, for example, the behavioural expectations in schools may be at odds with the dominant norms of the communities they serve. This takes us back to the basic question of what we are trying to achieve in relation to children's behaviour and school, rather than into the well-rehearsed and often sterile debate about schools promoting middle-class values. The bottom line, in terms of many behaviour policies in schools, relates to children not fighting or stealing, taking turns and behaving in a polite way towards adults and each other. Schools are also expected to take a strong stance against bullying. Many behaviour-management policies emphasise the role and duties of adults in schools, as well as children. Most policies emphasise pretty basic social norms, although the issue of children fighting and being involved in bullying can cause differences in opinion about the accuracy of accounts of events as well as the nature of the response from schools (Hayden and Dunne, 2001).

As we noted in Chapter 2 and earlier in this chapter, schools are centre stage as *the* universal service for all children and as a key service around which other children's services might be colocated and planned. It is a vision with a great deal to recommend it; although it is a vision that may take some time to realise. Some key areas of instability are apparent in this vision. Quite apart from the workload concerns noted earlier, there are other practical problems such as space, particularly in some inner-city primary schools. Further, the availability of appropriately trained and skilled personnel varies by area – specifically, the evidence of teachers leaving the profession and of the drift of those who move jobs from the schools in the most adverse circumstances, to those that are easier places to work. Simply, schools that need staff most have the most difficulty recruiting. Inclusive schools are self-evidently better for individual children, as well as the communities they serve. However, it is plain that the ability of schools to be inclusive varies. Indeed, the ongoing concern about behaviour in schools is evidence of the problems of coping with the 'core business' that already exists.

Of course, other universal services such as primary care teams also have an important role to play in being alert to children and families who need help and in pointing them towards the help available. Primary care teams might be seen as crucial for children under the age of 3, important for children under school age, but of decreasing importance for the great majority of children thereafter. Indeed, most services are likely to have much less regular contact with children and families in comparison with schools (particularly primary schools in relation to contact with parents and carers).

Exclusion from services, whether universal or targeted, is an extremely serious action to take against children. We hear most about exclusion from school, discussed at some length in this volume; however, other services also exclude children. Young people are, in effect, excluded from youth and community facilities, as well as care placements. In relation to the latter, 'placement breakdown' is the term used. The behaviour of children is a frequent reason why care placements break down (see, e.g. Hayden *et al.*, 1999). Children in most trouble often have complex problems and not all of them are in control of their behaviour. For example, we already know that many of those in receipt of ASBOs are people with special educational needs and/or mental health problems. Yet the dominant response to what is seen as anti-social behaviour is to punish and exclude. Exclusion and labelling can move the problem somewhere else, rather than dealing with the issue. ASBOs can move the problem behaviour out of one area and into another, and in some cases back into the home. The various ways we respond to the most problematic behaviour of young people tends to emphasise rejection.

The complexity of the circumstances of children and young people in most trouble presents a strong case for a more thoughtful response to trying to meet all of their needs in the same environment or centre, at least for a time. It is obvious that mainstream schools cannot cater for children with the most extreme behaviour and that in these cases the criminal·justice system is often the end result of the failure of welfare agencies to provide the support needed. Further, when many children leave YOIs there can be difficulties getting an educational placement, or picking up where they left off in their studies. Some of this is about the scarcity of welfare-based residential resources (both institutional and in specialist foster care) for the minority of very complex cases; as illustrated in the research study on out-of-area placements in Chapter 4. It is also an issue of recognising the need for a continuum of responses to a continuum of needs.

Balancing Populism with Positive Change

It is often easy for the majority to see children in trouble as somebody else's children, who, like anti-social behaviour, are problems presented by other people, not us. Yet it is also obvious that how we respond to children in trouble is important to the wider community. The competing desires to control or protect children are often strong, but the arguments for preventing children's problems continuing into adulthood are also well appreciated. The gulf in perception and understanding of the issues and language used is exemplified in the opening quotations. Academics often put forward the tolerant or analytical view, leaving the rants to the media, elected members, or members of the general public. The reality of the political process means that government will always be subjected to such competing perspectives and imperatives. The government needs to be seen to be doing something and appeasing a range of viewpoints. For example, Burney (2002) views ASBOs as a microcosm of the political processes involved in the governance of law and (dis)order. This view sees the electorate as suffering to an unknown extent from some tangible objects of censure and fear, such as noisy neighbours, unruly children, and so on. Following the identification of these issues as 'a problem', laws are passed subsuming them under some all-embracing category – in this case, 'anti-social behaviour'. Structures are put in place – Crime and Disorder Reduction Partnerships – thus demonstrating a response to the issue.

The book started with a brief look at how we have understood and responded to children in trouble. Figure 8.1 focuses on the changes and enduring themes from the 1980s onwards. The ongoing nature of the balances, compromises and tensions are obvious. So while the 1980s might be characterised as 'the Thatcher years', which were commonly understood to be a period of right-wing government, the response to children and young people in serious trouble with the law was, in the main, diversionary. The focus was on keeping them in the community and out of institutions, although this may in part have been about cutting costs in the public sector, as much as concern about child welfare. The Children Act 1989, enacted after 10 years of right-wing government, was widely interpreted as a progressive piece of legislation with child welfare at its heart. On the other hand, the mainstream educational reforms of this period have been widely criticised for creating a pressurised, exclusionary environment in which the needs of the most vulnerable children are not well met. Yet it was also during the 1980s that arguments for inclusive education began to take root and the concept of maladjustment was replaced with special educational needs, specifically emotional and behavioural difficulties (now referred to as SEBD).

Schools, and particularly teaching unions, were concerned about pupil behaviour throughout this period. In the 1980s this took the form of concern about 'discipline' in schools, and the 1990s saw mounting evidence about exclusion from school with a shift in emphasis from the individual 'pupils with problems' in 1994 to the broader circumstances of SIPS by 1999, with a change in government. From 1997 there was a rapid shift in emphasis in how pupil behaviour was understood – sadly, it was not a shift that sufficiently took into account the perspectives of schools. Secondary head teachers are said to have been instrumental in the numerous amendments to SIPS that have, in effect, shifted the balance of power back to schools and exposed the tensions in the social inclusion agenda envisaged for schools.

1980s	The Thatcher years	Ongoing tensions
1981	Education Act (following Warnock)	*Children and young people –*
1982	Criminal Justice Act	*dangerous or vulnerable?*
1983	Further development of Intermediate Treatment (LAC, 83, 3)	
1986	Physical punishment ended in state schools	
1988	Education Reform Act	
1989	The Children Act Elton Report – *Discipline in Schools* United Nations Convention on the Rights of the Child (ratified in the UK in 1990)	
1990s	*Changing perspectives*	*Rights or responsibilities?*
1992	First national figures on school exclusion	
1993	Death of Jamie Bulger	
1994	DfE guidance: *Pupils with Problems*	
1997	Home office White Paper: *No More Excuses* New Labour elected: 'education, education, education' as the priority	
1998	Human Rights Act Crime and Disorder Act (established YOTs, ASBOs) Physical punishment ended in private schools Social Exclusion Unit established	*Individual needs or group needs?*
1999	Youth Justice and Criminal Evidence Act Youth Justice Board established DfES/DoH/Home Office guidance: *Social Inclusion, Pupil Support*	
2000s	*Responsibilisation*	*Care or control?*
2000	The Children's Fund established as a millennium project	
2002	First parent jailed for child's non-attendance at school	
2003	Anti-Social Behaviour Act DfES green paper: *Every Child Matters*	
2004	The Children Act and *Change for Children*	
2005	Task force and report on discipline in schools: *Learning Behaviour* Appointment of a Children's Commissioner DfES Green Paper: *Youth Matters*	*Inclusion or exclusion?*

Figure 8.1 Children in trouble – key legislation, guidance, enquiries and events (1980–2005)

Overall the 1990s was a decade of some major shifts in thinking about children in trouble in which many have argued that the death of Jamie Bulger in 1993 was influential (see, e.g., Muncie, 2004). A move to a 'no more excuses'-type of approach towards the most problematic and criminal behaviour from children and young people was established. At the same time the emphasis on social inclusion later in the decade, coupled with the passing of the Human Rights Act 1998, presents a more progressive thread to the changes in process.

By 2005 we are back to a concern about 'discipline', with the language of 'zero tolerance' being put forward as the appropriate response to problem behaviour in schools. There is a growing use of terms such as 'violence' and 'anti-social behaviour' to describe behaviour in schools, as part of a wider discourse on these latter issues and young people in the community. The potential crime-prevention role of schools has become more explicit, not least with police officers working with schools in crime hot spots (see for example Hayden, 2005b). Parents have increasingly been made accountable for the behaviour of their children – starting with parenting agreements and contracts, moving to orders and even imprisonment for failure to ensure a child's attendance at school. These moves have been interpreted as part of a wider 'responsibilisation' strategy, a concept that has been used to encapsulate the way in which governments seek to achieve their law and order ends by relying on non-criminal justice agencies; such as schools, 'communities' and other non-law and order agencies. The ascendancy of the concept of 'anti-social behaviour' and its popular association with young people has brought with it further monitoring and incursions into the lives and behaviour of ordinary young people in poor areas, or indeed any young people aged under 16 in some city and town centres, an action that led to a successful legal challenge to the use of child curfews by a 15-year-old, on the basis of human rights legislation (Barkham, 2005). 'Governmentality', or government by proxy, has been used to conceptualise some of these shifts in responsibility from government to communities, with communities setting the agenda for whatever behaviour they censure.

The overall picture may appear contradictory, and in some ways it is. But it is also understandable in terms of balancing the competing priorities of care and control of young people throughout this period.

The Move to Integrated Services for Children

Much of the argument and research evidence in this book has emphasised the way that children in most trouble often have high levels of need within their family and community, as well as in relation to their education. Figure 1.3 in Chapter 1 looked at how different agencies might construct and respond to aggressive and impulsive behaviour. These single tracks or routes through a particular agency, the problem construction and response should in theory be a thing of the past, with a move to integrated children's services. Certainly thinking and response had become much less rigid in 2005, in comparison with 1995. However, children's services as a whole still have to work largely with people trained in particular professional backgrounds and ways of working, with different explanations and responses to the way children behave. In many complex cases there will be several possible explanations and potential responses to a child's behaviour. The perspective and response that are accorded primacy in these situations may well be the most powerful ones, but they may not work in practice. In a sense that was part of the problem with the JSFST, reported upon in Chapter 5. Here an educational psychologist had a model of working that was well evidenced (an ecosystemic approach), but under-resourced and, most importantly, not fully supported by all the schools who actually had day-to-day contact and responsibility for the most problematic children. In essence, schools prioritised group work over individual work and were critical of JSFST staff who had difficulties working with groups of children (as opposed to one to one work). There was a credibility problem as well as a problem about agreed priorities and approaches to working.

On the other hand, there has been a strong move towards establishing new integrated services for children from the late 1990s onwards and there are instances where this way of working is now well established. The most obvious services set up as integrated services include YOTs, YISPs, Sure Start and Connexions. YOTs are an example of established integrated care-management teams for children already in trouble. They use a validated instrument, 'ASSET', to assess risk and protective factors for young people, although there has been some resistance from staff to completing this (largely because of the length and detail required). Yet it has been found to be a good predictive instrument (where completed) for level of risk and reoffending (Baker *et al.*, 2003). Staff should be trained to use and interpret this instrument effectively, as is the case with most such instruments. However, YJB research on YOT and YISP work with persistent young offenders indicates that this training is not happening or is not effective. The YJB research also notes that 'inter-agency relationships were limited', partly because work with social services and education agencies was viewed as out-of-date and not sufficiently targeted on offending behaviour; partly because work with these agencies was seen as 'difficult and time-consuming' (Arnull *et al.*, 2005, p. 6). Sure Start centres are an example of an integrated and largely preventative service that co-ordinates the response to families and children's need for support in the early years (see Chapters 4 and 7 for more detail). Connexions is an umbrella service that, in theory, is available to any young person from the age of 13 to 19 who needs advice or assistance. It sets out to 'join up' the work of youth, careers, drugs advice, sexual health and homelessness services, integrating the work of statutory, voluntary and private agencies.

Following the Children Act 2004, the appointment of Directors of Children's Services has accelerated the process of integration. The overall aim of the Act is to encourage integrated planning, commissioning and delivery of children's services, as well as improvements to multi-disciplinary working. The expectation is that this should remove duplication. Information-sharing is key to these developments. Indications from research on identification, referral and tracking systems in 'trailblazer authorities' show some achievements, but there are also familiar problems with new initiatives to do with short-term

funding, ambiguity over the legal aspects of information-sharing, local practicalities to do with space and location, and inconsistent representation from
agencies and other resource pressures within particular agencies, as well as
resistance to change (Cleaver *et al.*, 2005).

The five key outcomes for all children put forward by the *Every Child
Matters* Green Paper (see Chapter 2) are an important direction in which all
children's services should go. These outcomes are easy to agree with, although,
as, ever, the devil may be in the detail of how such outcomes can be achieved
and measured. An important issue to highlight here is whether the views and
priorities and the specific role of individual government departments are really
co-ordinated in the first place and whether they have taken account of the
realities for local authorities and their dealings with professional groups and
organisations. Common problems for people trying to deliver services in this
context are the amount of paperwork and requirements for monitoring,
numerous performance targets and short-term funding and consequent staffing
problems, as well as the pace of change. New legislation, regulation and 'guidance' continue to create irritation amongst many professionals who have to try
and work within a situation in which there is too much 'complexity, confusion
and inconsistency in the law' (Clayton, 2005, p. 32).

Nevertheless, the relative simplicity of the five key outcomes for children is
welcome, as are the concepts of integrated children's services and children's
trust arrangements. Various options on integrating services have been outlined
by Miller and McNicholl (2003), as well as 'children's trust arrangements'
(Miller, 2005). The rationale for these developments is obvious from the
content of this book, as is the evidence about the need for structures to be
workable (with at least some medium-term stability in funding) for those deliver-
ing the services. It seems reasonable to conclude with a cautious optimism
about the general direction of change in some aspects of the response to children in trouble – specifically the efforts in the early years and the move towards
extended schools. However, we need to take much greater care about how
we treat the rights of ordinary young people – reflect for a moment about
how adults might feel if they were told to keep away from areas in the
evening because of the action of a minority of adults who are criminal or
anti-social. Adults, after all, account for most of the abusive, anti-social and
criminal behaviour in society, and they lay the foundations of the problems
of the next generation. As Rod Morgan has argued, we should distinguish
between young children who can't choose their parents, neighbourhoods or
circumstances, and can't walk away from them and young adults who do
have more choice (Bright, 2005b). Finally, a great deal more needs to be
done for the most difficult and vulnerable young people while they are in
young offenders institutions and when they leave.

References

Allen, D. (ed.) (2002) *Ethical Approaches to Physical Interventions*. Kidderminster: BILD.

Altheide, D. L. (2002) Children and the discourse of fear, *Symbolic Interaction*, 25(2), pp. 229–50.

Ames Reed, J. (1995) Young Carers. *NCB Highlight 137*. London: National Children's Bureau.

Ariès, P. (1960) *Centuries of Childhood*. Harmondsworth: Penguin.

Arnull, E., Eagle, S., Gammampila, A., Archer, D., Johnston, V., Miller, K. and Pitcher, J. (2005) *Persistent Young Offenders*. London: YJB.

ASBU, Anti-Social Behaviour Unit (2003) *The ASBU One-Day Count of Reported Anti-Social Behaviour*. London: ASBU.

Audit Commission (1996) *Misspent Youth: Young People and Crime*. London: Audit Commission.

Audit Commission (2004) *Youth Justice 2004: A Review of the Reformed Youth Justice System*. London: Audit Commission.

Baker, K., Jones, S., Roberts, C. and Merrington, S. (2003) *The Evaluation of the Validity and Reliability of the Youth Justice Board's Assessment for Young Offenders*. Probation Studies Unit, Centre for Criminological Research, University of Oxford. London: YJB.

Bandura, A. (ed.) (1995) *Self-Efficacy in Changing Societies*. Cambridge: Cambridge University Press.

Barkham, P. (2005) Liberty challenges child curfews and dispersal orders in landmark case, *Guardian*, 27 May, www.guardian.co.uk/humanrights/story/0,,1493319,00.html (accessed 25 November 2005).

Barlow, J. (1999) *Systematic Review of the Effectiveness of Parent-Training Programmes in Improving Behaviour Problems in Children Aged 3–10 years*. Oxford: Health Services Research Unit, University of Oxford.

Barlow, J., Parsons, J. and Stewart-Brown, S. (2002) *Systematic Review of the Effectiveness of Parenting Programmes in the Primary and Secondary Prevention of Mental Health Problems*. Oxford: Health Services Research Unit, University of Oxford.

Basini, A. (1981) Urban schools and 'disruptive pupils': a study of some ILEA support units, *Educational Review*, 33(3), pp. 191–205.

Beck, U. (1992) *Risk Society: Towards a New Modernity*. London: Sage.

Beedell, C. (1993) *Poor Starts, Lost Opportunities, Hopeful Outcomes*. London: Charterhouse Group.

Behr, R. (2005) R-E-S-P-E-C-T, *Observer*, 22 May, pp. 16–17.

Beinart, S., Anderson, B., Lee, S. and Utting, D. (2002) *Youth at Risk? A National Survey of Risk Factors, Protective Factors and Problem Behaviour*

Among Young People in England, Scotland and Wales. London: Communities that Care.

Bentley, T. (1997) *Learning to Belong, the Wealth and Poverty of Networks: Tackling Social Exclusion.* Demos Collection 12. London: Demos.

Blunkett, D. (2000) Influence or irrelevance: can social science improve government?, *Research Intelligence*, 71, pp. 12–21.

Blunkett, D. (2003) *A Civil Society – Are We Nearly There Yet?* London: IPPR.

Bottoms, A., Brown, P., McWilliams, B., McWilliams, Nelliw, M. in collaboration with Pratt, J. (1990) *Intermediate Treatment and Juvenile Justice.* London: HMSO.

Bowcott, O. (2005) The *Guardian* Profile: Louise Casey, *Guardian Unlimited*, 9 September, www.guardian.co.uk/guardianpolitics/story/0,,1566099, 00. html (accessed 21 November 2005).

Bowlby, J. (1951) *Maternal Care and Mental Health.* Geneva: World Health Organisation.

Bradford, S. (2005) Modernising youth work: from the universal to the particular and back again, in Harrison, R. and Wise, C. (eds) *Working with Young People.* London: Sage Publications with Open University Press, pp. 57–69.

Bradshaw, J. (2003) Child poverty and child health in international perspective, in Hallet, C. and Prout, A. (eds) *Hearing the Voices of Children: Social Policy for a New Century.* London: Routledge-Falmer, pp. 213–36.

Brent, J. (2001) Trouble and tribes: young people and community, *Youth and Policy*, 73, Autumn, pp. 1–19.

Bright, M. (2005a) Children with autism the target of Asbos, *Observer*, 22 May, p. 7.

Bright, M. (2005b) Crime czar: stop calling children 'yobs', *Observer*, 22 May, p. 7.

Britten, N., Campbell, R., Pope, C., Donovan, J., Morgan, M. and Pill, R. (2002) Using meta-ethnography to synthesis qualitative research: a worked example, *Journal of Health Services Research and Policy*, 7(4), pp. 209–15.

Brown, A. P. (2004) Anti-social behaviour, crime control and social control, *Howard Journal of Criminal Justice*, 43(2), May, pp. 203–11.

Budd, T., Sharp, C., Weir, G., Wilson, D. and Owen, N. (2005) *Young People and Crime: Findings from the 2004 Offending, Crime and Justice Survey.* Home Office Statistical Bulletin 10/05, November. London: Home Office.

Burney, E. (2002) Talking tough, acting coy: what happened to the Anti-Social Behaviour Order?, *Howard Journal*, 41(5), pp. 469–84.

Burt, C. (1925) *The Young Delinquent.* London: University of London Press.

Cabinet Office (1999) *Modernising Government.* Cm 4310. London: HMSO.

Cahill, C. (2000) Street literacy: urban teenagers' strategies for negotiating their neighbourhoods, *Journal of Youth Studies*, 3(3), pp. 251–77.

Callaghan, A. (2004) Anti-Social Behaviour Act 2003, *NCB Highlight 209*. London: National Children's Bureau.

Campbell, S. (2002) *A Review of Anti-Social Behaviour Orders.* Home Office Research Study no. 236. London: Home Office.

Canter, L. and Canter, M. (1992) *Assertive Discipline.* Bristol: Behaviour Management Ltd.

Charlton, T., Abrahams, M. and Jones, K. (1995) Prevalence rates of emotional and behavioural disorder among nursery class children in St Helena, South Atlantic: an epidemiological study, *Journal of Social Behaviour and Personality*, 10(1), pp. 273–80.

Cherlin, A. J., Furstenburg, F. F., Jr., Chase-Lansdale, P. L., Kiernan, K. E., Robons, P. K., Ruane Morrison, D. and Teitler, J. O. (1991) Longitudinal studies of effects of divorce on children in Great Britain and the United States, *Science*, 252, 7 June.

Clayton, G. (2005) Show a little respect, *The Teacher*, July/August. London: NUT, p. 3.

Cleaver, H., Barnes, J., Bliss, D. and Cleaver, D. (2005) *Developing Identification, Referral and Tracking Systems: An Evaluation of the Processes Undertaken by Trailblazer Authorities – Early Findings.* Brief no. RB521. London: DfES.

Clegg, M., Finney, A. and Thorpe, K. (2005) *Crime in England and Wales: Quarterly Update to December 2004.* Home Office Statistical Bulletin 07/05. London: Home Office.

Coates, D. and Silburn, R. (1971) *Poverty: The Forgotten Englishman.* Harmondsworth: Penguin.

Coleman, J. (1997) The parenting of adolescents in Britain today, *Children & Society*, 11(1), April, pp. 43–52.

Coles, B., England, J. and Rugg, J. (2000) Spaced out? Young people on social housing estates: social exclusion and multi-agency work, *Journal of Youth Studies*, 3(1), pp. 21–33.

Cooper, P. (1998) Developments in the understanding of childhood emotional and behaviour problems since 1981, in Laslett, R., Cooper, P., Maras, P., Rimmer, A. and Law, B. (eds.) *Changing Perceptions. Emotional and Behavioural Difficulties since 1945.* East Sutton: AWCEBD.

Cooper, P. and Upton, G. (1990) An ecosystem approach to emotional and behavioural difficulties in schools, *Educational Psychology*, 10, pp. 302–21.

Cooper, P. (1999) (ed.) *Understanding and Supporting Children with Emotional and Behavioural Difficulties.* London: Jessica Kingsley.

Cope, S. and Goodship, J. (1999) Regulating collaborative government: towards joined-up government?, *Public Policy & Administration*, 12(2), pp. 3–16.

CPPRG, Conduct Problems Prevention Research Group (1992) A developmental and clinical model for the prevention of conduct disorder: The FAST Track Program, *Development and Psychopathology*, 4, pp. 509–27.

CRAE, Children's Rights Alliance for England (2004) *State of Children's Rights in England 2004.* London: Children's Rights Alliance for England (www. crae.org.uk).

Craine, S. and Coles, B. (1995) Alternative careers: youth transitions and young people's involvement in crime, *Youth and Policy*, 48, pp. 6–27.

Cramer, H. and Carter, M. (2002) *Homelessness: What's Gender Got to Do with It?* London: Shelter.

Crawford, A. (1998) *Crime Prevention and Community Safety: Politics, Policies and Practices*. London: Longman.

Crow, I., France, A., Hacking, S. and Hart, M. (2004) *Does Communities that Care Work? An Evaluation of a Community-Based Risk-Prevention Programme in Three Neighbourhoods*. York: Joseph Rowntree Foundation.

CtC, Communities that Care (2005) *Findings from the Safer London Youth Survey 2004*. July. London: Communities that Care.

Cullingford, C. and Morrison, J. (1997) The relationship between criminality and home background, *Children & Society*, 11(3), pp. 157–72.

Currie, J. and Thomas, D. (2000) School quality and the long-term effects of Head Start, *Journal of Human Resources*, Fall, 35(4), pp. 755–74.

Davies, S., Nutley, M. and Smith, P. C. (eds) (2000) *What Works? Evidence-Based Policy and Practice in Public Services*. Bristol: The Policy Press.

Derzon, J. H. and Wilson, S. J. (1999) An empirical review of school-based programs to reduce violence, paper presented at the American Society of Criminology Conference, Toronto, Canada, November.

De Silva, N. (2005) *Sentencing Statistics 2003, England and Wales*. 0505 RDS NOMS. February. London: RDS, Home Office.

DES/WO, Department of Education and Science/Welsh Office DES/WO (1978) *Special Educational Need: Report of the Committee of Enquiry into the Education of Handicapped Children and Young People*. London: HMSO (Warnock Report).

DES/WO, Department of Education and Science and the Welsh Office (1989) *Discipline in Schools. Report of the Committee of Enquiry Chaired by Lord Elton*. London: HMSO (Elton Report).

DfE, Department for Education (1992) *Exclusions – A Discussion Paper*. London: DfE.

DfEE, Department for Education and Employment (1999) *Social Inclusion: Pupil Support*. London: The Stationery Office.

DfES, Department for Education and Skills (2002a) *Safer School Partnerships. Guidance*. Issued jointly by the DfES, Home Office, YJB, Association of Chief Education Officers, ACPO. London: DfES.

DfES (2002b) *Transforming Youth Work*. London: DfES.

DfES (2003a) *Every Child Matters*. London: DfES.

DfES (2003c) *Youth Cohort Study: The Activities of 17-Year-Olds: England and Wales 2003*. SFR 35/2003, London: DfES.

DfES (2004) *Outcome Indicators for Looked-After Children. Twelve months to 30 September 2004: England*. SFR 13/2004. London: DfES.

DfES (2005a) *Youth Matters*. London: DfES.

DfES (2005b) *Permanent and Fixed-Period Exclusions from Schools and Exclusion Appeals in England, 2003/04*, SFR 23/2005, 23 June. London: DfES.

DfES (2005c) *Statistics of Education: Referrals, Assessments and Children and Young People on Child Protection Registers: Year Ending 31 March 2004.* London: TSO.

DH, Department of Health (1995) *Child Protection. Messages from Research.* London: Department of Health.

DH (1998) *Modernising Social Services: Promoting Independence, Improving Protection.* Cm 4169. London: HMSO.

DH (2002) *Children Looked After in England; 2001/02.* Bulletin 2002/22. London: Department of Health.

DH (2005) *Background – the evolution of policy.* www.dh.gov.uk/PolicyAndGuidance/HealthAndSocialCareTopics/ChildrenServices (accessed 17 October 2005).

Dopson, S., Locock, L., Gabbay, J., Ferlie, E. and Fitzgerald, L. (2003) Evidence-based medicine and the implementation gap, *Health: An Interdisciplinary Journal for the Social Study of Health, Illness and Medicine*, 7(3), pp. 313–30.

Dryfoos, J. G. (1994) *Full-Service Schools: A Revolution in Health and Social Services for Children, Youth and Families.* San Francisco: Jossey-Bass.

DSRU, Dartington Social Research Unit (2004) *Refocusing Children's Services Towards Prevention: Lessons from the Literature.* Research Report RR510, London: DfES.

East, K. and Campbell, S. (2001) *Aspects of Crime: Young Offenders 1999*, London: Home Office.

Edwards, S. J. L., Lilford, R. J., Braunholtz, D. A., Jackson, J. C., Hewison, J. and Thornton, J. (1998) The ethics of randomised controlled trials from the perspective of patients, the public, and healthcare professionals, *British Medical Journal*, 317, pp. 1209–12.

Estrada, F. (2001) Juvenile violence as a social problem, *British Journal of Criminology*, 41, pp. 639–55.

Etzioni, A. (1995) *The Spirit of Community.* London: Fontana.

Falshaw, L., Friendship, C., Travers, R. and Nugent, F. (2003) *Searching for 'What Works': An Evaluation of Cognitive Skills Programmes.* Findings 206. London: Home Office.

Farrington, D. (1978) The family backgrounds of aggressive youths. In Hersov, L., Berger, M. and Shaffer, D. (eds) *Aggression and Anti-Social Behaviour in Childhood and Adolescence.* Oxford: Pergamon, pp. 73–93.

Farrington, D. (1991) Childhood aggression and adult violence: early precursors and later life outcomes, in Pepler, D. J. and Rubin, K. H. (eds) *The Development and Treatment of Childhood Aggression.* Hillsdale, NJ: Lawrence Erlbaum, pp. 5–29.

Farrington, D. (1996) *Understanding and Preventing Youth Crime*, York: York Publishing Services Ltd/Joseph Rowntree Foundation.

Farrington, D. P. (2002) Risk factors for youth violence, in Debarbieux, E. and Blaya, C. (eds) *Violence in Schools and Public Policies*, Oxford: Elsevier Science, pp. 13–32.

Farrington, D. P. and West, D. J. (1990) The Cambridge Study in Delinquent Development: a long-term follow-up of 411 London males, in Kaiser, G. and Kerner, H-J. (eds) *Criminality, Personality, Behavior, and Life History*. Berlin: Springer-Verlag.

Ferguson, T. (1966) *Children in Care and After*. London: Oxford University Press.

Fergusson, D. and Lynskey, M. (1997) Physical punishment/maltreatment during childhood and adjustment in young adulthood, *Young Person Abuse and Neglect*, 21(7), pp. 617–30.

Fergusson, R. (2004) Discourses of exclusion: reconceptualising participation amongst young people, *Journal of Social Policy*, April, 3(2), pp. 289–320.

Field, F. (2003) *Neighbours from Hell: The Politics of Behaviour*. London: Politico's.

Fielding, M., Bragg, S., Craig, J., Cunningham, I. Eraut, M., Gillinson, S., Horne, M., Robinson, C. and Thorpe, J. (2005) *Factors Influencing the Transfer of Good Practice*. Brief Number RB 615. London: DfES.

Fitz-Gibbon, C. (2000) Education: realising the potential, in Davies, H. T. O., Nutley, S. M. and Smith, P. C. (eds) *What Works? Evidence-based Policy and Practice in Public Services*. Bristol: The Policy Press, pp. 69–92.

Forbes, A. and Griffiths, P. (2002) Methodological strategies for the identification and synthesis of 'evidence' to support decision-making in relation to complex healthcare systems and practices, *Nursing Enquiry*, 9(3), pp. 141–55.

Foster, J. (1990) *Villains*. London: Routledge.

Fortin, L. and Bigras, M. (1997) Risk factors exposing young children to behaviour problems, *Emotional and Behavioural Difficulties*, 2(1), pp. 3–14.

Foucault, M. (1977) *Discipline and Punish*. London: Penguin Books.

Friendship, C., Blud, L., Erikson, M. and Travers, R. (2002) *An Evaluation of Cognitive Behavioural Treatment for Prisoners*. Findings 161. London: Home Office.

Frosh, S., Phoenix, A. and Pattman, R. (2002) *Young Masculinities*. Basingstoke: Palgrave.

Frost, S. and Liabo, K. (2003) The 'What Works for Children?' project: promoting research informed practice amongst Children's Fund Programmes, paper presented at the *Social Policy Association Conference*, 15–17 July, University of Teesside.

Furlong, A. and Cartmel, F. (1997) *Young People and Social Change*. Buckingham: Open University Press.

Garces, E., Thomas, D. and Currie, J. (2002) Longer-term effects of head start, *American Economic Review*, September, pp. 999–1012.

Giddens, A. (1998) *The Third Way*. Cambridge: Polity Press.

Gill, M. and Hearnshaw, S. (1997) *Personal Safety and Violence in Schools*. DfEE Research Report, RR21, London: DfEE.

Gillen, S. (2002) Government looks to toughen guidelines on school exclusions, *Community Care*, 31 January–6 February, pp. 18–19.

Glass, N. (2005) Surely some mistake? *Guardian Unlimited*, 5 January www.education.guardian.co.uk/earlyyears/story/0,,1383617,00.html (accessed 29 November 2005).

Goldson, B. (1997) Children, crime, policy and practice: neither welfare nor justice, *Children & Society*, 11, pp. 77–88.

Goldson, B. (2000) Youth Justice and the Criminal Evidence Act 1999, *NCB Highlight 175*, London: NCB/Barnardo's.

Goldson, B. (2002) *Vulnerable Inside: Children in Secure and Penal Settings*. London: The Children's Society.

Goldson, B. and Peters, E. (2000) *Tough Justice. Responding to Children in Trouble*. London: The Children's Society.

Goodman, R. (1997) The Strengths and Difficulties Questionnaire: a research note, *Journal of Child Psychology and Psychiatry*, 38, pp. 581–6.

Graham, J. and Bowling, B. (1995) *Young People and Crime*. Home Office Research Study 145. London: HMSO.

Green, E., Mitchell, W. and Bunton, R. (2000) Contextualising risk and danger: an analysis of young people's perceptions of risk, *Journal of Youth Studies*, 3(2), pp. 109–26.

Grier, A. and Thomas, T. (2004) A war for civilisation as we know it, *Youth and Policy*, 82, pp. 1–15.

Grimshaw, R. with Berridge, D. (1994) *Educating Disruptive Children: Placement and Progress in Residential Special Schools for Pupils with Emotional and Behavioural Difficulties*. London: National Children's Bureau.

Hagell, A. and Newburn, T. (1994) *Persistent Young Offenders*. London: Policy Studies Institute.

Hall, S., Hobson, D., Lowe, A. and Willis, P. (1991) *Culture, Media, Language*. London: Routledge.

Hambleton, R., Essex, S., Mills, L. and Razzaque, K. (1996) *The Collaborative Council: A study of inter-agency working in practice*. York: LGC Communication/Joseph Rowntree Foundation.

Hammersley, M. (2001) On 'systematic' reviews of research literatures: a 'narrative' response to Evans and Benfield, *British Educational Research Journal*, 27(5), pp. 543–54.

Hansard, House of Commons 6 May 2003, Col. 142, Written Answer on Child Protection.

Hargreaves, D., Hestor, S. and Mellor, F. (1975) *Deviance in Classrooms*. London: Routledge & Kegan Paul.

Harker, R. M., Dobel-Ober, D., Berridge, D. and Sinclair, R. (2004) *Taking Care of Education. An evaluation of the education of looked-after children*. London: National Children's Bureau.

Hawkins, D., Catalano, R. and Arthur, W.(2002) Promoting science-based prevention in communities, *Addictive Behaviours*, 27, pp. 951–76.

Hayden, C. (2000) Exclusion from school in England: the generation and maintenance of social exclusion, in Walraven, G., Parsons, C., van Veen, D. and Day, C. (eds) *Combating Social Exclusion through Education*. Leuven-Appledoorn: Garant/EERA.

Hayden, C. (2001) Social exclusion and exclusion from school in England, in Visser, J., Daniels, H. and Cole, T. (eds) *Emotional and Behavioural Difficulties in Mainstream Schools*. International Perspectives on Inclusive Education, Vol. 1, pp. 113–28. London: JAI/Elsevier Science.

Hayden, C. (2005a) More than a piece of paper? Personal Education Plans and looked-after children in England, *Child and Family Social Work*. 10(3), pp. 173–87.

Hayden, C. (2005b) Crime prevention: the role and potential of schools, in Winstone, J. and Pakes, F. (eds) *Community Justice. Issues for Probation and Criminal Justice*. Cullumpton: Willan, pp. 142–64.

Hayden, C. and Dunne, S. (2001) *Outside, Looking In. Children and Families' Experiences of Exclusion from School*. London: The Children's Society.

Hayden, C., Goddard, J., Gorin, S. and van der Spek, N. (1999) *State Child Care. Looking After Children?* London: Jessica Kingsley.

Hayden, C., Williamson, T. and Webber, R. (2006) Schools, pupil behaviour and young offenders: using postcode classification to target behaviour support and crime prevention programmes, *British Journal of Criminology*.

Haydon, D. and Scraton, P. (2000) 'Condemn a little more, understand a little less': the political context and rights implications of the domestic and European court rulings in the Venables–Thompson Case, *Journal of Law and Society*, 27(3), pp. 416–48.

Hirsch, D. and Miller, J. (2004) *Labour's welfare reform: Progress to date*, Findings 44. York: Joseph Rowntree Foundation.

HMSO (1969) *Children in Trouble*. Cmnd 3601. London: HMSO.

HM Treasury (1998), *Modern Public Services for Britain: Investing in Reform – New Public Spending Plans 1999–2002*. CM4011. London: HMSO.

HM Treasury/DTI (2003) *Balancing work and family life: Enhancing choice and support for parents*. London: HMSO.

Hogan, C. D. and Murphey, D. A. (2000) *Towards an 'Economic of Prevention': illustrations from Vermont's experience*. The Finance Project. Waterbury, Vermont: Vermont Human Services Agency. www.financeproject.org/publications/vermont.htm (accessed 21 November 2005).

Home Office (1998) *Draft Guidance Document: Anti-Social Behaviour Orders*. London: Home Office.

Home Office (2003) *A Guide to Anti-Social Behaviour Orders and Acceptable Behaviour Contracts*. London: Home Office.

Home Office (2004) *Anti-Social Behaviour* www.homeoffice.gov.uk/crime/antisocialbehaviour/index/html (accessed 30 May 2004).

Hopkins, B. (2004) Restorative justice in schools, *Support for Learning*, 17(3), pp. 144–9.

Hough, M. and Roberts, J. V. (2004) *Youth Crime and Youth Justice: Public Opinion in England and Wales.* Bristol: The Policy Press.

Howard League (2002) *96% of Teenagers are Victims of Crime.* 11 April, www.howardleague.org/press/2002/11402.html (accessed 2 July 2004).

Hudson, B. (2002) Punishment and control, in Maguire, M., Morgan, R. and Reiner, R. (eds) *The Oxford Handbook of Criminology* (3rd edition). Oxford: Oxford University Press, pp. 233–63.

Hughes, G., McLaughlin, E. and Muncie, J. (eds) (2002) *Crime Prevention and Community Safety. New Directions.* London: Sage in association with the Open University.

Humphreys, C., Mullender, A., Lowe, P., Hague, G., Abraham, H. and Hester, M. (2001) Domestic violence and child abuse: developing sensitive policies and guidance, *Child Abuse Review*, 10(3), pp. 183–97.

Hunter, C. and Nixon, J. (2001) Taking the blame and losing the home: women and anti-social behaviour, *Journal of Social Welfare and Family Law*, 23(4), pp. 395–410.

Hyland, J. (1993) *Yesterday's Answers. Development and Decline of Schools for Young Offenders.* London: Whiting & Birch.

Jackson, S. (1987) *The Education of Children in Care.* Bristol Papers. Bristol, SAUS.

James, O. (2005) Kindergarten cop, *Observer Magazine*, 10 July, p. 74.

Jones, D. (2001) 'Misjudged Youth' a critique of the Audit Commission's reports on Youth Justice, *British Journal of Criminology*, 41, pp. 362–380.

Jones, S. (2001) *Criminology.* (2nd ed.) Trowbridge: Butterworth.

Kennedy, H. (2004) Playing the victim lets Blair erode our liberty, *Guardian Student*, 2 December, p. 10.

Kilkelly, U. (2001) The Human Rights Act 1998 and Children, *NCB Highlight no. 183.* London: NCB.

Kolvin, I., Miller, F. J., Scott, D. McI., Gatzanis, S. R. M. and Fleeting, M. (1990) *Continuities of Deprivation.* ESRC/DHSS Studies in Deprivation and Disadvantage No. 15. Aldershot: Avebury.

Labour Party Manifesto (2005) *Britain Forward, Not Back.* www.labour.org.uk

Land, H. (2004) Children, families, states and changing citizenship, in Scott, J., Treas, J. and Richards, M. (eds) *The Blackwell Companion to The Sociology of Families.* Oxford: Blackwell, pp. 54–68.

Laslett, R. (1998) Changing perceptions, in Laslett, R., Cooper, P., Maras, P., Rimmer, A. and Law, B. *Emotional and Behavioural Difficulties since 1945.* East Sutton: AWEBD.

Lauritsen, J. and Quinet, K.(1995) Repeat victimisation among adolescents and young adults, *Journal of Qualitative Criminology*, 11(2), pp. 143–66.

La Valle, I., Arthur, S., Millward, C., Scott, J. and Clayden, M. (2002) *Happy Families? Atypical Work and its Influence on Family Life.* Bristol: Policy Press.

Leach, P. (1999) Physical punishment of children in the home, *NCB Highlight 166.* London: NCB/Barnardo's.

Leach, R. (2003) Children's participation in family decision-making, *NCB Highlight no. 196*. London: NCB/Barnardo's.

Lemert, E. (1951) *Social Pathology*. New York: McGraw Hill.

Linfoot, K., Martin, A. J. and Stephenson, J. (1999) Preventing conduct disorder: a study of parental behaviour management and support needs with children aged 3 to 5 years, *International Journal of Disability, Development and Education*, 46(2), pp. 223–46.

Lipscombe, J. (2003). Another side of life: foster care for young people on remand, *Youth Justice*, 3(1), pp. 35–48.

Lipsey, M. W. (1992) Juvenile delinquency treatment: a meta-analytic inquiry into the variability of effects, in Cook, T. D. *et al.* (eds) *Meta-Analysis for Explanation: A Casebook*. New York: Russell Sage Foundation.

Lipsey, M. W. (1995) What do we learn from 400 research studies on the effectiveness of treatment with juvenile delinquents?, in McGuire, J. (ed.) *What Works: Reducing Offending. Guidelines from Research and Practice*. Chichester: John Wiley, pp. 63–78.

Lipsey, M. W. and Wilson, D. B. (1998) Effective intervention for serious juvenile offenders: a synthesis of research, in Loeber, D. P. and Farrington, R. (eds) *Serious and Violent Juvenile Offenders: Risk Factors and Successful Interventions*. Thousand Oaks: Sage, pp. 313–45.

Lister, R. (2003) Investing in the citizen-workers of the future: transformations in citizenship and the state under New Labour, *Social Policy and Administration*, 37(5), pp. 427–43.

Little, M. with Kelly, S. (1995) *A Life Without Problems? The Achievements of a Therapeutic Community*. Aldershot: Arena.

Little, M., Kogan, J., Bullock, R. and Van Der Laan, P. (2004) An experiment in multi-systemic responses to persistent young offenders known to children's services, *British Journal of Criminology*, 44, pp. 225–40.

Lloyd, R. and Ching, C. (2003) *School Security Concerns*. DfES Research Report RR419. London: DfES.

Loader, I., Girling, E. and Sparks, R. (1998) Narratives of decline: youth, dis/order and community in an English 'middletown', *British Journal of Criminology*, 38(3), Summer, pp. 388–403.

Loader, I. and Sparks, R. (2002) Contemporary landscapes of crime, order, and control. Governance, risk and globalization, in Maguire, M., Morgan, R. and Reiner, R. (eds) *The Oxford Handbook of Criminology* (3rd ed). Oxford: Oxford University Press, pp. 83–111.

London Health Observatory, LHO (2000) *Common Mental Health Problems*. London: London Health Observatory.

Lucky Duck (2002) *What is Circle Time Really About?* www.luckyduck.co.uk (accessed 23 November 2005).

Lupton, C. and Nixon, P. (1999) *Empowering Practice? A Critical Appraisal of the Family Group Conference Approach*. Bristol: Policy Press.

Lupton, C. and Stevens, M. (1998) Planning in partnership? An assessment of process and outcome in UK Family Group Conferences, *International Journal of Child Family Welfare*, 98(2), pp. 135–48.

McCann, J., James, A., Wilson, S. and Dunn, G. (1996) Prevalence of psychiatric disorders in young people in the care system, *British Medical Journal*, 313, pp. 1529–30.

McCarthy, P., Laing, K. and Walker, J. (2004) *Offenders of the Future? Assessing the Risk of Children and Young People Becoming Involved in Criminal or Antisocial Behaviour*. DfES Research Report RR545. London: DfES.

MacDonald, R. and Marsh, J. (2001) Disconnected youth?, *Journal of Youth Studies*, 4(4), pp. 373–91.

McGuire, J. (ed.) (1995) *What Works: Reducing Offending. Guidelines from Research and Practice*. Chichester: John Wiley.

McKey, H. R., Condelli, L., Ganson, H., Barrett, B., McConkey, C. and Palntz, M. (1985) *The Impact of Head Start on Children, Families and Communities. Final report of the Head Start Evaluation, Synthesis and Utilisation Project*. The Head Start Bureau. Administration for Children, Youth and Families, Office of Human Development Services, US Department of Health and Human Services, Washington, DC.

McManus, M. (1989) *Troublesome Behaviour in the Classroom. A Teacher's Survival Guide*. London: Routledge.

Malek, M. (1993) *Passing the Buck. Institutional Responses to Controlling Children with Difficult Behaviour*. London: Children's Society.

Managing Schools Today (2005) Sure Start – where next?, March/April, pp. 10–11.

Marrin, M. (2005) A few good (brawny) men could pacify our schools, *Sunday Times*, 6 February, p. 19.

Martin, P. Y. and Jackson, S. (2002) Educational success for children in public care: advice from a group of high achievers, *Child and Family Social Work*, 7(2), pp. 121–30.

Martin, T. (2002) *Foster Care Payment and Accreditation Scheme Evaluation: Interim Report*. Research Unit, Social and Caring Services: West Sussex County Council.

Martinson, R. (1974) What works? – questions and answers about prison reform, *The Public Interest*, 10, pp. 22–54.

Marx, K. and Engels, F. (1968) *Selected Works*. London: Laurence & Wishart.

Matthews, R. (2005) The myth of punitiveness, *Theoretical Criminology*, 9(2), pp. 175–201.

Meltzer, H., Gatward, R., Goodman, R., and Ford, T. (2000) *Mental Health of Children and Adolescents in Great Britain*. London: Office for National Statistics.

Mendel, R. (2000) *Less Hype More Help. Reducing Youth Crime: What Works and What Doesn't?* Washington, DC: American Youth Policy Forum.

Micklewright, J. (2002) *Social Exclusion and Children: A European View for a US Debate*. Casepaper 51. London: Centre for Analysis of Social Exclusion, London School of Economics.

Miller, C. (2005) *Children's Trust Arrangements: Developing Local Ways Forward*. London: OPM.

Miller, C. and McNicholl, A. (2003) *Integrating Children's Services: Issues and Practice*. London: OPM.

Minow, M. (1996) Rights for the next generation: a feminist approach to children's rights, in Ladd, R. (ed.) *Children's Rights Revisioned: Philosophical Readings*. London, New York and Belmont: Wadsworth.

MORI (Market and Opinion Research International) (2004) *MORI Youth Survey 2004*. London: Youth Justice Board.

Mosley, J. (1993) *Turn Your School Round*. Wisbech: LDA.

Muncie, J. (2004) *Youth and Crime* (2nd ed.). London: Sage.

NACRO (2003) The sentencing framework for children and young people, *Youth Crime Briefing*, December. London: NACRO (www.nacro.org.uk).

NACRO (2004) Some facts about young people who offend – 2002, *Youth Crime Briefing*, March. London: NACRO.

NAO (National Audit Office) (2005) *Improving School Attendance in England*. London: The Stationery Office.

NAS/UWT (National Association of Schoolmasters/Union of Women Teachers) (2003) *NAS/UWT Report on Violence and Indiscipline* (available from www.teachersunion.org.uk (accessed 27 March 2003).

Neill, S. R. St. J. (2002) *Unacceptable Pupil Behaviour: A Survey Carried Out for the National Union of Teachers*. Institute of Education: University of Warwick.

Newburn, T. (2002) Young people, crime and youth justice, in Maguire, M., Morgan, R. and Reiner, R. (eds) *The Oxford Handbook of Criminology* (3rd ed.). Oxford: Oxford University Press, pp. 531–78.

Newburn, T. and Shiner, M. (2005) Mentoring Plus, *YJB/BSC Youth Justice Research Methodologies Workshop*, 19 July, London.

Newman, J. (2001) *Modernising Governance – New Labour, Policy and Society*. London: Sage.

Newman, J. and Nutley, S. (2003) Transforming the Probation Service: 'what works', organisational change and professional identity, *Policy and Politics*, 31(4), October, pp. 547–63.

Newsom, J. and Newsom, E. (1989) *The Extent of Parental Punishment in the UK*. London: Approach.

Nobes, G. and Smith, M. A. (1997) Physical punishment of children in two-parent families, *Clinical Child Psychology and Psychiatry*, 2(2), pp. 271–81.

Noblit, G. W. and Hare, R. D. (1988) *Meta-Ethnography: Synthesizing Qualitative Studies*. Qualitative Research Methods, Series 11. London: Sage.

Nutley, S. and Webb, J. (2000) Evidence and the policy process, in Davies, H. T. O., Nutley, S. and Webb, J. (eds) *What Works? Evidence-based Policy and Practice in Public Services*. Bristol: Policy Press.

Nuttall, C., Goldblatt, P. and Lewis, C. (1998) *Reducing Offending: An Assessment of Research Evidence on Ways of Dealing with Offending Behaviour.* Research Study 187. London: Home Office.

Oakley, A. (2000) *Experiments in Knowing. Gender and Method in the Social Sciences.* Oxford: Polity Press.

Office for National Statistics (ONC) (2000) *Psychiatric Morbidity among Young Offenders in England and Wales.* London: Department of Health and National Assembly.

O'Hara, M. (1995) *Children and Domestic Violence.* NCB Highlight no. 139. London: NCB.

Oliver, C., Smith, M. and Barker, S. (1998) Effectiveness of early intervention, paper prepared for the *Comprehensive Spending Review: Cross-Departmental Review of Provision for Young Children.* Supporting Papers Vol. 1. London: HM Treasury.

Parsons, T. (1939) *The Structure of Social Action.* New York: Free Press.

Passmore, B. (2002) Shock prison sentence raises truancy stakes, *Times Educational Supplement,* 17 May, p. 15.

Pawson, R. and Tilley, N. (1997) *Realistic Evaluation.* London: Sage.

Payne, L. (2003) Anti-social behaviour, *Children & Society,* 17, pp. 321–4.

Petrosino, A., Turpin-Petrosino, C. and Buehler, J.(2002) *'Scared Straight' and Other Juvenile Awareness Programs for Preventing Juvenile Delinquency.* Cochrane database of systematic reviews, Issue 4 (available at www.Campbell. collaboration).

Pinchbeck, I. and Hewitt, M. (1969) *Children in English Society, Volume One: From Tudor Times to the Eighteenth Century.* London: Routledge & Kegan Paul.

Piper, C. (2001) Who are these youths? Language in the service of policy, *Youth Justice,* 1(2), pp. 30–9.

Pitts, J. (2001) *The New Politics of Youth Crime: Discipline or Solidarity?* Lyme Regis: Russell House.

Popper, K. R. (1959) *The Logic of Scientific Discovery.* London: Hutchinson.

Postman, N. (1982) *The Disappearance of Childhood.* New York: Delacorte Press.

Power, A. and Tunstall, R. (1997) *Dangerous Disorder: Riots and Violent Disturbances in Thirteen Areas 1991–92.* York: Joseph Rowntree Foundation/ York Publishing Services.

Pugh, G. (1998) Children at risk of becoming socially excluded: an introduction to the 'problem', paper prepared for *Comprehensive Spending Review. Cross-Departmental Review of Provision for Young Children.* Supporting Papers. Treasury Seminar on Social Exclusion, 21 January. London: HM Treasury.

Richards, S. (1998) An institutional framework for provision for young children, paper prepared for *Comprehensive Spending Review – Cross-Departmental Review of Provision for Young Children.* Supporting Papers, Volume 1. London: HM Treasury.

Rickford, F. (2000) First Steps, *Community Care,* Issue 1327, 22–28 June, pp. 20–1.

Roberts, H., Liabo, K., Lucas, P., Dubois, D. and Sheldon, T. A. (2004) Mentoring to reduce antisocial behaviour in childhood, *British Medical Journal*, 328, pp. 512–14.

Rodham, H. (1973) Children under the law, *Harvard Educational Review*, 43, p. 487.

Royal College of Psychiatrists (2004) *Surviving Adolescence – A Toolkit for Parents*. London: Royal College of Psychiatrists.

Rutter, M. (1981) *Maternal Deprivation Re-Assessed*. London: Penguin.

Rutter, M. (1985) Family and school influences: meanings, mechanisms and implications, in Nichol, A. R. (ed.) *Longitudinal Studies in Child Psychology and Psychiatry*. Chichester: John Wiley.

Rutter, M., Giller, H. and Hagell, A. (1998) *Antisocial Behaviour by Young People*. Cambridge: Cambridge University Press.

Rutter, M., Maughan, B., Mortimore, P. and Ouston, J. (1979) *Fifteen Thousand Hours. Secondary Schools and their Effects on Children*, Shepton Mallet: Open Books Publishing.

Rutter, M. and Smith, D. J. (eds) (1995) *Psychosocial Disorders in Young People. Time Trends and their Causes*. Chichester: John Wiley, published for Academis Europaea.

Safe on the Streets Research Team (1999) *Still Running: Children on the Streets in the UK*. London: The Children's Society.

Schweinhart , I. and Weikart, D. (1980) *Young Children Grow Up: The Effects of the Perry Pre-School Program on Youths Through Age 15*. Monographs of the High/Scope Educational Research Foundation, No. 7. Ypsilanti, MI: USA.

Scott, S., Knapp, M., Henderson, J. and Maughan, B. (2001) Financial cost of social exclusion: follow-up study of antisocial behaviour into adulthood, *British Medical Journal*, 323(191), 28 July (www.bmj.bmjjournals.com).

Sereny, G. (2005) Ridiculous assumption that ignores child's needs, *The Times*, 13 June, p. 20.

SEU (Social Exclusion Unit) (1998) *Truancy and Exclusion from School*. London: Cabinet Office.

SEU (2000) *Report of Policy Action Team 8: Anti-Social Behaviour*. London: Social Exclusion Unit.

SEU (2001) *A New Commitment to Neighbourhood Renewal*. London: Cabinet Office.

SEU (2002) *Young Runaways*. London: SEU.

Sherman, L. W., Gottfredson, D., Mackenzie, D., Eck, J., Reuter, P. and Bushways, S. (1997) *Preventing Crime: What Works, What Doesn't, What's Promising*. Office of Justice Programs report. Washington DC: US Department of Justice.

Sibley, D. (1995) *Geographies of Exclusion*. London: Routledge.

Sinclair, I. and Gibbs, I. (1998) *Children's Homes: A Study in Diversity*. Chichester: John Wiley.

Skevik, A. (2003) Children of the welfare state: individuals with entitlements, or hidden in the family, *Journal of Social Policy*, 32(3), pp. 423–40.

Smith, D. J. and McVie, S. (2003) Theory and method in the Edinburgh study of youth transitions and crime, *British Journal of Criminology*, 43, pp. 169–95.

Smith, M. L. and Glass, G. V. (1977) Meta-analysis of psychotherapy outcome studies, *American Psychologist*, 32, pp. 752–60.

Smith, P. K. (2002) School bullying, and ways of preventing it, in Debarbieux, E. and Blaya, C. (eds) *Violence in Schools and Public Policies*. Oxford: Elsevier Science, pp. 117–28.

Smith, P. K. and Myron-Wilson, R. (1998) Parenting and school bullying, *Clinical Child Psychology and Psychiatry*, 3(3), pp. 405–17.

Spence, J. (2005) Concepts of youth, in Harrison, R. and Wise, C. (eds) *Working with Young People*. London: Sage with the Open University, pp. 46–56.

St James-Roberts, I., Greenlaw, G., Simon, A. and Hurry, J. (2005) *Mentoring Schemes 2001–2004*. Summary report. London: Youth Justice Board.

Steer, Sir A. (Chair) (2005) *Learning Behaviour. The Report of The Practitioners' Group on School Behaviour and Discipline*. Nottingham: DfES.

Stephen, D. E. and Squires, P. (2003) *Community Safety, Enforcement and Acceptable Behaviour Contracts. An Evaluation of the Work of the Community Safety Team in the East Brighton 'New Deal for Communities' Area*, September, Health and Social Policy Research Centre. Brighton: University of Brighton.

Stephen, D. E. and Squires, P. (2004) 'They're still children and entitled to be children': problematising the institutionalised mistrust of marginalized youth in Britain, *Journal of Youth Studies*, 7(3), pp. 351–69.

Stephenson, M., Bates, F. and Hay, C. (2001) *An Audit of Education Provision within the Juvenile Secure Estate. A Report to the Youth Justice Board*. London: Youth Justice Board.

Straw, J. and Michael, A. (1996) *Tackling the Causes of Crime: Labour's Proposal to Prevent Crime and Criminality*, London: Labour Party.

Sullivan, J. and Beech, A. (2002) Professional perpetrators, *Child Abuse Review*, 11, pp. 153–67.

Sundell, K., Vinnerljung, B. and Ryburn, M. (2001) Social workers' attitudes towards family group conferences in Sweden and the UK, *Child and Family Social Work*, 6, pp. 327–36.

Sutton, C., Utting, D. and Farrington, D. (2004) *Support from the Start: Working with Young Children and Their Families to Reduce the Risks of Crime and Anti-social Behaviour*. DfES Research Report 524. London: DfES.

Taite, G. (1995) Shaping the 'at risk youth': risk, govermentality and the Finn Report, *Discourse: Studies in the Cultural Politics of Education*, 16, pp. 123–4.

Taylor, C. (2003) Justice for looked after children?, *Probation Journal*, 50(3), pp. 239–51.

Taylor, M. (2005) Task force to tackle discipline in schools, *Education Guardian*, 21 May, www.education.guardian.co.uk/schools/story/0,,1489004,00. html (downloaded 7 June 2005).

Team-Teach (2003) *Team-Teach Work Book*. St Leonards-on-Sea: Steaming Publications.

Thompson, A. E. and Pearce, J. B. (2001) Attitudes towards and the practice of discipline amongst parents of pre-school children in Nottingham, *Children & Society*, 15, pp. 231–6.

Tubbs, N. (1996) *The New Teacher. An Introduction to Teaching in Comprehensive Education*. London: David Fulton.

TUC/MORI (2001) *Half a Million Kids Working Illegally*. London: TUC, 21 March.

Tunstill, J., Allnock, D., Akhurst, S. and Garbers, C. (2005) Sure Start local programmes: implications of case study data from the national evaluation of Sure Start, *Children & Society*, 19, pp. 158–71.

Utting, D. (1995) *Family and Parenthood: Supporting Families, Preventing Breakdown*. York: Joseph Rowntree Foundation.

Utting, D. (1998) Suggestions for the UK: an overview of possible action, paper prepared for *Comprehensive Spending Review – Cross-Departmental Review of Provision for Young Children*. Supporting Papers Vol. 1. London: HM Treasury.

Utting, D., Bright, J. and Henricson, C. (1993) *Crime and the Family. Improving Child-Rearing and Preventing Delinquency*. Occasional paper 16. London: Family Policy Studies Centre.

Vennard, J., Hedderman, C. and Sugg, D. (1997) *Changing Offenders' Attitudes and Behaviour: What Works?* Research Findings No. 61. London: Home Office Research and Statistics Directorate.

Walby, S. and Allen, J. (2004) *Domestic Violence, Sexual Assault and Stalking: Findings from the British Crime Survey*. HOR Study 276. London: Home Office.

Ward, L. (2005) Doubts over value of £3bn Sure Start, *Guardian*, 13 September, p. 1.

Watkins, C. (2004) Reclaiming Pastoral Care, *Pastoral Care in Education*, 22(2), pp. 3–6.

Webster-Stratton, C. (1999) Researching the impact of parent training programmes on child conduct problems, in Lloyd, E., *Parenting Matters*. Illford: Barnardo's.

Wells, L. E. and Rankin, J. H. (1991) Families and delinquency: a meta-analysis of the impact of broken homes, *Social Problems*, 38(1), pp. 71–89.

West, D. J. and Farrington, D. P. (1973) *Who Becomes Delinquent?* London: Heinemann.

Westinghouse Learning Corporation (1969) *The impact of Head Start: an evaluation of the effects of Head Start on children's cognitive and affective development*. Report to the Office of Economic Opportunity. Washington, DC: Clearing House for Federal, Scientific and Technical Information.

Whipple, E. E. and Richey, C. A. (1997) Crossing the line from physical discipline to child abuse: How much is too much?, *Child Abuse & Neglect*, 21(5), pp. 431–44.

Whiting, E. and Harper, R. (2003) *Young People and Social Capital.* London: Office for National Statistics.

Whittle, S. (2004) Alone and afraid, *Children Now*, 20–26 October, London: NCB, pp. 20–1.

Whyte, B. (2002) *Restorative Justice.* CJSW Briefing No.4. Edinburgh, CJSW Development Centre for Scotland.

Williams, F. (2004) What matters is who works: why every child matters to New Labour. Commentary on the DfES Green Paper 'Every Child Matters', *Critical Social Policy*, 24(3), pp. 406–27.

Wilson, D. B., Gottfredson, D. C. and Najaka, S. S. (2001) School-based prevention of problem behaviours: a meta-analysis, *Journal of Quantitative Criminology*, 17(3), pp. 247–72.

Wilson, D. B., MacKenzie, D. L. and Mitchell, F. N. (2005) Effects of correctional boot camps on offending, *Campbell Collaboration Systematic Review* (www.aic.gov.au/campbellcj/reviews/titles.html).

Wilson, S. J. and Lipsey, M. W. (2000) Wilderness challenge programmes for delinquent youth: a meta-analysis of outcome evaluations, *Evaluation and Planning*, (23), pp. 1–12.

Wilson, S. J. and Lipsey, M. W. (2006) The effectiveness of school-based violence prevention programmes for reducing disruptive and aggressive behaviour: a meta-analysis, *International Journal on Violence in Schools*, 1, May. www.ijvs.org/1-6053-Article.php?id=16&tarticle=0 (accessed 25 May 2006).

Wilson, S. J., Lipsey, M. W. and Derzon, J. H. (2003) The effects of school-based intervention programs on aggressive behaviour: a meta-analysis, *Journal of Consulting and Clinical Psychology*, 71(1), pp. 136–49.

Wolke, D. F. H. (1999) *Research Report Submitted to the ESRC*, September.

Wood, M. (2004) *Perceptions and Experiences of Anti-Social Behaviour.* Findings 252. London: Home Office.

Wood, S., Hodges, C. and Alijunied, M. (1996) The effectiveness of assertive discipline training, *Educational Psychology in Practice*, 12(3), pp. 175–81.

Wright, C. (1986) School processes: an ethnographic study, in Eggleston, S., Dunn, D. and Anjali, M. (eds) *Education for Some.* Stoke-on-Trent: Trentham Books.

WWFC (What Works for Children) (2003) *Group-Based Parenting Programmes Can Reduce Behaviour Problems of Children Aged 3–10 Years.* www.whatworksforchildren.org.uk

YJB (2001a) *Risk and Protective Factors Associated with Youth Crime and Effective Interventions to Prevent It.* London: Youth Justice Board.

YJB [Hobbs and Hook Consulting] (2001b) *Research into Effective Practice with Young People in Secure Facilities.* London: Youth Justice Board.

YJB (2004) *Youth Justice Annual Statistics 2003/04.* London: YJB.

Young, J. (2002) Crime and social exclusion, in Maguire, M., Morgan, R. and Reiner, R. (eds) *The Oxford Handbook of Criminology* (3rd ed.). Oxford: Oxford University Press, pp. 457–90.

Young, M. and Halsey, A. H. (1995) *Family and Community Socialism.* London: Institute for Public Policy Research.

Young Minds (2005) *Mental Health.* London: Young Minds.

Zingraff, M. T., Leiter, J., Johnsen, M. C. and Myers, K. A. (1994) The mediating effect of good school performance on the maltreatment–delinquency relationship, *Journal of Research in Crime and Delinquency,* 31(1), pp. 62–91.

Index